Social Classes and So

Social Classes and
Social Credit in Alberta

EDWARD BELL

Foreword by Maurice Pinard

McGill-Queen's University Press
Montreal & Kingston • London • Buffalo

© McGill-Queen's University Press 1993
ISBN 0-7735-1168-7 (cloth)
ISBN 0-7735-1169-5 (paper)

Legal deposit second quarter 1994
Bibliothèque nationale du Québec

Printed in Canada on acid-free paper

This book has been published with the help of a grant
from the Social Science Federation of Canada, using
funds provided by the Social Sciences and Humanities
Research Council of Canada.

Canadian Cataloguing in Publication Data

Bell, Edward A. (Edward Allan), 1955–
  Social classes and Social Credit in Alberta
  Includes bibliographical references and index.
  ISBN 0-7735-1168-7 (bound). –
  ISBN 0-7735-1169-5 (pbk.)
  1. Alberta – Social Credit League – History.
  2. Alberta – Politics and government – 1935–1971.
  I. Title.
  JL339.A57B45 1994   971.23'02   C94-900179-1

Typeset in Palatino 10/12 by
Caractéra production graphique inc., Quebec City.

In loving memory of my parents,
Edward William Bell and Josephina Salveig Kristjanson

Contents

Tables   ix

Maps   xi

Foreword by Maurice Pinard   xiii

Acknowledgments   xvii

1 Introduction   3

2 A Brief History of Alberta to 1935   8

3 The Conventional Wisdom   19

4 The Douglas Social Credit Philosophy   37

5 The Alberta Social Credit Philosophy   61

6 The 1935 Election: Cities, Towns, and Countryside   86

7 Social Credit in Power   107

8 The 1940 Election: Cities, Towns, and Countryside   129

9 Social Credit in Alberta: An Alternative Perspective   140

Notes   165

References   183

Index   193

Tables

3.1 Macpherson's Breakdown of the Alberta Work-Force 22

3.2 Alberta's Class Structure, 1931 (Males Only) 25

3.3 Social Credit Vote in the 1935 Provincial Election, Four Largest Cities 31

3.4 Social Credit Vote in the 1935 Provincial Election, for Urban Areas with Populations from 1,000 to 5,000 32

6.1 Vote in Calgary in the 1935 Provincial Election, by Area 93

6.2 Vote in Calgary in the 1930 Provincial Election, by Area 93

6.3 Vote in Lethbridge in the 1935 Provincial Election, by Area 97

6.4 Vote in Lethbridge in the 1930 Provincial Election, by Area 97

6.5 Vote in Medicine Hat in the 1935 Provincial Election, by Area 100

6.6 Vote in Medicine Hat in the 1930 Provincial Election, by Area 100

6.7 Quebec Federal Social Credit Vote, 1962, by Class 102

x   Tables

6.8 Vote in the 1935 Provincial Election, for Urban Areas with Populations from 1,000 to 5,000   103

8.1 Vote in Calgary in the 1940 Provincial Election, by Area   130

8.2 Vote in Lethbridge in the 1940 Provincial Election, by Area   133

8.3 Vote in Medicine Hat in the 1940 Provincial Election, by Area   135

8.4 Vote in the 1940 Provincial Election, for Urban Areas with Populations from 1,000 to 5,000   136

Maps

6.1 Calgary Provincial Polling Subdivisions, 1935   90

6.2 Lethbridge Provincial Polling Subdivisions, 1935   96

6.3 Medicine Hat Provincial Polling Subdivisions, 1935   99

6.4 Alberta Electoral Divisions 1935, Showing North-South Boundary   105

8.1 Alberta Electoral Divisions 1940, Showing North-South Boundary   138

Foreword

For some forty years now, a great number of Canadian social scientists have considered the rise of the Social Credit movement in Alberta during the mid-1930s to be a political phenomenon whose general characteristics have been well analysed and explained. For them, it never presented any puzzle to start with and no further examination or revision of the received wisdom regarding it appeared necessary. Almost unanimously, they shared the view that the Social Credit doctrine was conservative, even reactionary, and aimed at preserving capitalism. More specifically, Social Credit was seen as fundamentally petit-bourgeois in its orientations and projects. Given such views, it did not surprise them that Social Credit should have had such success in a prairie province characterized (falsely) as having a relatively high degree of class homogeneity and dominated by the petite bourgeoisie of "independent commodity producers," whether farmers or the urban self-employed. Indeed, they believed that it was precisely the supposedly confused members of this intermediate class, located between the bourgeoisie and the working class, who had propelled the Alberta Social Credit Party to power in 1935.

Unfortunately, despite the very wide "scientific" consensus, that interpretation gives every indication of being wrong in almost every respect. In the future, no one will be able to hold a cogent discussion of the Social Credit movement without tackling, one way or another, Edward Bell's pathbreaking re-analysis of it. His study is outstanding not only in its results, which are sharply at variance with conventional

xiv Foreword

views, but also in the exemplary nature of his efforts at empirical verification and his new interpretation of the movement.

From C.B. Macpherson's allegedly classic *Democracy in Alberta*, originally published in 1953, to the many analysts who have since adhered to his views, with at most only minor variations, one is struck by the paucity – if not the total absence – of empirical evidence that has been provided to support the received claims regarding the Social Credit movement. In sharp contrast, Professor Bell's study is striking in the rigorous, often very painstaking, efforts that he has made to empirically assess the various claims advanced previously.

Foremost in this regard is his return to the archival electoral data to ascertain the distribution of support for Social Credit and other parties in both the 1935 and the 1940 provincial elections for each of the polling subdivisions in most of the main cities in Alberta, and his mapping of those results on to areas representing various social classes in those cities. He has also assessed the support received in small towns and in the countryside – the latter as a measure of the farm vote. With no less rigour, he has scrutinized Major Douglas's statements as well as Alberta Social Credit philosophy to assess the extent to which they agreed with the characterizations of them in the extant literature. Finally, he has carefully analysed the actions and legislation of the Social Credit government between 1935 and 1940 to establish whether it really was a conservative, petit-bourgeois administration.

The author's efforts to ground his analysis empirically have not been in vain. None of his data on class voting support the assertion that the class basis of the movement's electorate was located in the petite bourgeoisie proper, or in the lower middle class as a whole, or even in the middle class in general. Nor was it located dispropor-tionately in small towns (presumably an important location for the petite bourgeoisie) and/or in purely rural agrarian areas. Instead, data for both the 1935 and 1940 elections reveal, first, that within the larger urban areas support was strongly inversely related to social class, with the working class providing particularly high levels of support, and, second, that in rural areas farmers provided strong support, although at a lower level than urban workers. As for those in small towns, their support was in fact slightly lower than in the province as a whole. Thus the movement, rather than being based in a single class, turns out to have represented a cross-class alliance of workers and farmers – which would also be the case some twenty-five years later with the Créditistes in Quebec.

As mentioned above, Professor Bell also carefully analyses both Douglas's original Social Credit doctrine and its Alberta variant in

Aberhart's movement; moreover, he also examines the beliefs that appear to have been behind the actions of the first Social Credit administration from 1935 to 1940. The interpretations he draws from that analysis are again sharply at odds with the prevailing consensus. Rather than simple conservative philosophies developed to promote the interests of the petite bourgeoisie or the capitalist system in general, he shows that these doctrines advocated radical transformations of the existing economic system, transformations that would have worked against both bourgeois and petit-bourgeois interests. Particularly interesting is the author's demonstration that, in contrast to the Progressives of the 1920s, the Alberta Social Credit movement did not originally espouse the recurrent anti-central-Canada views of many western Canadians. As for Aberhart's first administration, Professor Bell argues that it was a combination of Douglas's Social Credit projects, most of which failed, and successful implementations of social-democratic economic reforms. To be sure, it might have been helpful if the author had provided a clearer distinction between the social and economic tenets of Social Credit, but this would not have altered the validity of the criticisms he levels at previous analyses.

But if previous interpretations have so little going for them, why have they been so widely accepted? Is there an alternative explanation for the sudden rise of Social Credit and for its class bases? The first question leads the author into a brief foray into the sociology of knowledge. As for the important second question, the author, in refreshing contrast to most previous analysts, grounds his interpretation in the literature on social and political movements, stressing, in particular, the high level of rationality behind the Social Credit preferences of so many workers and farmers. (See, for example, the author's interpretation of these voters' choice of Social Credit over social democratic alternatives.) More generally, Professor Bell argues that serious economic grievances (very high levels of unemployment among workers, falling agricultural prices compounded by farmers' inability to repay their mortgages and loans); an uncomplicated ideology rooted in Christian beliefs; a charismatic leader and the conversion of his radio broadcasts from religion to politics; and an important organizational substructure, the Calgary Prophetic Bible Institute, were key determinants of the movement's ability to forge a cross-class alliance around common interests, leading to overnight electoral success. Here the reader may regret that the author did not examine some of the political factors conducive to this success and, more generally, did not provide a brief comparative analysis of this and other economic protest movements.

xvi Foreword

All in all, however, Professor Bell's contribution to our understanding of this and similar movements is invaluable. His research carries an important lesson for all of us – that we should not uncritically accept the prevailing received wisdom on many issues in the social sciences. This is a very significant book; it clearly deserves the attention of all Canadian social scientists.

Maurice Pinard
McGill University
November 1993

Acknowledgments

The author is grateful for the funding received while writing this book, in particular Social Sciences and Humanities Research Council of Canada doctoral and post-doctoral fellowships, a post-doctoral fellowship from the Calgary Institute for the Humanities, and a grant from Brescia College, University of Western Ontario, to produce the maps. Additional thanks go to the departments of sociology at McGill University and the University of Calgary, where the SSHRC fellowships were held, and to the taxpayers of Canada, who subsidize SSHRC and the country's universities.

I owe a rather large intellectual debt to Richard Hamilton. His work on the lower middle class in Germany and the United States was the inspiration for this study. Whatever merit the class analyses have in this project stems largely from his earlier insights. Professor Hamilton also provided valuable comments on previous drafts of the book.

Maurice Pinard read the entire text of this study and provided valuable critical commentary. Richard Ogmundson, Axel van den Berg, Michael R. Smith, Thomas Flanagan, and Tom Langford kindly read various chapters, offering helpful criticism and suggestions. Also to be acknowledged are the comments provided by Morton Weinfeld, Jerome Black, Donald Von Eschen, and Harry Hiller, and two anonymous reviewers selected by McGill-Queen's University Press. Copy editor Susan Kent Davidson should be commended as well for her attention to detail and matters of style.

xviii Acknowledgments

Thanks are also due to City of Calgary archivists Brian Owens and Neil Watson, who helped to locate election materials and provided extensive information on Calgary. Alex Johnston and Greg Ellis of the Galt Museum, Lethbridge, provided historical information on the neighbourhoods of that city. Donny White and Kathy Dirk of the Medicine Hat Museum and Art Gallery offered valuable historical advice concerning Medicine Hat's neighbourhoods. The staff of the Provincial Archives of Alberta, Edmonton, and the Glenbow Museum and Archives, Calgary, were most helpful as well.

A special note of gratitude goes to my wife, Jennifer Wakefield, who assisted with the word processing and, more importantly, provided the kind of support that is indispensable to human happiness.

The responsibility for the shortcomings of this study, of course, rests with the author.

Social Classes and Social Credit in Alberta

1 Introduction

The Social Credit movement in Alberta provided some of the most intriguing and controversial episodes of Canadian history. It was from the beginning a movement that evoked the strongest emotions, both positive and negative. It achieved a remarkable notoriety in the short period preceding its electoral victory in 1935 and once in power received extensive international attention.

What really captured people's imaginations was the movement's promise that it could solve the problems of the Depression. Social Credit represented one of several programs competing for acceptance in a world desperately looking for solutions. The other competitors included socialism, communism, fascism, liberalism, and conservatism, as well as combinations of these. Much of the English-speaking world watched to see if Social Credit in Alberta could offer any hope.

The Social Credit doctrine was a major part of the controversy. To some it was an epochal scientific discovery that would finally bring about an end to "poverty in the midst of plenty." To others it was merely the utopian maunderings of an eccentric British military officer. Yet somehow even the most sceptical were drawn to it.

Other facets of the Alberta movement contributed to the fascination. A fiery lay preacher orchestrating a mass movement through an exciting new medium – radio – was a spectacle in itself. The persona of Alberta Social Credit leader William Aberhart aroused much interest as well. Movement supporters looked upon him with the reverence and awe due a prophet or saviour, while those opposed claimed he was a charlatan who threatened to immobilize the province under a blizzard of worthless credit certificates.

In addition to the immediate popular interest, Social Credit attracted the attention of intellectuals who endeavoured to chronicle and make theoretical sense of the movement. In the late 1940s the Canadian Social Science Research Council, with funding from the Rockefeller Foundation, sponsored a series of ten full-length monographs dealing with the background and development of the movement.[1] Social Credit became the topic of further books as well as myriad journal articles, commentaries, dissertations, and theses, and continues to generate academic interest to this day.

The legacy of these studies is rich. The authors writing on Social Credit have made valiant, even heroic efforts to capture the essence of this era of Canadian life, and students of Canadian society are forever in their debt. None the less, it will be argued here that some of these works were misguided in some crucial respects.

This study seeks to determine the nature of the Social Credit movement and offer a new theoretical interpretation of it by examining three interrelated elements: the Social Credit ideology, the class basis of its mass support, and the actions taken by the first Social Credit government. The interpretation offered here challenges many of the major works on the movement, but none more than C.B. Macpherson's *Democracy in Alberta* (1962 [1953]).

Macpherson's monograph has been very influential in our understanding of Alberta politics and prairie society in general. Shortly after *Democracy in Alberta* was published in 1953, a reviewer stated that it "belongs among the best books yet written by Canadian social scientists" (Ward 1955, 61). Twenty years later it was described as "the best political analysis in the Marxist tradition undertaken in Canada" (Panitch 1977, 10) and "the best historical explanation of the rise of political movements in Alberta" (Long and Quo 1972, 24). In a commemorative essay following the author's death in 1987, *Democracy in Alberta* was referred to as "a classic account of the contradictions of the petit-bourgeoisie in liberal societies" (Drache and Kroker 1987, 24). The book has recently been translated into Japanese.

Macpherson views the rise of Social Credit as part of an ongoing reaction of Alberta's petite bourgeoisie (composed mainly of independent farmers) to its "quasi-colonial" position in Canada's economic and political system (1962, 6–10). Exploited by the railway, manufacturing, and financial interests of central Canada, Alberta's petite bourgeoisie, he argues, acted in a fashion typical of this class by pressing for Social Credit (219–30). Macpherson claims that

5   Introduction

although Social Credit was ostensibly a radical movement, the petit-bourgeois class position of its supporters and activists predisposed them to take a conservative position on the issue of property rights. This limited the goal of the movement to improving the petite bourgeoisie's position within the capitalist system. A truly radical movement, having a different class base, he suggests, would have been free to call capitalism itself into question. In Macpherson's words, the Social Credit movement was that of a "quasi-colonial society of independent producers, in rebellion against eastern imperialism but not against the property system" (220).[2] The petite bourgeoisie was able to rule Alberta, he explains, because the province was a "community of independent commodity producers" with a "relatively homogeneous" class structure (21, 205, 236). Since no other classes existed in sufficient numbers to clash with the petite bourgeoisie, it was relatively easy for it to hold power.

Macpherson's work was the star that many others followed with regard to Social Credit's ideology, popular class basis, and behaviour in office. With some notable exceptions, many writers have adopted Macpherson's interpretation of Social Credit as a conservative, petit-bourgeois movement bent on redressing regional grievances.

Macpherson's portrayal of the Social Credit movement is based on a body of theoretical literature on the petite bourgeoisie that has its origins in the *Communist Manifesto* (Marx and Engels 1967 [1848], 88–91). Essentially, this school of thought maintains that as capitalism develops, the petite bourgeoisie (self-employed people hiring few or no employees apart from family members) finds that it cannot compete with the big bourgeoisie, given the latter's capital advantages, economies of scale, use of machinery, and so forth. Driven out of business by the bourgeoisie, members of the petite bourgeoisie "sink gradually into the proletariat" (88). The recognition that they are losing their once-predominant position in society through this downward mobility is said to create feelings of insecurity and alienation. The psychological malaise becomes manifest in staunchly conservative attitudes and a desire to reverse the social changes that are undermining their position. This leads the petite bourgeoisie to become fundamentally opposed to the central features of advanced capitalist society, such as the growth of big corporations, trade unionism, and government "interference" in the economy. Macpherson, for example, argues that the various segments of the petite bourgeoisie "are all in varying degree vestigial," and that members of this class "have a delusive understanding of the nature of society, of the economy, and of their place in it. They conceive society in their own image, not realizing or not admitting that the day of that society is past" (1962, 225, 226). Proponents of the theory sometimes maintain that the petite bourgeoisie vacillates between radicalism and conservatism, arguing that its intermediary position between labour and capital creates constant confusion as to its true interests in a mature capitalist society.

Lenin (1972 [1895]) adopted the Marxian view of the petite bourgeoisie in his analysis of the Narodniks, a movement active in Czarist Russia. The theory became increasingly popular among European scholars in the inter-war period, especially in Weimar Germany. Many writers of this era grouped the lower-income, white-collar occupations together with the independent petite bourgeoisie under the rubric "lower middle class," to which was attributed all the characteristics of the petite bourgeoisie proper. A large body of literature emerged that interpreted Nazism as an attempt by the lower middle class to forestall its decline in advanced capitalism.[3] In the 1950s and early 1960s North American writers used the theory in an effort to explain a number of right-wing extremist movements in the United States (e.g., Trow 1958).

Several writers have challenged the idea that the petite bourgeoisie is destined to disappear, but virtually all now agree that it has declined in size relative to the other classes. Some recent Marxist writings provide a variety of new definitions for the various class categories, although the original formulations are still popular. The attitudinal and behavioural traits generally attributed to the petite bourgeoisie – either staunch conservatism or a confused oscillation between conservatism and radicalism – have remained remarkably true to the original position as both Marxist and non-Marxist scholars continue to uphold the theory[4] with few exceptions. The exceptions include Richard Hamilton (1972, chap. 5; 1975, chaps. 2 and 3; 1982), who, unlike most proponents of the theory, brings a wealth of evidence to bear on the issue.

The works interpreting Social Credit in Alberta as a petit-bourgeois movement, then, should be viewed in the context of the established intellectual tradition on this class. Broadly speaking, the movement has been viewed as a Canadian manifestation of petit-bourgeois alienation and confusion.[5]

It often happens that ideas gain considerable prominence in the social sciences without ever having been examined empirically. Theories pertaining to the class basis of the Social Credit movement are a case in point. The situation is rather like a group of early cartographers agreeing that a particular river drains into the Great Lakes without anyone's ever having taken a voyage to the river's end. Yet under such circumstances, strange things may often be encountered

7   Introduction

once the first voyage is underway. This study was conducted under similar circumstances. For the first time, extensive empirical evidence was brought to bear on the issue of the class basis of Social Credit, and unexpected things were discovered. In fact, the map of Alberta's class structure and class politics in the 1930s may have to be redrawn.

The next chapter presents a brief history of Alberta to 1935, placing Social Credit in the larger context of the province's historical development. Chapter 3 reviews the literature pertaining to the class basis of the movement's popular support. Some preliminary empirical findings are reported here that reveal serious problems with most accounts of the movement's popular class basis.

Chapter 4 examines the social philosophy of the founder of Social Credit, Major C.H. Douglas. An analysis of Douglasism is provided because, to understand Alberta Social Credit, one must first understand Douglas. In chapter 4 I argue that part of the reason Alberta Social Credit has been misunderstood is that many analysts have misunderstood Douglas. Chapter 5 discusses the Social Credit doctrine as interpreted and propagated by Alberta Social Credit leader William Aberhart. Here again the standard positions taken in the literature are seen to be problematic.

An ecological analysis of the results of the 1935 breakthrough election is performed in chapter 6 in order to arrive at a measure of the pattern of class voting. The suspicions aroused in earlier chapters regarding the class basis of popular support for Social Credit are borne out by this analysis. Chapter 7 examines Social Credit's first term of office, comparing the government's actions with existing theoretical accounts of its goals and motives. In chapter 7 it is suggested that the standard portrayal of Social Credit as an anti-imperialist government dedicated to the upholding of property rights seriously distorts the real *raison d'être* of the first Aberhart administration. In chapter 8 the results of the 1940 election are analysed, providing a second look at the class basis of Social Credit's mass support. The final chapter offers an alternative theoretical interpretation of the movement.

Although Social Credit remained in power in Alberta from 1935 to 1971, this study does not examine the period after the 1940 election. The decision to conclude the analysis at this point was taken because the purpose of this study is to analyse the Social Credit *movement*. By 1940 Social Credit was well on its way to institutionalization, resembling a conventional political party more than a popular movement.[6]

I begin, then, with a brief history of Alberta.

2 A Brief History of Alberta to 1935

The pages that follow review, in broad outline, the political history of Alberta to 1935. The chapter is designed mainly for those who are unfamiliar with western Canadian history, in particular the immediate circumstances surrounding the rise of the Social Credit movement. Chapter 7 examines the period from 1935 to 1940, Social Credit's first term of office.

EARLY HISTORY

When Social Credit formed the government in 1935, the province of Alberta was only thirty years old, although the region had been a part of Canada since 1870. Its human history, however, dates back several thousand years. Native peoples had lived in the area for at least eleven thousand years prior to the arrival of Europeans, hunting the bison that once roamed the great inland plains of North America (MacGregor 1972, 13).

The first whites to enter what is now Alberta were fur traders who arrived in 1754. In the latter half of the eighteenth century, Hudson's Bay and North West Company fur traders established several trading stations in the region, such as Fort Edmonton and Rocky Mountain House (Palmer and Palmer 1990, 13–14). The non-native population remained sparse until a major wave of immigration began in the closing years of the nineteenth century.

A crucial turning-point in the history of what came to be western Canada was reached with the ceding of Rupert's Land and the North-

West Territories to the Canadian government in 1870. This vast tract of land, which included all areas draining into Hudson Bay plus all British lands to the north and west, excluding British Columbia, had been under the domain of the Hudson's Bay Company. Since the HBC's main interest in the region was the fur trade, its presence led to little European settlement and no immediate threat to native people. All this was to change after 1870, when the Canadian government embarked on its policy of railway building and settlement in the west.

The arrival of the Canadian Pacific Railway in 1883 led to the development of railway towns such as Medicine Hat, and greatly expanded the commerce and population of Calgary and Edmonton. The commercial coal mines that had begun operations near present-day Lethbridge a few years earlier also received a boost from the presence of the railway. Beef was needed to feed the North-West Mounted Police troops stationed in the area as well as the men building the railway, which provided the impetus for ranching in southern Alberta, where large tracts of land are ideal for cattle raising. Ranching remained the main economic activity in the region until an influx of immigrant farmers finally outnumbered the ranchers around the turn of the century (Palmer and Palmer 1990, 51–61).

In 1875 the area that would become the province of Alberta had a total population of only 30,000. By 1901, after four years of vigorous effort to bring immigrants to the west by Canada's minister of the Interior Clifford Sifton, the population had more than doubled, reaching 73,022. Within another five years it had doubled again (MacGregor 1972, 13).

PROVINCEHOOD

The increase in population was accompanied by a drive to achieve provincial status, which was granted in 1905. Full provincial status was denied, however, as the federal government retained jurisdiction over natural resources. This was to remain a sore point until 1930, when federal authorities finally transferred control over natural resources to the province.[1]

The Liberal Party formed the first Alberta government, under the leadership of Alexander Rutherford. According to L.G. Thomas (1959, 205), the Liberal victory was more the result of there being a Liberal government in Ottawa than strong support for Liberal policy. Perhaps more so than today, having ties to the ruling party in Ottawa made it easier to become a beneficiary of federal largesse. The only serious competitors to the Liberal Party at this time were the Conservatives, who received 37 per cent of the vote in 1905 compared to the Liberals' 58 per cent (Alberta 1983, 10).

The first decade for the fledgling province was one of economic boom and continued rapid immigration. Alberta's Liberal government, which won re-election in 1909, 1913, and 1917, set about establishing the provincial infrastructure, most notably guaranteeing bonds for railroad expansion and setting up a provincially owned telephone system. Schools, hospitals, and other community services also had to be constructed. Some idea of the magnitude of the task at hand can be got by considering again the growth in the province's population. By 1914 Alberta's population had reached about 470,000 (MacGregor 1972, 196), almost sixteen times what it had been twenty years earlier. The rapid immigration made the province's population ethnically diverse, as native peoples and settlers of French and British origin were joined by immigrants from Scandinavian countries, eastern and western Europe, southern Europe, Asia, the United States, and other areas. The rapid development had another important effect on the province – it produced a high level of public and private debt. This problem was to weigh most heavily upon Albertans in the 1920s and 1930s.

Rapid population growth and economic expansion are often accompanied by government scandal. Alberta proved to be no exception. In 1910 the opposition Conservatives alleged that some Liberal members of the legislature had personally profited from the sale of the railway bonds guaranteed by the province. The scandal split the Liberal Party and resulted in the resignation of Premier Rutherford, although a royal commission later concluded that financial mismanagement rather than corruption had taken place. The episode reduced the Liberals' popularity in the province, but not enough to bring about a change of government.

The success of the Liberal Party in Alberta has been attributed to a number of factors. In addition to the ability to dispense patronage, the federal Liberals had overseen the mass immigration to the west beginning in 1896, which tended to make the party popular among immigrants. Also, the party's policy of free trade endeared it to farmers, who maintained that high tariffs lowered their standard of living. These policies contrasted with those of the Conservatives, who favoured high tariffs and expressed some misgivings about non-British immigration (Palmer and Palmer 1990, 136–7).

The early years of provincehood also witnessed Alberta's first oil boom. In 1914 at Turner Valley, near Calgary, the Dingman well began producing oil, which led to an investment frenzy involving the creation of over five hundred oil companies and a capitalization

11   Alberta to 1935

exceeding $83 million, although fewer than fifty companies actually drilled for oil (Foran 1978, 124). This established Calgary as the administrative and financial centre of the provincial oil industry, which facilitated the spectacular and much larger oil boom that was set off in Alberta some thirty years later. Prior to the Turner Valley discovery, both natural and synthetic gas had been produced commercially in southern Alberta.

As the number of farmers in the province increased, it became apparent that the concerns of farmers required greater political representation. In 1909 two rival farm organizations, the Alberta Farmers' Association and the Society of Equity, merged to form "The United Farmers of Alberta, 'Our Motto Equity,'" better known as the UFA. In its early years the UFA did not advocate direct political action for the organization but acted instead as a farmers' lobby to the ruling provincial Liberals. It achieved considerable success in this regard. According to L.G. Thomas (1959, 206) the UFA convention had a stronger voice in provincial affairs than the Alberta legislature.

A move to direct political involvement on the part of farm organizations began in 1917, when the Alberta Non-Partisan League, patterned after a North Dakota movement of the same name, fielded four candidates in the provincial election, two of whom were elected. The league had a "strong socialist flavour" (Thomas 1959, 178), advocating regional economic development through co-operatives and government-owned industries. UFA locals supported the NPL in 1917 and demanded that the UFA executive implement a policy of direct involvement in electoral politics, to which the leadership reluctantly assented. In 1919 the Non-Partisan League formally merged with the UFA.

The UFA's political activities formed part of the larger Progressive movement in Canada. The Progressives achieved their greatest successes in the period immediately after the First World War, when many issues that had been developing before the war again came to the fore. The market price of agricultural commodities dropped in the years after the war, while the costs of farm production increased. The movement advocated the removal of import tariffs on manufactured goods and the reduction of freight rates for farm produce. If enacted, such policies would have allowed farmers to purchase farm implements and consumer goods at a cheaper price and given them a higher return on the goods they sold.

The Progressives also came to believe that the two traditional parties, the Liberals and Conservatives, were the instruments of big-business interests in central Canada and that neither party would ever represent the interests of farmers. They also developed a critique of the party system itself, proposing that it be replaced with a system of delegate democracy wherein those elected to Parliament would voice the concerns of their constituents without an obligation to support a political party. People in the Progressive movement often supported various other reform movements, such as those favouring women's suffrage and prohibition.

The first electoral victory for the Progressives came in 1919, when the United Farmers of Ontario, with the help of the Labour members of the legislature, formed the provincial government. This was followed by a victory for the United Farmers of Alberta in 1921 and the United Farmers of Manitoba in 1922. On the federal scene the Progressives' best showing was in the 1921 election, in which they won 65 of the 235 seats in the House of Commons (Morton 1950, 128).

A major achievement of the UFA's first term of office was the establishment of the Alberta Wheat Pool. During the First World War, the federal government had marketed Canadian grain using its own agencies, first the Board of Grain Supervisors and then the Canadian Wheat Board, in order to co-ordinate the distribution of foodstuffs to allied nations. This proved to be very beneficial to farmers, giving them a consistently high price for their produce, but the practice was discontinued in 1920. The Alberta Pool was designed to have the same effect as the federal organizations by once more obviating the vagaries involved in dealing with the Winnipeg Grain Exchange. Wheat pools operated under the slogan "orderly marketing" (Richards and Pratt 1979, 29). Farmers deposited their wheat with the Pool and received a partial payment for it. When the wheat was sold they received a second payment, the size of which was determined by the selling price of the wheat. The establishment of the Alberta Pool in 1923 was followed by good crop years and comparatively high grain prices (MacGregor 1972, 255).

The UFA's zeal in opposing the party system waned after a few years in office. Party solidarity and cabinet rule began to replace delegate democracy as the de facto system of government in Alberta. Another significant change occurred after the UFA had been in power for some time: the party chose a non-farmer to be its leader. John Brownlee, an established Calgary lawyer who had been attorney general in the first UFA administration, replaced Herbert Greenfield, the original UFA premier, who had served for four years. The UFA under Brownlee won re-election in 1926, taking 43 of 61 seats with 40 per cent of the popular vote (Alberta 1983, 12). The Liberals took seven seats with 26 per cent, the Conservatives five with 22 per cent, and Labor five with 8 per cent (12).

13   Alberta to 1935

The second UFA term of office was characterized by prosperous times until 1929, when the price of wheat declined sharply. This had a disastrous effect on the Pool, as it had paid farmers more than it could get for the crop that year. Other areas of the economy also began to suffer. None the less, Brownlee's government guaranteed the debts of the Pool and otherwise retained enough public confidence to win the 1930 election. The party's popularity declined slightly to 39 per cent; it took 39 of 63 seats (Alberta 1983, 12).

The economic decline was, of course, the beginning of the Depression. As it deepened, the government came under increasing pressure to take steps to end it. It was inundated with schemes from people claiming that they had the answer to the province's economic woes. One plan that the government learned it could not ignore was Social Credit, popularized by Calgary high school principal and radio evangelist William Aberhart.

ORIGINS AND DEVELOPMENT OF THE
SOCIAL CREDIT MOVEMENT

Aberhart had arrived in Calgary from his native province of Ontario in 1910, taking a teaching position in a city school. He then served as principal of various schools until his appointment as principal of Crescent Heights High School in 1915, where he was to remain until he became premier in 1935 (Irving 1959, 13).

Aberhart had always had a fervent interest in religious activities and continued these pursuits as a lay preacher in Calgary. A spirited and charismatic orator, he had little difficulty in drawing crowds to his meetings, although his interpretations of scripture were often controversial. He was associated with a number of fundamentalist churches before he and his colleagues established the Calgary Prophetic Bible Institute in 1927, which later became the headquarters for the Social Credit movement.

In 1925 Aberhart made the fateful decision to broadcast his sermons over a Calgary radio station. His programs had a large audience, reaching as far north as Edmonton and into parts of British Columbia, Saskatchewan, and Manitoba, as well as into some of the northern states of the American midwest. Mixing his Bible message with plenty of homespun humour, Aberhart became a radio celebrity.

Before the Depression Aberhart had shown little interest in politics, but as conditions worsened he began to search for a solution to the crisis. Like so many others, he was appalled by the economic devastation wreaked upon the province and the rest of the world at this time. Things were so bad that plummeting prices for agricutural products caused the net income per farm in Alberta to drop from $1,975 in 1927 to only $54 in 1933 (Barr 1974, 20). The situation for farmers was particularly serious in areas suffering from drought. In southeastern Alberta as in adjacent parts of Saskatchewan, years of drought made conditions so desperate that the Canadian Red Cross found it necessary to conduct a national drive for food and clothing for the people in this area (20). Life in the cities was harsh as well. Unemployment in Calgary and Edmonton was approximately 25 per cent, while those fortunate enough to work often did so at very low wages. Most cities had areas in which large groups of unemployed people lived in makeshift shacks. "Relief," the social assistance available for the destitute, was barely enough to satisfy basic needs and often required that the recipient perform hard labour. The social stigma of being on relief was enormous as well.

These problems were compounded by debt. Many Albertans could not meet mortgage payments on their homes or farms, or could not pay back the loans they had taken out to purchase farm machinery. In addition to private debt there was heavy public debt – about half the provincial government's annual revenues in the mid-1930s were required to pay the interest on the provincial debt. It should also be made clear, as Irving (1959, 335–9) illustrates, that these physical hardships were accompanied by psychological turmoil, as for many Albertans the Depression was a profoundly humiliating experience.

After being coaxed by a fellow teacher into reading a book on Social Credit, Aberhart became convinced that the program originated by British engineer Major C.H. Douglas could be used to bring prosperity back to Alberta. As we shall see in greater depth in chapter 4, Douglas claimed that economic crises were caused by a lack of purchasing power on the part of the consuming public. He argued, among other things, that there is never enough money in circulation to buy all the goods and services on the market, suggesting that additional funds in the form of "social credit" be issued to make up the difference between the existing money supply and the value of all items available. This would, according to Douglas, increase the standard of living of the general public and allow the economy to thrive and expand to its true potential. Douglas also claimed that the banks were, by far, the most powerful and exploitative organizations in the world.

In 1932 Aberhart took the dry monetary theories of Major Douglas and expressed them in popular form. Part of their popularization involved the claim that twenty-five dollars a month could be paid to each adult in the province under a Social Credit system. While

15   Alberta to 1935

twenty-five dollars a month would be a pittance today, it was a considerable amount of money in the 1930s. As Barr (1974, 57) points out, at that time eggs sold for five cents per dozen, roasts for seventy-five cents, accommodation could be rented for nine dollars a month, and men's made-to-measure three-piece suits cost about twenty-five dollars.

Using his professional training as a teacher and the enthusiasm he generated for his religious broadcasts, Aberhart organized Social Credit study groups that were to spread throughout the province. He published Social Credit booklets and, most importantly, carried the discussion of Social Credit into his radio broadcasts. Aberhart's original plan was to remain aloof from party politics; he wanted existing parties to take up the Social Credit cause and urged his followers to support only those politicians in favour of the scheme.

A groundswell of support for Social Credit developed among several groups. Rank and file members of the UFA as well as some party officials expressed keen interest. The provincial Liberal leader took the position that Douglas's system should be investigated, while the Alberta Federation of Labor demanded that Douglas Social Credit advocates be allowed to speak before members of the provincial legislature. Even some newspapers thought the plan should be examined, although they expressed some scepticism (Irving 1959, 86–7).

Although this was a promising beginning, it became apparent that no political party was about to embark on a Social Credit crusade. The UFA government called several witnesses, including both Aberhart and Douglas, before a legislative committee to consider the Social Credit plan, but after patiently listening to weeks of testimony it decided to take no action.

The decision to ignore Social Credit did not meet with unanimous approval from government supporters. In fact, by 1934 the UFA was badly fragmented into a number of competing factions. The premier and his Cabinet wanted to continue with the status quo, seeing little merit in any major change of policy. A monetary reform group including UFA MP William Irvine wanted Social Credit to be part of the UFA's election platform. A third faction was comprised of committed socialists who thought the Douglas plan was worthless; they favoured the social democracy of the Co-operative Commonwealth Federation, which UFA activists had helped to establish at the Calgary meetings of 1932 and the Regina conference of 1933. The UFA annual convention of January 1933 voted in favour of affiliation with the CCF (Johnson 1979, 97), and the socialists carried the day at the 1934 convention as well by passing a motion endorsing the CCF (Irving 1959, 69). The division within the UFA caused by pro-Social Crediters was evident at the latter convention, however, as a motion demanding an investigation into Douglasism was passed as well.

In addition to fragmentation over policy, the government was rocked by a scandal in which Premier Brownlee was accused of seducing a young secretary from the attorney general's office. Although some people believed the premier had been falsely accused (see Barr 1974, 32–6), public opinion apparently favoured the young woman. Brownlee resigned the premiership in the summer of 1934 as a result of the scandal, to be replaced by R.G. Reid. From this point on, the government's tarnished reputation stood in stark contrast to that of the pious Aberhart, who for many Albertans personified moral rectitude.

A final attempt by Aberhart to get official support from the UFA for a Social Credit scheme was made as late as January 1935, only seven months before the 1935 election. He made an impassioned speech before the UFA convention but could not convince a majority of the delegates to adopt his Social Credit program. The UFA later hired Major Douglas as "principal reconstruction adviser" to the government, but this was seen by many as a token gesture designed to silence the demands for the implementation of Social Credit.

The other parties also refused to make Social Credit the cornerstone of their policy. The Liberals kept promising to study it and avoided any direct condemnation of it. Labor would not jump on Aberhart's bandwagon either but instead, like the UFA, affiliated with the CCF. The Conservatives were unequivocally opposed to Social Credit and made this clear from the beginning.

In order to bring his plans to fruition, the Alberta Social Credit leader had no choice but to organize his own party. He did not have to start from scratch, however, as by 1935 the network of Social Credit study groups that he had started had already expanded into large portions of the province. Aberhart also had a very able lieutenant in the young Ernest Manning, a graduate of the Prophetic Bible Institute, and he had his radio broadcasts.

The future premier used all his resources to full advantage. The radio he used relentlessly. The other parties, particlarly the UFA, also put their best speakers on the airwaves, but none, it seems, could match Aberhart's rhetorical skills. Aberhart also saw to it that Social Credit speakers continued their tours of the province, and he kept up his own hectic schedule of personal appearances. In a controversial move, he arranged for the party's candidates to be selected by an advisory board that included himself rather than having them elected by constituency associations. Under this candidate-selection process, each riding association presented a small number of prospective candidates to the board, which would then pick the persons to represent the party in the election. This procedure had been vigorously debated, but none the less approved, by Social Credit conventions. Aberhart drew harsh criticism from his opponents for this method of selecting candidates, which they claimed was dictatorial.

Social Crediters enjoyed many advantages that were not of their own making. To begin with, they were challenging incumbents who had been in power for five years of depression. With these years of futility behind them, it was difficult for the UFA to convince voters that Social Credit could do a worse job of governing the province. Also, the UFA failure to improve economic matters, coupled with their affiliation with the CCF, made it difficult for other socialist-oriented parties such as Labor to make any headway with the public. The socialists had been in power for some time, it was believed, yet the condition of the province was showing no improvement.

Moreover, both the UFA and Labor had shown little sympathy for protesters voicing their opposition to the way the UFA government was handling the economic crisis. This was revealed in the parties' responses to a large hunger march in Edmonton in 1932, which drew people from various regions of the province. The provincial authorities tried to prevent participants from entering the city, while the Labor-dominated city council denied the marchers a permit to stage their demonstration. Some two thousand people went ahead with the march anyway, only to be "viciously attacked by the police" (Finkel 1984, 119). Literally adding insult to injury, the *Alberta Labor News*, the official organ of the Alberta Federation of Labor, then denounced the hunger marchers (119). Another factor that worked to the advantage of the Social Crediters was the general climate of opinion in favour of monetary reform in the early 1930s, a matter that will be examined more fully in chapter 9.

A final issue concerning the campaign of 1935 to be discussed at this point involves the press. Apart from an early period of curiosity about Social Credit, the major newspapers in the province were openly hostile to the movement. Near the end of the campaign, front-page editorials were published outlining the chaos that would result from the implementation of social credit. The *Edmonton Bulletin* (17 August 1935, 1), for example, referred to social credit as "the craziest and most fallacious scheme ever put before an electorate in any part of the British Empire." Political cartoons also appeared on the front pages of the major dailies, lampooning the provincial Social Credit leader. Irving (1959, 326) states that in the month leading up to the election, not a single editorial favourable to the movement was published in any of the six dailies in Alberta. The attacks did not have the effect intended, however, as they made a martyr of Aberhart; he and his followers interpreted the abuse as evidence that high finance was desperately trying to kill the movement.

When election day arrived, Social Credit scored a decisive victory. It won 56 of 63 seats, taking 54 per cent of the popular vote. The Liberals took five seats with 23 per cent, the Conservatives two with 6 per cent. The UFA did not elect a single member but received 11 per cent of the vote. Labor also lost all legislative representation, receiving only 2 per cent of all votes cast (Alberta 1983, 13).

Before considering in depth the program that Social Credit advocated and analysing of the pattern of class voting, it is worthwhile to review the leading academic positions regarding the class basis of the movement's popular support. This is the topic of the next chapter.

3 The Conventional Wisdom

Here I shall examine three claims regarding the class basis of mass support for Social Credit in Alberta: that the movement was essentially a farmers' movement, that it was a petit-bourgeois movement, and that the movement had a cross-class, lower-middle–working-class appeal. The petit-bourgeois thesis will be especially closely scrutinized since it is often claimed that Social Credit appealed primarily to members of this class, that Douglasism and the Aberhartite adaptation of it were essentially "petit-bourgeois ideology," and that the movement's behaviour in office was distinctly petit-bourgeois. My main concern in this chapter will be with the quality of the evidence, if any, provided to substantiate the claims pertaining to Social Credit's popular class basis.

SOCIAL CREDIT PORTRAYED AS A FARMERS' MOVEMENT

The earliest academic accounts of Social Credit in Alberta suggest that the movement was essentially a farmers' protest organized to deal with the economic crisis brought about by the rapid decline in the price of wheat. A.R.M. Lower, for example, writes that "through countless [Social Credit] 'study groups' the Albertan farmers, hopeless of a solution from Ottawa, had set out to find their own cure for their ills" (1946, 518).

Social Credit is also portrayed as a farmers' movement by S.M. Lipset in *Agrarian Socialism* (1971 [1950]). He argues that Alberta,

North Dakota, and Saskatchewan, which he describes as three "wheat areas," "elected agrarian radical governments as a result of the depression" (153–4). Lipset claims that "Social Credit, the NPL [Non-Partisan League], and the CCF were like responses to very similar conditions. Each movement represented an attack by western farmers on the economic power of eastern big business and sought to preserve their economic and social status by preventing foreclosures of farm mortgages" (154).

Neither Lower nor Lipset offers any evidence that support for the movement was restricted to farmers, or that farmers accepted Social Credit in disproportionate numbers relative to people in other occupations. Also, since no other occupational group is mentioned in these accounts, the reader is led to assume that non-agrarian classes constituted only an insignificant proportion of the class structure. But the stereotypical image of Alberta in the 1930s as a province made up almost entirely of farmers seriously distorts the real picture of the province's class composition. Farm proprietors, including unpaid family workers, made up less than half (46 per cent) of the male work-force in Alberta in 1931. If paid farm labourers are added to this category, which would then include all agricultural occupations, the total would be 56 per cent (Canada 1936, 579).[1] To be sure, this is a large portion of the work-force, but we should not disregard what it leaves out. It does not follow from these figures that all movements in the province at this time were necessarily *farm* movements. In sum, those arguing that Social Credit was a mass movement of agrarians do not provide evidence for this position.

SOCIAL CREDIT PORTRAYED AS A PETIT-BOURGEOIS MOVEMENT

An early association of Social Credit with the petite bourgeoisie was made in 1933 by Maurice Dobb, who claimed that the British Social Credit movement had the effect of "canalizing *petit-bourgeois* discontent with capitalism, instead of into revolutionary politics based on a Marxist understanding of the process of history, harmlessly against certain sham 'bogeys'" (1933, 556). Dobb's piece, which includes no substantiating evidence regarding the movement's class base, foreshadowed the works that were to appear later on Social Credit in Alberta.[2]

Social Credit in Alberta was not treated as a petit-bourgeois movement, in the sense that it was explicitly interpreted in terms of the received theory of this class, until Macpherson's *Democracy in Alberta*

21 The Conventional Wisdom

was published in 1953. Since Macpherson is the leading theorist in this school, a close look at his work is useful.

One of Macpherson's first tasks in presenting the petit-bourgeois thesis is to demonstrate that Alberta, like the other prairie provinces, had a class structure substantially different from the other regions of the country by virtue of its relatively large petite bourgeoisie. He defines the latter as "those whose living comes neither from employing labour nor from selling the disposal of their labour" (1962, 225). He also uses the term "independent commodity producers" to describe this class in the context of the prairie provinces. "Independent commodity producers" are "farmers and farmers' sons working on the family farm, and those in other occupations working on their own account" (15–16).

Using census data, Macpherson establishes that farmers made up 32 per cent of the gainfully occupied population of Alberta in both 1931 and 1941. He adds to this figure unpaid family workers on the farm, which raises these percentages to 42 for 1931 and 41 for 1941.[3] The non-agricultural petite bourgeoisie for these years, he states, constituted 7 per cent of those gainfully employed. When these are added to the farmers and unpaid family workers, he arrives at raw totals of 49 and 48 per cent of the labour force engaged in "independent commodity production" for 1931 and 1941 respectively.

However, Macpherson questions whether all farmers in Alberta should be placed in the "independent commodity producer" category, since some were subsistence farmers not producing goods for the market and some hired farm labour to produce the goods they sold. He estimates that normally only 5 per cent of all farms were subsistence farms and that another 5 per cent hired a sufficient amount of labour to be excluded from his definition of "independent commodity producer." He subtracts 10 per cent of the 32 per cent of the work-force who were farm proprietors to account for this, which reduces the latter percentage to 29. His adjusted figure for the proportion of the work-force that was petit-bourgeois in 1941 is 45 per cent – 29 per cent farm proprietors, 9 per cent unpaid family workers, and 7 per cent non-agricultural self-employed (Macpherson 1962, 19 n 18). He summarizes his breakdown of the Alberta work force as follows:

In the whole economy of Alberta, independent commodity producers (farmers and others) have, until 1941, outnumbered industrial employees, the former being about 45 per cent, the latter 41 per cent, of the gainfully occupied population in 1941. This is sufficiently different from the prevalent proportion in Canada as a whole, where independent producers were less

22 Social Classes and Social Credit in Alberta

Table 3.1
Macpherson's Breakdown of the Alberta Work-Force

	1931 %	1941 %
PETITE BOURGEOISIE		
Petit-bourgeois farm proprietors	29	29
Unpaid family-farm workers	10	9
Non-agricultural petite bourgeoisie	7[a]	7[b]
Total petite bourgeoisie	46.0	45.0
OTHERS		
Industrial employees	41.0	41.0
Paid farm labourers	9.0	8.0
Non-farm employers	1.5[c]	1.5[c]
Subsistence farmers	1.6[d]	1.6[d]
Farmers hiring substantial amounts of labour	1.6[d]	1.6[d]
Totals	100.7	98.7

Source: Macpherson 1962, 15, 19 n 18. Percentages do not add up to 100 because some figures have been approximated from the text.

[a] Given as "from 6 to 7 per cent" (15).

[b] Given as "from 6 to 7 per cent" on 15 and as "7 per cent" on 19 n 18.

[c] Given as "between 1 and 2 per cent" (15).

[d] Macpherson states that in 1931 and 1941, farm proprietors made up 32 per cent of the work-force (15). His estimate that normally 5 per cent of all farms are subsistence farms and another 5 per cent hire substantial amounts of labour was used to arrive at the 1.6 per cent figure given here (5 per cent of 32 is 1.6).

than 30 per cent and industrial employees some 60 per cent, that we should not be surprised to find some difference in political behaviour. (20)

Macpherson defines "industrial employees" as "wage and salary workers in every occupation except agriculture" (15). In order to give a more complete picture of Macpherson's depiction of Alberta's class composition, Table 3.1 was constructed from the figures he cites.

A number of observations should be made at this point. The first pertains to Macpherson's definition of the key terms used in his analysis. When one encounters the term "independent commodity producers" in the context of the Alberta of the 1930s, one naturally thinks of *agricultural* producers. But it must be emphasized that he also includes the non-agricultural petite bourgeoisie in this class.[4] This latter group includes merchants, repair-shop owners, some independent professionals, etc. To call such people "commodity producers" is a rather curious use of language. And as we shall see

23   The Conventional Wisdom

below, it has led some readers of Macpherson to believe that the term "independent commodity producers" includes only farmers.

It is important to consider the non-agricultural petite bourgeoisie for another reason. According to Macpherson, the petite bourgeoisie as a whole is heterogeneous and lacks "any consciousness of class" (1962, 226). He adds, however:

What is true of the whole heterogeneous class is not necessarily true of one fairly homogeneous section of it.

... The western farmers, being more homogeneous than the *petite-bourgeoisie* as a whole, have been able to organize both politically and economically to promote their immediate interests, and in the course of this organization they have developed a vigorous consciousness of common interests. But it is an agrarian consciousness, not a class consciousness; it emphasizes the common interests of agrarian producers and their difference from all other producers.   (227)

Much of Macpherson's discussion of class is couched in terms of the western *farmer* (220–30). Although he states that the Social Credit movement "spoke directly to townsmen as well as to farmers" (3), he makes no attempt to account for the politics of the restaurateur, shopkeeper, or any other element of the non-agrarian petite bourgeoisie. The reader would do well to remember that Macpherson's figures indicate that the agrarian petite bourgeoisie (including unpaid family members) made up only 39 per cent of the work-force in Alberta in 1931.

Macpherson uses another term that may be misleading. This is "industrial employees," which as mentioned above he defines as "wage and salary workers in every occupation except agriculture." This term and its definition may confuse for two reasons. First, the use of the word "workers" in the definition may lead some to equate "industrial employees" with "working class," which would be erroneous if the latter is defined as all employees doing manual work. Macpherson's "industrial employees" includes not only the non-farm working class but also bank employees, school teachers, civil servants, and all other non-manual employees in both the public and private sectors. Secondly, as Macpherson's "industrial employees" category includes all people employed in the public sector and in financial institutions, it is not confined to those employed in *industry*. To reiterate, this term includes *all* non-farm employees.

Also, one may question Macpherson's characterization of Albertan society as derived from his statistical breakdown of the province's class composition. Throughout *Democracy in Alberta* the reader finds the province referred to as "a society of independent producers" or a "community of independent commodity producers" (220, 236, 239); and one finds Alberta portrayed as having a "relatively homogeneous" class structure (21, 205). But these comments are not justified by the data he provides. If we combine his "industrial employees" with the paid agricultural labourers into a class of "wage and salary earners," which would be in keeping with Macpherson's usage of Marxist class categories, then this class, not the petite bourgeoisie, was the largest class in Alberta when Social Credit came to power. Wage and salary earners, according to Macpherson's data, made up 50 per cent of the work-force in 1931 (49 per cent in 1941; see Table 3.1 above). Yet wage and salary earners do not figure at all in his analysis of Social Credit. As Jackson (1977, 12) puts it, in *Democracy in Alberta* "wage and salary earners disappear from sight entirely."

Regardless of how those outside the petite bourgeoisie are classified, the fact remains that those *not* in petit-bourgeois occupations formed a majority of the occupational structure for the period in question. (Macpherson's figures are 54 per cent for 1931, 55 per cent for 1941.) In light of this fact, his depiction of Alberta as a "society of independent producers" appears exaggerated. It also reveals that an analysis of the behaviour of those outside the petite bourgeoisie is crucial to our understanding of the movement's popular support. Similarly, his characterization of the class structure as "relatively homogeneous" is problematic. That Alberta had an atypically large petite bourgeoisie at this time is true, but to assert homogeneity from the figures he cites is unjustified. Such a description is like calling a group of people made up of 50 men and 46 women a "relatively homogeneous community of women."[5]

An alternative portrayal of Alberta's class structure is provided in Table 3.2.[6] An important difference between Table 3.2 and Macpherson's breakdown is that in the table the size of Alberta's salaried middle classes and working class are estimated.

Another issue to be considered is that Macpherson's argument for the petit-bourgeois basis of Social Credit is not backed up with any direct evidence of disproportionate support. He simply states that since Alberta had an atypically high proportion of "independent commodity producers" compared to Canada as a whole, "we should not be surprised to find some difference in political behaviour." His reasoning appears to be that since the province's class structure was "relatively homogeneous" (i.e., comprised largely of "independent commodity producers") and since the "conservative" Social Credit movement captured 89 per cent of the seats in the 1935 election, any

25   The Conventional Wisdom

Table 3.2
Alberta's Class Structure, 1931 (Males Only)

		%
Upper class[a]		1
Upper middle class[b]		7
Salaried lower middle class[c]		9
Petite bourgeoisie		
Agrarian[d]	42	
Non-agrarian[e]	6	
		48
Working class		
Agrarian[f]	10	
Non-agrarian[g]	20	
		30
Farm employers[h]		2
Subsistence farmers[h]		2
TOTAL		99[i]

Source: Government of Canada 1936, 156–69.

[a] Defined as the owners of the major non-agricultural means of production.

[b] Calculated as the 40 per cent of salaried non-manual employees with the highest incomes, plus 1 of the 2 per cent of non-farm employers.

[c] Calculated as the 60 per cent of salaried non-manual employees with the lowest incomes.

[d] Calculated as 90 per cent of all farm proprietors plus 90 per cent of all agricultural unpaid labour.

[e] Calculated as the total of all non-agrarian occupations classified as "own account" or "no pay" in the census.

[f] Includes only those whose principal occupation is paid farm labour.

[g] Defined as all non-agricultural employees doing manual work.

[h] Calculated as 5 per cent of all farm proprietors and unpaid farm labour.

[i] Percentages do not add up to 100 due to rounding.

further attempt to demonstrate petit-bourgeois support for the party would be superfluous.

The petit-bourgeois argument, however, begins to look somewhat doubtful if we consider the percentage of the popular vote for Social Credit[7] and compare it with the proportion of the work-force that was petit-bourgeois. In 1935 Social Credit captured 54 per cent of the popular vote; according to Macpherson, 46 per cent of the work force were petit-bourgeois in 1931 (48 per cent using the data in Table 3.2). If one assumes that the class composition of the labour force approximates the class composition of the electorate, given the popular-vote figure and no additional data, it is theoretically possible that virtually every petit-bourgeois voter voted *against* Social Credit in 1935. Although it will be demonstrated later that this did not occur, the fact that such a statement can be made is an indication of the looseness of fit between the petit-bourgeois argument and the evidence generally provided.

This looseness of fit is even more striking if we consider that the United Farmers of Alberta received 11 per cent of the popular vote (but no seats) in 1935. It is reasonable to assume that a large majority of these votes were cast by farmers, since the UFA's theory of occupational "group government" discouraged the solicitation of support from non-farmers. (In 1935 only one UFA candidate ran in an urban constituency.)[8] Assuming further, as Macpherson does, that 90 per cent of all farmers were petit-bourgeois, the UFA attracted a substantial proportion of the petit-bourgeois vote. If, hypothetically, 75 per cent of the UFA vote came from petit-bourgeois farmers, then 8.25 of the 11 per cent of the total vote won by the UFA would have come from petit-bourgeois farmers.[9] This would reduce the size of the petite bourgeoisie that was free to bring Social Credit to power to 37.75 per cent of the work-force[10] (39.75 per cent if we use the data in Table 3.2).

It is also important to consider the number of petit-bourgeois *farmers* who would have been free to vote Social Credit in 1935, since much of Macpherson's discussion of class focuses on farmers and many authors contend that Social Credit was a movement of independent farmers. The above scenario of farmer support for the UFA would reduce the proportion of the work-force composed of petit-bourgeois farmers who were free to bring Social Credit to power to 30.75 per cent[11] (33.75 per cent using the data in Table 3.2). Surely, if we consider that Social Credit captured 54 per cent of the popular vote in 1935, these figures indicate that any accurate account of the class basis of Social Credit must involve an analysis of those outside the petit-bourgeois class, especially those who were not petit-bourgeois farmers. It should also be borne in mind that the above scenario does not consider petit-bourgeois support for the Liberal, Conservative, or Communist parties, which would lower the proportion of those in this class who were free to support Social Credit even further. As mentioned in chapter 2, the Liberals provided the strongest competition for Social Credit in the 1935 provincial election, winning 23 per cent of the popular vote.[12]

Much of the commentary on the class basis of popular support for Social Credit that has appeared since the publication of *Democracy in Alberta* involves either a restatement of Macpherson's position or minor variations on his main theme. J.R. Mallory, whose book followed Macpherson's in the Social Science Research Council series on

27   The Conventional Wisdom

Social Credit, writes that the party's support "came from agrarian and lower middle class sources" (1954, 183). Mallory does not define "lower middle class," nor is the claim backed up with any evidence or reference to other studies. In his foreword to Mallory's book S.D. Clark states, "It is significant ... that the movement had appealed in particular to the small-town middle classes in Alberta, to people who, while quite dismayed and exasperated by economic conditions, did not really envisage or desire to see established a new economic order in the province" (viii). No supportive reference is given.

Walter D. Young characterizes Social Credit as "a movement of the lower middle class, the *petite bourgeoisie*, of people not normally active in any sort of public body but driven by despair and drawn by Aberhart's conviction to the ranks of Social Credit" (1978, 97). Young offers no evidence for his assertions regarding the class basis of the movement.

Kenneth McNaught argues that, "led by William Aberhart, a radio evangelist, the Social Credit Party spoke directly to farmers and ranchers hard-pressed for mortgage payments" (1969, 249). Here again we have the assumption that Social Credit supporters were farm proprietors, and no evidence that popular support for the movement was confined to this minority of the work-force.

R.T. Naylor asserts that both the CCF in Saskatchewan and Social Credit in Alberta had "objective appeal" for "the petit bourgeois class as a whole" (1972, 253), but again the claim is made without any empirical foundation. Like the other writers in this school, Naylor fails to consider how the other classes in Alberta responded to Social Credit and thus ignores a majority of the work-force.

J.F. Conway advances the argument that "populism, as a political movement in self-defence on the part of a threatened agrarian petit-bourgeoisie, is what fundamentally characterized the CCF and Social Credit" (1978, 124). Elsewhere he makes a similar case, noting however that in 1935 Social Credit "also appealed successfully to the working class and the urban and small town *petit-bourgeoisie*" (1979, 84). In a later piece he defends the petit-bourgeois thesis by asking, "Was it accidental that Aberhart, who certainly received large support among the working class and the urban *petite bourgeoisie* in 1935, won the 1940 election in the rural areas?" (1990, 373). Conway too does not bolster his case with data; his comments on the 1940 election are considered again in chapter 8.

Not surprisingly, the class perspective reviewed here has made its way into Canadian sociology textbooks. In one textbook students are told:

28   Social Classes and Social Credit in Alberta

Perhaps the most important provincial manifestation of farmers' political concerns was the emergence of the Social Credit party in Alberta and the CCF in Saskatchewan ... scholars have stressed the common class base of these two movements and have concluded, generally, that both the Social Credit and the CCF should be viewed as populist responses (of independent commodity producers) to the domination by eastern financial and industrial interests.   (Grayson and Grayson 1983, 520)

The Graysons cite Naylor (1972), Sinclair (1975), and Conway (1978) here, but such writers offer only assertions, not evidence.[13]

In another textbook it is written that Social Credit "appealed to western farmers and small-town businessmen who wanted to believe that their troubles resulted from the control of the economy by eastern financial interests" (Sam Clark 1982, 352). Again, Clark does not provide his readers with evidence. A third textbook portrays Social Credit as a movement of agrarian "petty commodity producers" (Bakker and Winson 1993, 506–7), once more without an evidentiary basis.

Robert Brym also makes the petit-bourgeois argument, although he does maintain that "Macpherson undoubtedly overemphasized the homogeneity of Alberta's class structure" (1986, 52). Brym suggests that Alberta farmers "coalesced" with "the small-town petit bourgeois element" in supporting Social Credit (1978, 345–6). He contrasts this with the situation in Saskatchewan, where, he argues, farmers united with workers in their support for the CCF.[14]

To establish his argument for the Alberta case, Brym provides quotations from an article by Jean Burnet (1947), whose work is often cited by students of the movement as illustrative of small-town support for Social Credit. He also presents an occupational breakdown of 1935 Social Credit MLAS, whose ranks, he reports, did not include any members of the working class, unlike the Saskatchewan CCF government of 1944. Similarly, some writers cite Social Credit's lack of support by labour leaders as evidence of a lack of support for the movement among workers.

Burnet's work will be discussed below. At this juncture it should be pointed out that a subsequent study by Larry Hannant (1985) has shown that in Calgary, the organizational centre for Social Credit until it came to power, large numbers of working-class people were active in the movement as secondary leaders and organizers. Hannant also suggests that electoral candidates for the Social Credit Party were from higher class backgrounds than activists in general (110–12).

29   The Conventional Wisdom

The class backgrounds of members of a movement elected to public office is an important element of the movement's class character, and it is a significant finding that no Social Credit MLAS were members of the working class. The issue of working-class support for the party as the mass level, however, cannot be resolved by examining the class backgrounds of its elected members. Many socialist parties, at least since the time of Marx, have drawn a large proportion of their leadership from the middle class. Conversely, large segments of the working class often support non-socialist parties whose leaders include few working-class people. In Alberta in the 1970s, for example, the Lougheed Conservatives, whose ranks included few if any working-class MLAS and who did not receive official support from organized labour, fared handsomely with the working class of Alberta.[15] Thus working-class support for Social Credit is by no means disproved by showing that no workers were elected under the party banner, or by the fact that the party was not openly embraced by organized labour.

Virtually no one doubts that large numbers of *farmers* supported Social Credit, in spite of the fact that the movement was rejected by the leading farmers' organization, the UFA. Far fewer analysts of the movement, however, consider that working-class support for Social Credit may have been high despite its rejection by labour organizations. Moreover, it would appear that the acceptance of Social Credit ideas by labour leaders has been underestimated. William Irvine, who in 1921 was elected as a Labor member of Parliament for Calgary East and who later served as both a UFA and a CCF MP, was a fervent exponent of the Douglas Social Credit doctrine. In fact he assisted in bringing Major Douglas to Ottawa to give testimony before the House of Commons Committee on Banking and Commerce in 1923. Significantly, although Irvine was not a supporter of Aberhart, he argued that Douglas's Social Credit doctrines and democratic socialism were not incompatible (Mardiros 1979, 146–7). Also, the Alberta Federation of Labor demanded that Douglas Social Crediters be allowed to speak before members of the Alberta legislature.

Only two empirically based studies evaluating the Macpherson-inspired position on the popular basis of Social Credit support are known to the author. One was conducted by Thomas Flanagan (1972; see also 1973, 1979), who divides Alberta into four geographic regions: the agrarian "heartland," which he defines as the region extending north from the United States border to Edmonton and west from Saskatchewan to the foothills of the Rocky Mountains (excluding Calgary and Edmonton); the Rocky Mountain and foothills area; the two major cities (Calgary and Edmonton); and the north, defined as the region north of Edmonton, which in the period in question "was even more rural and just as agrarian as the southern heartland" (1972, 154).[16]

Flanagan argues that the "basis of Social Credit became, with one modification, the same heartland voters with whom the UFA had done so well" (1972, 157). The modification was that Social Credit's political philosophy, unlike that of the UFA, did not prevent it from seeking election in non-agrarian regions of the province. Flanagan contends, however, that "in spite of this broadened appeal, Social Credit showed relative weakness in the same areas where the UFA had been weak" (157–8). Breaking down the popular vote for Social Credit in 1935 by region, he arrives at the following percentages:

Heartland	61%
Mountain	49%
Cities (Calgary and Edmonton)	48%
North	46%

The first thing to note about Flanagan's findings is that the two rural regions, which contain high concentrations of farm (i.e., petit-bourgeois) voters, the heartland and the north, show both the highest and the lowest levels of support for Social Credit, although support in the latter region was only marginally lower than in the city and mountain regions. If we combine the two agrarian regions into one, we find that 56 per cent of the voters in this composite area voted Social Credit (Alberta 1983), which is only two percentage points higher than the party's province-wide figure of 54 per cent.

Flanagan's inclusion of Alberta's cities in his analysis should be lauded, since most of the adherents of the petit-bourgeois theory ignore the Social Credit presence in the cities entirely.[17] In asserting that Social Credit was a rural and "small-town" phenomenon, such accounts commonly imply that the success of Social Credit was negligible in the cities.

A good case can be made to include Medicine Hat and Lethbridge in any discussion of Alberta cities. The size of their urban populations (in 1931 they were the third and fourth largest cities in the province, after Calgary and Edmonton)[18] and their economic activity made them quite different from the smaller communities and the ranching and grain-growing regions that surround them.[19] The politics of these two cities also set them apart; as Flanagan points out, the UFA normally did not even run candidates in Medicine Hat and

31   The Conventional Wisdom

Table 3.3
Social Credit Vote in the 1935 Provincial Election, Four Largest Cities[a]

	% Social Credit	N
Edmonton	37	37,267
Calgary	58	38,443
Lethbridge	53	5,798
Medicine Hat	62	4,582
PROVINCE	54	301,752

Sources: For Calgary, Calgary Herald, 23 August 1935, 20. For Lethbridge and
Medicine Hat, Statement of Vote for the 1935 election, Provincial Archives of
Alberta. For Edmonton, Government of Alberta 1983.

[a] Figures are for the cities proper, except for Edmonton, which includes the entire
constituency of Edmonton; but see Table 6.5, n b, below. Figures for the city of
Edmonton proper are not available.

Lethbridge.[20] Describing these two communities as "cities" would
also be consistent with Macpherson's use of this term.[21]

If we include Medicine Hat and Lethbridge in the "cities" category,
we get the pattern of Social Credit support shown in Table 3.3.
Looking at the per cent Social Credit column, we see that Flanagan's
figure of 48 per cent for Calgary and Edmonton masks a fairly large
difference in support between the two cities. Surprisingly, the 58 per
cent figure for Calgary places it four percentage points above the
province-wide mark. Lethbridge and Medicine Hat, it should be
noted, also had high levels of Social Credit voting. Hence it appears
that Flanagan's claim that "Social Credit showed relative weakness in
the same areas where the UFA had been weak" cannot be substantiated for three of the four largest cities in the province.

The difference in support for Social Credit in the two largest cities
probably reflects the fact that the movement originated in Calgary,
that the organizational headquarters of the movement were there,
that Social Crediters were active in promoting the cause much earlier
in Calgary than in Edmonton, and that the movement's founder and
leader was a Calgary resident. As chapter 6 will show, not only
Edmonton but the entire northern region of the province, which like
Edmonton itself was not exposed to the same level of Social Credit
mobilization as the south, had lower levels of support for Social Credit
in 1935 than did the southern region.[22]

The success of the party in the four cities casts doubt on the idea
that Social Credit was a petit-bourgeois movement, since only about
11 per cent of the work-force in these cities was petit-bourgeois.[23]

32   Social Classes and Social Credit in Alberta

Table 3.4
Social Credit Vote in the 1935 Provincial Election, for Urban Areas with
Populations from 1,000 to 5,000[a]

	Population 1931	% Social Credit
Blairmore	1629	45
Camrose	2258	46
Cardston	1672	69
Claresholm	1156	54
Coleman	1704	63
Drumheller	2987	55
Edson	1547	35
Fort Saskatchewan	1001	31
Grande Prairie	1464	30
Hanna	1490	78
High River	1459	50
Innisfail	1024	50
Lacombe	1259	39
Lloydminster	1516	45
Macleod	1447	56
Magrath	1224	55
Olds	1056	49
Pincher Creek	1024	46
Raymond	1849	66
Redcliff	1192	66
Red Deer	2344	49
Stettler	1219	56
Taber	1279	70
Vegreville	1659	45
Vermillion	1270	53
Wainright	1147	35
Wetaskiwin	2125	60
PROVINCE		54

Source: Statement of Vote for the 1935 election, Provincial Archives of Alberta.
[a] Excluding Beverly, for which data are not available.

As noted above, the popularity of the movement in the cities is often neglected. This is a serious oversight since one quarter (26 per cent) of the province's population lived in these four cities in 1931 (Canada 1933, 464–82). The success of the party in the cities, especially Calgary, also brings into question the popular idea that Social Credit, as far as urban areas were concerned, was a "small-town" movement. Further doubt on the "small-town" hypothesis is cast by the data in Table 3.4, which lists the results for the 1935 election in urban areas having a population from 1,000 to 5,000, a range consistent with Macpherson's characterization of Alberta "towns."[24] If we define these

33   The Conventional Wisdom

communities as the small towns, only 11 of the 27 small towns had a Social Credit popular vote that exceeded the provincial average.

Table 3.4 may also help to explain how many observers came to contend, erroneously, that the small towns were bastions of Social Credit support. The field-work for the studies that are often cited as illustrative of small-town support for Social Credit (Burnet 1947, 1951) was conducted in Hanna, which had the highest level of support of any small town, with 78 per cent in favour!

The second empirically based study was conducted by Grayson and Grayson (1974). They examined the support for Social Credit in urban Alberta – that is, in all municipalities with a population of 1,000 or more. The authors address Macpherson's interpretation of Social Credit, but they seem to have misconstrued his position to some extent. They quote the following sentence from *Democracy in Alberta*, where Macpherson is discussing the UFA and Social Credit: "The radicalism of both was that of a quasi-colonial society of independent producers [farmers], in rebellion against eastern imperialism but not against the property system" (293, interpolation added by Grayson and Grayson). But we have seen above that, for Macpherson, "independent producers" includes both the agricultural and non-agricultural segments of the petite bourgeoisie, not just farmers. The authors further state that "Macpherson regards position in the productive process as his independent variable" (293). But Macpherson is much more specific than this, focusing his analysis of Social Credit on one particular class – the petite bourgeoisie.

Grayson and Grayson's divergence from Macpherson on these points leads them to make a somewhat confused critique of his position. They quote Macpherson's statement that Social Credit was a revolt "by farmers and townsmen," claiming that, "clearly, then, Social Credit support came not only from 'independent producers' on the land but from townsmen as well" (1974, 293). They argue that "further refinement" of Macpherson's theory is thus required, suggesting that urban unemployment may have been a "crucial variable" (294).

In their findings the Graysons first note that there does not appear to have been a rural-urban cleavage in support for the provincial Social Credit Party in 1935. It received 32.8 per cent of its total support from urban areas, which made up 31.1 per cent of the province's population. The correlation coefficent they calculate for community size and the provincial Social Credit vote, contrary to popular expectation, is *positive* at .10; its beta weight is .02. From the regression analysis reported, this variable explains 0 per cent of the variance (302). This suggests that a small-town dynamic did not contribute to popular support for Social Credit. (This observation does not form part of the Graysons' analysis.)

The authors' ethnic variables together explain 9 per cent of the variance, the religious variables 8 per cent. Surprisingly, the per cent fundamentalist variable by itself explains only 2 per cent of the variance. The percentage of unemployed males variable had the largest impact of those considered, explaining 35 per cent of the variance. Grayson and Grayson conclude that economic factors are more important than religious ones in accounting for Social Credit support in urban areas. Their arguably loose interpretation of Macpherson, however, appears to have led them to view this assessment as supporting his account of Social Credit. They write: "Such an interpretation is consistent with Macpherson's analysis of the movement. Because of the depression and consequent unemployment, the position in the productive process of large numbers of farmers and townsmen alike was changed. This, in turn, led to a propensity to support a new movement preaching economic as well as religious salvation" (309).

It must be stressed that Macpherson does not consider unemployment to be the key variable determining support for Social Credit. This is an idea advanced by the Graysons. Actually, it diverges considerably from Macpherson's position. He argues that Social Credit was a confused response of the petite bourgeoisie to its exploitation by the bourgeoisie of central Canada. This is something quite distinct from unemployment, a condition suffered mainly by wage and salary earners. The latter, presumably, do not suffer the delusions said to be inherent in the petit-bourgeois class position, which allegedly predisposed people to support Social Credit.

Also, it should be noted that although farmers suffered miserably during the Depression, the vast majority of them stayed on the farms. (With the high rate of unemployment across the country, they had little choice.) While urban areas experienced population loss during this period, the number of farmers in Alberta actually increased.[25] The number of occupied farms in Alberta increased from 77,130 in 1926 to 97,408 in 1931, and to 100,358 in 1936; in 1941 the total was 99,732 (Macpherson 1962, 11). Thus it seems that the unemployed appearing in the Graysons' data, which are based on the 1931 census, included only a very small number of recently dispossessed farmers.

In summary, despite its popularity in the literature, the petit-bourgeois thesis is not bolstered by evidence of disproportionate support from members of this class.

SOCIAL CREDIT PORTRAYED AS A CROSS-CLASS MOVEMENT

As early as 1959, John Irving claimed that, "if the Social Credit movement was a rural and small town movement, it was equally a lower middle and working class movement" (244). Irving's analysis of the class basis of Social Credit is based on numerous open-ended interviews but lacks systematically gathered aggregate data. Schultz (1960, 2) and Barr (1974, 54) provide accounts of the class basis of Social Credit that are similar to Irving's but also lack aggregate data. And the Grayson and Grayson study suggests that the urban unemployed as well as the petite bourgeoisie supported Social Credit. Comparable depictions of Social Credit as a cross-class movement are provided by Finkel (1989, 8, 210)[26] and Palmer and Palmer (1990, 261, 276).

Those authors maintaining that Social Credit was a cross-class movement argue a plausible case, but the dearth of aggregate data means that it is essentially another untested hypothesis. Also, like the other assertions regarding the movement's class basis, the magnitude of the alleged support is not specified. If the party received support from these classes, how high was that support? Neither do these studies address the issue of whether some supportive classes were more favourable to Social Credit than others. In addition, most of the generalizations about the class basis of Social Credit have tended to ignore the class support of parties in competition with the movement, which received 46 per cent of the popular vote in 1935. Similarly, little attention has been given to the question of which parties were endorsed by the more affluent classes.

CONCLUSIONS

A key finding of this chapter is that Alberta's class composition was substantially different from the portrayal commonly found in the literature. That a solid majority of the work-force in 1931 fell outside the agrarian petit-bourgeois class means that the analysis of other occupational groups should not be considered some kind of side-show to the great agrarian drama but a main event. Other key points raised in this chapter include the high level of support for Social Credit in Calgary, Lethbridge, and Medicine Hat, and that the latter two centres should be included in any discussion of Alberta cities. Another important finding is that, contrary to many established accounts, a small-town dynamic did not contribute to Social Credit support.

Since the various positions taken in the literature on the class basis of Social Credit lack the needed aggregate data, and since the class structure was more diverse than is commonly believed, a comprehensive empirical account of how *all* classes reacted to Social Credit is clearly called for, in conjuction with a discussion of how each class responded to the parties in competition with Social Credit. Such an analysis is provided in chapter 6 for the 1935 election and in chapter 8 for the election of 1940. But before turning to an analysis of the class pattern of the vote, it is necessary to examine the Social Credit philosophy, for in order to explain why people voted for Social Credit we must know what the movement stood for. Most accounts of the Social Credit philosophy maintain that it was inherently conservative, that it was a reflection of the petit-bourgeois dilemma outlined in chapter 1. The received tradition also suggests that strong anti-central-Canadian-imperialist sentiment formed an integral part of the movement's ideology. In the next two chapters the argument will be made that these accounts have not provided an accurate portrayal of the Social Credit ideology.

4 The Douglas Social Credit Philosophy

Just what was this "social credit" that so easily stirred the emotions? What kind of a society did Social Crediters want to create? Here I begin to address these questions by examining the doctrine of the founder of Social Credit, Major C.H. Douglas. By examining the original Social Credit theories, we can begin to make sense of the Alberta Social Credit movement as well as the larger international movement of which it was a part.

THE DOUGLAS DOCTRINE

Major Douglas's theories of society are expressed in numerous books, pamphlets, and articles. Like many social theorists, he did not write a comprehensive treatise explaining how all the elements of his philosophy relate to one another, although a general social theory is discernible that integrates his various works.

Douglas's ideas gained considerable notoriety after several of his articles were published in the *New Age* shortly after the 1914–18 war. The *New Age* was a popular British avant-garde periodical whose contributors included Arnold Bennett, G.B. Shaw, H.G. Wells, Katherine Mansfield, G.K. Chesterton, Ezra Pound, and Wyndham Lewis (Finlay 1972, 66–7). Its editor, A.R. Orage, became a convert to Social Credit, believing Douglas to be a "mastermind" and "the Einstein of economics" (Selver 1959, 75–6). Pound also became a Social Crediter, once claiming that "Gibbon's History of Rome is a meaningless jumble till a man has read Douglas" (Pound 1935, 5).[1]

38   Social Classes and Social Credit in Alberta

The starting point of the Major's analysis is his championing of "the supremacy of the individual considered collectively, over any external interest" (1920, 5). This statement, particularly the "individual considered collectively" part, is typical of much of Douglas's prose in that it is turbid and difficult to follow. Douglas himself admitted that his style of presentation was problematic and that it may partially explain the limited appeal of his doctrine.[2] Significantly, Alberta Social Credit leader William Aberhart became a convert to the movement not by reading Douglas but by reading a book on Social Credit by Maurice Colbourne (1928). Also, because the relationship between individual and collective rights expressed in the phrase "the individual considered collectively" was never adequately resolved by Douglas, it has been the subject of much confusion among Social Credit scholars.

Douglas believed that individual freedom is suppressed in modern society by a growing concentration of economic, political, and military power. In his early writings Wilhelmian Germany and the Soviet Union are singled out as examples of societies where personal liberty is ruthlessly suppressed; later, Nazi Germany and Fascist Italy are so described. He warned that the democratic countries were beginning to resemble these societies and that, unless a massive effort were made to reverse this trend, they would become just like them.

The liberation Douglas proposed involved freeing people from the necessity of working full time, through the application of "science and mechanism." He believed that it is technically possible for modern industrial societies to satisfy the material needs of all their citizens without having to employ fully all those able to work. He even went so far as to claim that science and technology, which he called the "cultural heritage," had progressed to the point where it would be possible to produce goods and services "at a rate very considerably greater than the possible rate of consumption of the world" (1933, 18). He advanced a number of estimates of the time and effort that would be needed to produce such material abundance with the technology already available. One estimate, which by no means exaggerates his position, suggests that this could be achieved by employing only 25 per cent of the available labour, working seven hours a day (18).[3]

Since only a minimal amount of work is needed to fulfil our material needs, mankind has the ability to free itself from the growing concentration of power. The universal wealth would liberate the population, allowing it to pursue "the interest of man which is self-development" (1920, 7).[4] Unlike many orthodox economists of his day, Douglas did not see employment as an end in itself but, at best, as a means to self-development. He believed that the world is

39   The Douglas Social Credit Philosophy

"working toward the Leisure State" in which "production, and still more the activities which are commonly referred to as 'business,' would of necessity cease to be the major interest of life and would, as has happened to so many biological activities, be relegated to a position of minor importance to be replaced, no doubt, by some form of activity of which we are not yet fully cognisant" (1931, 78–9). Douglas spoke openly of the "millennium which is easily possible" (84).[5]

Why, then, are so few free from the need to work full time? What is preventing us from living in the type of society Douglas believed possible?

The A + B Theorem

According to Major Douglas, there is an inherent shortage of consumer purchasing power in all industrial societies. He came to this conclusion while performing his duties as assistant superintendent of the Royal Aircraft Works at Farnborough during the First World War. In reviewing its payroll procedures, he noticed that the amount of money paid out to employees was far less than the value of the goods produced. He reasoned that if this were true for one productive enterprise, it must be true for all. This idea evolved into his famous A + B theorem, the central assumptions of which form the core of the Social Credit monetary doctrine.

The theorem states that payments made by any business firm are of two types: "A" payments, made to individuals, which comprise wages, salaries, and dividends; and "B" payments, made to other firms, such as those for raw materials, bank charges, and so on. A chronic shortage of consumer purchasing power exists because "the rate of flow of purchasing-power to individuals is represented by A, but since all payments go into prices, the rate of flow of prices cannot be less than A + B" (Douglas 1921, 22). In other words, all A payments made in a given period represent the money income available to individuals, yet the collective price of all goods on the market in this period is equal to A *plus* the value of all B payments. Since A can never equal A + B, the public is able to purchase only a small and constantly decreasing fraction of all goods produced. In making this assertion Douglas claims that the modern industrial system is extremely effective in *producing* goods, but not in distributing them: "Distribution and not manufacture is the real economic problem and is at present quite intolerably unsatisfactory" (1921, 87).

In order to compensate for the chronic shortage of purchasing power that he believed is revealed in the A + B theorem, Douglas proposed to reform the monetary system. "Credit" is to be made available to consumers in amounts at least equal to all B payments so that consumers can purchase all the goods and services available; with this credit the public would then have incomes equal to A + B. Credit distribution is to be implemented through two mechanisms: the "national dividend" and the "just" or "assisted" price, discussed below.

Like other social theorists, Douglas expounded at length on the problems of society but was vague and evasive when it came to explaining in concrete terms how his solutions were to be implemented. However, in his "Draft Social Credit Scheme For Scotland" (1933, 205–12) he does give some indication of the action to be taken.

With regard to the national dividend, it seems that the national government, through its own financial institution, should create an account based on the "real credit" of the nation, which is to be founded on the ability of the society to deliver goods and services (1921, 105–6). Douglas had the idea that the value of all capital assets of a country, such as minerals, buildings, land, machines, and so on, should be added up, with "no distinction between public and private property" (1933, 205). Added to this figure is the "capitalized value of the population," which appears to mean the potential earning power of all citizens. The total of these two amounts is to constitute the country's capital account, from which "credit" is to be granted. In Douglas's scheme, "Money and Real assets are on opposite sides of the account (and should balance) not, as in a commercial account, on the same side of the account" (212). Dividends are to be paid to all citizens on a regular basis out of the national credit, equalling, he estimates, roughly 1 per cent of the capital account each year. The dividends are to be granted in perpetuity and are not to be paid back or taxed.

In addition to dividends, consumers are to receive the benefit of the just price for goods. In keeping with the reasoning of the A + B theorem, the just price would permit firms to sell all their products below cost price (1921, 91).[6] The difference between the unadjusted price and the just price is to be taken out of the national credit: "The capital account will be 'depreciated' by such sums, and 'appreciated' by all capital development" (210). Douglas predicts that this would result in a discount of 25 per cent on retail prices. As the just price would be lower than the regular price, he also considers the former to be a bulwark against inflation, which critics contend would be created by the scheme. In answering the inflation charge, Douglas claims that the credit issued would not exceed the difference between the value of the goods and services available and the amount of money in the hands of consumers, and so would not be inflationary.

41   The Douglas Social Credit Philosophy

A reasonable amount of profit would be possible and permitted under a Social Credit system, but excessive profits would not. Douglas believed, however, that the adverse effect of profit-taking is "over-rated" since profits account for only a small proportion of the cost of goods; they are insignificant when compared to "B" costs (1920, 68; 1922a, 58–9).

Technical Critique of the A + B Theorem

Although sound arguments may exist that capitalist societies do not adequately distribute the goods they produce, the A + B theorem is not one of them. In claiming that without "credit" incomes can never equal production costs, Douglas demonstrates that he completely misunderstood the relationship between costs and incomes. As one Social Credit critic puts it, "the relationship between costs and incomes is one of identity ... every element in a producer's cost is an element in someone's income" (Durbin 1934, 47). Put somewhat differently, a proportion of the B payments made to other firms is paid out in the form of wages, salaries, and dividends by these other firms, and so constitutes a source of personal income or A payments; thus the two kinds of payment are not mutually exclusive.

Looked at another way, the theorem maintains that consumers' incomes must equal the total payments of all firms at all stages of production, which is false. Individuals receive A payments at each stage of production, but pay for the A and B payments of the final stage only (Hiskett and Franklin 1939, 29). For example, A payments are made to loggers felling trees, to workers in a sawmill processing the logs, and to clerks in a furniture store where the final product is sold. Consumers pay for the A and B payments of the furniture store in the price of the goods, but not for these payments *plus* the sawmill's B payments *plus* the logging firm's B payments; the latter two B payments are included in those of the furniture store. The A + B theorem implies that all B payments, added together, are to be paid by consumers.

Durbin estimates that B payments constitute approximately 90 per cent of all payments made (1934, 42). A corollary of this estimate is that Douglas's solution (issuing "credit" in amounts equal to all B payments) would result in an enormous increase in the money supply, and so would be highly inflationary. None the less, as the reader will appreciate, the A + B theorem is not easily understood and therefore not easily refuted.

As the A + B theorem became well known and subject to intense criticism, Douglas and his followers, like devotees of other social

42 Social Classes and Social Credit in Alberta

theories subject to public condemnation, introduced twists and turns in it that in effect yielded four or five separate theorems, although the original remained the most popular and was never officially renounced. The innovations introduced include the idea that in stating that A cannot equal A plus B, the former A refers to all sources of income to individuals, while A + B refers to payments made by retailers only; that although A payments are received at all stages of production, they are not in the hands of consumers when the goods are placed on the market; that the deficiency in purchasing power is caused by producers setting money aside to cover depreciation charges; and that the shortage of purchasing power is caused by too much expenditure on the production of capital goods rather than consumer items (see Gaitskell 1933, 347–75). These elaborations made it difficult to criticize the theorem, as supporters could always deny that the critic had understood it, then invoke a contrary interpretation. Despite these variations, Douglas maintained to the end that there was a gross discrepancy between the amount of money in the hands of consumers and the collective price of all goods and services available.[7]

Money, Banks, and Credit

Douglas also provided a unique interpretation of the role of the banks in issuing credit and creating money. According to Douglas, banks can create money at will. This idea is conveyed in his famous dictum that money is created "by a stroke of the banker's pen" (1931, 17). He believed that banks can create money for their own use or for loan simply by forming an account and crediting it with whatever amount they desire: "Deposits are created, to a major extent, by purely book-keeping transactions on the part of banking institutions. It is therefore correct to say that banking institutions are in a position to create, claim as their property, and to lend upon their own terms, effective demand" (1935, 105). Banks acquire other assets in the same way: "A bank acquires securities for nothing, in the same way that a central bank, such as the Bank of England, may be said to acquire gold for nothing. In each case, of course, the institution concerned writes a draft upon itself for the sum involved, and the general public honours the draft by being willing to provide goods and services in exchange for it" (1931, 15).

Although he was "very much laughed at" for this analysis of the banking system, Douglas suggested that "instead of the banking institutions and the other financial institutions getting those securities for nothing, the public [should] get them for nothing" (Alberta

1934, 88, 94). When the newly elected William Aberhart asked him for advice in implementing a Social Credit program in Alberta, Douglas told him to begin by asking the banks for $5 million (1937, 129–30). Douglas claimed that the money did not have to be paid back because the banks can create money at will. Aberhart was instructed to "make an arrangement with any existing banking institution by which it will hand over to you, *not as a loan* but as a creation on your behalf and subject only to the disposition of your Government, sums of financial credit as may be required from time to time, being merely paid one sum for the book-keeping transaction of creating such credits, and possibly a small sum additionally to cover the book-keeping of accounts which may be based upon such credits" (1937, 145, emphasis added). Douglas's advice to Aberhart also helps to illustrate the Douglasite view that anything that is physically possible is financially possible. According to the Major, "the idea that a physical policy cannot be carried out unless there is, as the phrase goes, sufficient money with which to do it is, as it has always been, an illusion fostered for interested purposes" (1931, 52).

Technical Critique of Douglas's Position on Money, Banks, and Credit

In order to make sense of Douglas's theories of money and "credit," it is necessary to consider some aspects of the banking system. Douglas is right in claiming that the banks can create money – that is, increase the money supply – but he appears to have misunderstood or ignored the banks' obligations in this process.

Banks can increase the amount of deposit money in existence by lending or investing funds in excess of their cash reserves. Actually, banks may create deposit money by a *multiple* of their cash reserves. This multiple is called the "money multiplier" and is the inverse of the reserve ratio, which itself is the ratio of cash to demand deposits (Archer 1973, 294). Thus, for example, with a reserve ratio of 6 per cent (which approximates the norm), an increase in cash reserves can increase the amount of desposit money in existence by up to 16.7 times the additional cash acquired (294).[8] This is possible because in granting a loan, a bank normally credits the borrower's account to the amount of the loan (i.e., creates deposit money) rather than issuing cash. Banks may purchase securities in a similar way – that is, by writing cheques drawn upon themselves. Deposit money can be created in amounts greater than the value of the cash possessed by the bank because those with bank accounts withdraw only a tiny proportion of their funds in cash. The commerce of advanced capitalist countries is conducted primarily through the use of cheques (and, in recent years, credit cards), with cash in comparatively low demand. Only a small proportion (in Canada approximately 10 per cent) of the money supply is made up of coin and paper currency; the vast bulk of it is comprised of chequeable bank deposits (222). Thus the banks can, within certain limits,[9] create money "by a stroke of the pen" by granting loans or writing cheques drawn upon themselves in excess of their cash reserves. But Douglas and his followers did not realize that in doing so, a bank simultaneously creates *liabilities* for itself.

When a bank creates deposit money for a loan or for its own investment, it also creates an obligation to *pay* that amount. The system of lending money described here can only work if virtually all the money loaned out is paid back. Hence the difference between bank credit and the "social" credit described by Douglas: bank credit must be paid back. Banks cannot, as Major Douglas implies, simply create deposit money and increase their net worth by the amount created. Banks make profits by collecting interest on loans and from income generated through other investments and service charges, not simply by creating deposit money and claiming it as their property. Also, of course, if a loan or investment fails, the bank is still obliged to honour the money it created and so suffers a net loss.[10] However, as with the A + B theorem, the complexities of the banking process make a quick refutation of Douglas's views in this regard difficult.

The Communal Nature of Production and Distribution under a Social Credit System

Douglas believed that the chronic shortage of consumer purchasing power he describes has very serious consequences, but in his opinion the solution is simply a matter of applying proper bookkeeping procedures to ensure that enough "credit" is being issued. However, he proposed social changes that went far beyond new accounting methods in his plan to solve a second problem that he considered to be inherent in capitalist societies. This second problem, which has been neglected by most Social Credit analysts, is that the existing system "makes the wrong things and so is colossally wasteful" (1922a, 24). Instead of producing the goods and services that people actually need, it merely produces things that will provide money for those in control of the productive process, who for Douglas are financiers. The producers of goods are dependent on bank credit to finance production, since they cannot sell much of what they produce, due to the shortage of consumer purchasing power. This allows

45   The Douglas Social Credit Philosophy

the banks to control the productive resources of society, "which in turn enables [them] ... to control both the quantity and variety of its output, and so maintain [their] control over prices" (1922b, 10). The banks' objective is to make money rather than useful goods, so a granting of credit "is not a reflection of an increase in potential capacity to deliver goods and services, but merely ... the potential capacity to deliver money" (1921, 129). The power of the banks allows them to appropriate the bulk of society's wealth, which Douglas calls the "unearned increment of association."[11]

Douglas also claims that "the tawdry 'ornament,' the jerry-built house, the slow and uncomfortable train service, the unwholesome sweetmeat, are the direct and logical consummation of an economic system which rewards variety, quite irrespective of quality, and proclaims in the clearest possible manner that it is much better to 'do' your neighbour than to do sound and lasting work" (1920, 78). In their effort to dispose of these shoddy goods, producers rely on "artificial demand created by advertisement; a demand, in many cases, as purely hypnotic in origin as the request of the mesmerised subject for a draught of kerosine" (1920, 76).[12]

Douglas also believed that in order to maintain the illusion of scarcity, finance sees to it that as few consumer goods as "will avoid revolution" are produced (1922b, 10). Capital goods are produced instead, which helps to perpetuate the myth that all must work long, hard hours. "The end of all this," according to Douglas, "... will leave the 'victors' with a mass of monetary wealth which will not induce the baking of a loaf of bread" (11).[13]

Douglas maintained that the problem of how wealth should be created and distributed would best be solved by introducing fundamental changes in the economy, changes that go far beyond the issuing of credit to consumers. His proposals in this regard have received very little academic attention to date, as most commentators have dwelt on his plans for monetary reform.

Douglas proposed a "new basis of credit – the *useful* (to human beings as such) productive capacity of society" (1922b, 128). He argues further that the "community," not the market or the state, should decide what to produce and in what amounts. In his new system, prices would also be determined "on the broad principles of use value, by the community as a whole operating by the most flexible representation possible" (154). For Douglas, a "workable financial system is far more in the nature of an accounting and order system than an exchange system" (1933, 187).

It must be made clear that what Douglas was proposing is not a market system but a command economy. However, unlike the

46 Social Classes and Social Credit in Alberta

economies of communist countries, where the state determines which goods are to be produced, the number of goods to be produced, and selling prices, in a Social Credit system these decisions would be made by the community. Douglas anticipated no decline in efficiency or productivity in such a system.[14]

In Douglas's new system, the producers of the goods and services, who are to obey the community's explicit demands,

stand fundamentally and unalterably on a basis of Service – it is their business to deliver the goods to order, not to make terms about them, because it is the basis of the whole arrangement that the general interest is best served by this relationship ...

The goods having been delivered to order, it is the business of the community, to whose order they were made, to dispose of them – not the business of the producers, who would never have been able to function without the consent of society.   (1922a, 35–6).

Douglas also held that since industrial technology has developed over the centuries through the labour of countless individuals, and since technology is such an important factor in the production of wealth, no single person or group of persons should have an exclusive claim on that wealth. "The chief owners, and rightful beneficiaries of the modern productive system," he writes, "can be shown to be the individuals composing the community, as such" (1933, 50). He claims that "the plant of civilization belongs to the community, not to the operators, and the community can, or should, be able to appoint or dismiss anyone who in its discretion fails to use that plant to the best advantage" (1922a, 41–2).

Douglas argues that since his plan is to carry out *community* policy using the most efficient organization possible, it will free humanity from the all-embracing control of finance. Once the full Social Credit plan is implemented, finance will no longer keep people poor, force them to work long hours to produce goods they don't need and in so doing prevent them from developing themselves as human beings.

Douglas never adequately resolves the conflicting notions of community control of production and distribution with his widely heralded belief in individual rights, the "supremacy of the individual considered collectively, over any external interest," mentioned at the beginning of this chapter. That is, he does not address the issue of the rights of workers or capitalists to refuse community directives. At times he even appears to place the rights of the community above those of the individual, as in the Draft Social Credit Scheme for Scotland, where he states that for a period of five years after the

47   The Douglas Social Credit Philosophy

initiation of the scheme, those refusing to accept employment in the occupational category they were in at the time of the last census could be denied dividends (1933, 211).

However, one may surmise that an answer to this dilemma, albeit a utopian one, can be found in his notion of co-operation. Under his system, "individuals will submit themselves voluntarily to the discipline of the productive process, because in the first place they know that it is operated for production and so gains their primary ends with a minimum of exertion, and in the second place because of the interest and satisfaction of co-operative, co-ordinated effort" (1922a, 39–40).[15]

Douglas's position on economic co-operation is another item that is rarely acknowledged in academic accounts of Social Credit. Co-operation, he claims, "is the note of the coming age," although he cautions that it must involve "reasoned assent" and must not be "oppressive to the individual" (1920, 8). At the international level, "the logical and inevitable end of economic competition is war ... an effective League of Free Peoples postulates the abolition of the competitive basis of society, and by the installation of the co-operative commonwealth in its place makes of war not only a crime, but a blunder" (145).

One problem with Douglas's proposals in this regard is that he does not explain just what the "community" is. Also, he is vehemently anti-statist, but does not explain how large numbers of people can make collective decisions and take collective action, in particular run a command economy, without an extensive state apparatus. And as mentioned, he does not address the issue of productivity in command economies.

Theory of Democracy

Douglas developed a rudimentary theory of democracy that he advocates both for popularizing the Social Credit plan and for governing society once Social Credit has been implemented. He believed that citizens have the right to demand the outcomes of their choice but should leave to experts or technicians the job of realizing those outcomes. Thus the populace is to demand a Social Credit system but is not to worry about the technical matters of its implementation, which are matters for experts. Similarly, as intimated above, producers are to yield to the community's wishes and are to engage their technicians in providing what the community desires, even if community policy is at variance with what the industrial experts advocate:

48 Social Classes and Social Credit in Alberta

Just as a political majority is likely to be right on a matter which truly comes within the domain of policy, but is probably wrong in its ideas as to how that policy can be made effective, so, conversely, it is undoubtedly true that the industrial technician ... is very apt to hold distorted views on the objective of the producing process in which he is so keenly interested; while being unquestionably the right and proper person to decide on the technique to be applied to a given programme of production. (1933, 181)[16]

Douglas's political philosophy is also characterized by a severe distrust of formal organizations of any kind. He believed that there is an "inevitable degradation which accompanies large organizations" (1942, 19) and held that any association having over three thousand members is not to be trusted (Finlay 1972, 238). Needless to say, Douglas's abhorrence of political organization was not an asset in mobilizing an international social movement like Social Credit.

It bears repeating that in Douglas's Social Credit system the "community," not the state, national or local, is to control production and distribution. The community control of production and distribution he envisaged is to take place spontaneously, with a minimum of formal organization and no coercion. Also, since production and distribution are to be "community" controlled rather than directed by a national authority, he assumes that there will be some kind of spontaneous integration of local, regional, national, and international economic activity.

Finlay (1972, 236–52) argues convincingly that Douglas's political philosophy is, broadly speaking, anarchist. The revulsion he expressed for government authority, his dislike of formal organizations, and his belief in free and spontaneous association give him much in common with adherents of this philosophy.

Views on Socialism

As is readily apparent, Douglas's philosophy relies considerably on collectivist and co-operative sentiments. In spite of this he was staunchly anti-socialist, claiming that socialism, whether Fabian or Bolshevist, was a major cause of the world's problems rather than a solution to them. He argued that socialism contributes to a growing concentration of power by making individuals subservient to the state; he also claimed, without drawing parallels with his own system, that socialism is economically inefficient. Public control of "credit" along with community control of production and distribution, rather than public ownership of the means of production, was to form the foundation of his new civilization.

49 The Douglas Social Credit Philosophy

International Strife, Crime, Financial Law

Douglas believed that the chief cause of war and other international conflict is the competition for foreign markets. Since no country can sell all its goods domestically due to the shortage of consumer purchasing power, military struggles ensue for markets. Douglas claims, however, that while "it is the reverse of true to accuse *Financiers* of planning or desiring war, the financial *System*, of which they are the defenders, is, beyond question, the chief cause of international friction" (1931, 75). Yet Douglas is not entirely consistent in his claim that the system, as opposed to certain individuals, creates international conflict, for he often claims that a hidden government of financiers is attempting to dominate the entire world.

Douglas also believed that "90 per cent of the crime in the world is directly due to the financial system" and that laws pertaining to finance "are broadly speaking almost entirely laws for the protection of the financial system as it exists at the present time" (Alberta 1934, 103, 83).

Ethno-Religious Prejudices

Douglas's anti-Semitism has become one of the better-known aspects of his thought. He appears to have had a dislike for Jews all his adult life, although these sentiments were expressed with greater frequency and vitriol in his later years. In 1922 he wrote:

We have a good many more Jews in important positions in this country than we deserve. And not only in this country, but in every country, certain ideas which are the gravest possible menace to humanity – ideas which can be traced through the propaganda of Collectivism to the idea of the Supreme, impersonal State, to which every individual must bow – seem to derive a good deal of their most active, intelligent support from Jewish sources, while at the same time a grim struggle is proceeding in the great financial groups, many of which are purely Jewish, for the acquisition of key positions from which to control the World-State when formed. We are anxious not to be misunderstood. We do not believe for a single instant that the average British Jew would countenance such schemes for a single moment. (1922a, 121–2)

According to the founder of Social Credit, much of the evil done throughout the centuries was either perpetrated by Jews or done with Jews lurking in the background, controlling things. The alleged Jewish menace he often linked to what he called the "hidden government" of financiers that was plotting to take over the world. His

50   Social Classes and Social Credit in Alberta

world-conspiracy theories grew more bizarre in the twilight of his life; eight years before his death in 1952 he believed that Western bankers were conspiring with communists to destroy Western civilization (1945, 81).

Douglas also harboured strong anti-German prejudices. "Germans are," he claims, "a godsend to warmakers, and a pest to Europe" (1942, 4). He believed that it is "more than a coincidence that at the periods to which I have referred, Finance and a particular type of culture, which you can call Prussianism if you wish to give it a name, have been dominant at one and the same time" (1934, 67). There is a "fundamental and irreconcilable antagonism," he writes, "between the German and the British, the socialist and the liberal ... conception of life ... The German, or socialist *proximate* objective is government *by* administration, whereas the English conception is government *of* administration" (1945, 51–2). At one point Douglas also expressed anti-Catholic views, but these were later abandoned when the Catholic Church took a firm stand against communism.

ACADEMIC INTERPRETATIONS OF
DOUGLASISM

It would be useful at this point to consider the leading academic analyses of Douglas's philosophy. This will allow us to round out the explication of his doctrine and present an alternative to the received wisdom on the topic.

Douglasism Portrayed as Not Altering Capitalist Relations of Production

According to C.B. Macpherson, whose interpretation is generally accepted as the definitive exegesis of the Douglas doctrine, in a Social Credit system "capitalist enterprise, profits, and private ownership could all be retained. All that was needed was to restore the control of credit to the people made really sovereign, and thus enable the simple monetary devices of social credit to be put into practice." The "introduction of social credit," Macpherson writes, "while destroying the financiers, would not interfere with the right of private ownership of capital or private management of industry or agriculture." And again, "social credit ... would provide new plenty for all *without touching existing private ownership*" (1962, 97, 113–14, 116, emphasis added).

The view that the Douglas scheme simply involved monetary tinkering that would leave the essentials of capitalism untouched is

51   The Douglas Social Credit Philosophy

commonplace in the scholarship on the movement. It is sometimes further suggested that Social Credit was a defence of the bourgeoisie or capitalism itself. Finkel (1989, 35), for instance, describes Douglas's ideas as "pro-capitalist." Osborne and Osborne (1986, 49) go further, seeing in Douglasism a "free enterprise utopia." But did Douglas really want to leave the capitalist system fundamentally untouched? Was he in fact "pro-capitalist"?

It would seem that both Marxist and non-Marxist accounts of Douglasism are misguided in their portrayals of Douglas's view of capitalism and the relations of production he envisaged for his Social Credit system. Douglas generally portrays the non-financial bourgeoisie as a helpless victim of finance. As discussed above, finance is said to dominate the entire society. Among other things, it absorbs the bulk of societal wealth, determines what is to be produced, and controls prices and profits. But once a Social Credit system comes into existence, this power is to pass from finance to the community. Although the formal ownership of all enterprises, including the banks, is to remain private, in Douglas's system the public is to control economic policy directly. In his words, there must be "public control of economic policy through public control of credit" (1921, 91). So long as the public controls the issuing of credit, it has the power to implement its will. The community, not the market or the bourgeoisie, determines what is produced and how much goods and services are to cost. And by usurping finance's control over production, the community is free to distribute the unearned wealth that is hoarded by the banks. For Douglas, "a solution of the more immediately pressing problems with which civilisation is confronted ... does in fact turn on the removal of the limitations to the distribution of wealth" (1933, 50). These are major departures from capitalism as we know it.

Hence in Douglas's new system, capitalists, large and small, were not to be removed from their place in the productive process; they were simply to have new masters: the community rather than finance. The argument that finance never did control the rest of the bourgeoisie in the manner described by Douglas may be true, but it does not detract from the fact that he had no intention of allowing the non-financial bourgeoisie to control production and distribution. Capitalists in a Social Credit system were to have a status closer to public employees than owners in the conventional sense.[17]

Macpherson is particularly critical of the idea that the "wage relation," a definitive aspect of the capitalist system, would not be altered by Douglas. He writes that the "possibility of implementing social credit was based on the possibility of separating the internal administration of industries, including apparently the determination of wages, from the fixing of prices. The former was to be left in the hands of private enterprise, the latter was to be placed in the hands of the community" (1962, 116).

Macpherson seems to have overlooked that part of the Douglas doctrine that states that "the distribution of cash credits to individuals shall be progressively less dependent upon employment. That is to say, that *the dividend shall displace the wage and salary*" (Douglas 1934, 42, emphasis added). "Not being dependent upon a wage or salary for subsistence" in a Social Credit system, Douglas writes, means that a person "is under no necessity to suppress his individuality" (1931, 81). Furthermore, since for Douglas societal wealth is created by a community of individuals applying the "cultural heritage" to the production process, the receipt of dividends is to inhere in one's membership in the community, not in one's contribution to production or ownership of its means:

The original conception of the classical economist that wealth arises from the interaction of three factors – land, labour, and capital – was a materialistic conception which did not contemplate and, in fact, did not need to contemplate, the preponderating importance which intangible factors have assumed in the productive process of the modern world. The cultural inheritance, and what may be called the "unearned increment of association" probably include most of these factors, and they represent not only the major factor in the production of wealth, but a factor which is increasing in importance so rapidly that the other factors are becoming negligible in comparison.

It is both pragmatically and ethically undeniable that the ownership of these intangible factors vests in the members of the living community, *without distinction*, as tenants-for-life. Ethically, because it is an inheritance from the labours of past generations of scientists, organizers, and administrators, and pragmatically because the denial of its *communal character* sets in motion disruptive forces, threatening, as at the present time, its destruction. If this point of view be admitted ... it seems clear that the money equivalent of this property, which is so important a factor in production, vests in and arises from the individuals who are the tenants-for-life of it. (1933, 189–90, emphasis added)

Douglas also claims that "the community can be regarded as a single undertaking (decentralized as to administration to any extent necessary) and every individual comprised within it is in the position of an equal bondholder *entitled to an equal share of product*" (1920, 114, emphasis added). And, as noted earlier, it was Douglas's belief that "the chief owners and rightful beneficiaries of the modern productive

53   The Douglas Social Credit Philosophy

system can be shown to be the individuals composing the community, as such." According to Major Douglas, "wealth is a central pool into which everybody is contributing, and the proper function of money is not to interchange between those separate producers of wealth, but to give the general community, by whom wealth is produced, the necessary power to draw from the central pool of wealth" (Alberta 1934, 116).

Thus, rather than leaving capitalism untouched in all fundamentals, Douglas would have the community control production and distribution directly in a command economy, and have wages and salaries replaced by equal dividends for all. Although one would never know it from reading most academic interpretations of his doctrine, Douglas's vision of future relations of production has much more in common with theories of communism than with the capitalism of his day.

Douglasism and Property Rights

The argument is often made that because Douglas did not favour the abolition of private property, he had a fundamental commitment to the capitalist system. This contention lies at the heart of Macpherson's influential analysis of Douglasism (1962, 113–18).

Douglas does plead for a Social Credit system while simultaneously claiming that it is not his intention to abolish private property. He argues that the abolition of private property "merely means absolute centralization of economic power" (1942, 49). However, he never adequately explains his philosophy of property. He once defined private property as "anything, no matter what its composition or nature, which, being in the possession of the individual, is necessary to enable him to carry on his normal life without interference" (1939, 1; quoted in Macpherson 1962, 114). Yet the property rights of all factions of the bourgeoisie would be severely curtailed under his system because the community would control production and distribution. What to produce, what to charge, and the setting of profit limits would be the prerogative of the community, not the bourgeoisie. Moreover, as noted, societal wealth is to be shared equally by all members of the community.

While in Alberta, Douglas was asked by a member of the Agricultural Committee of the provincial legislature to explain "how we can administer wealth which is privately owned? Does not ... the Douglas system [involve] ... social ownership?" (Alberta 1934, 104). Douglas replied, "I am perfectly certain there is no difficulty whatever in distributing socially privately produced production" (104). Similarly,

54 Social Classes and Social Credit in Alberta

another committee member read a prepared statement claiming that Douglas is "urging us to recapture complete constitutional and legal control over all the institutions that sell currency or credit so that the issue of the tickets by means of which, alone, goods and services can circulate, will be subject to public policies of general welfare rather than to considerations of private profit." To this Douglas replied, "Broadly speaking, subject to reading it carefully, I should agree with that statement" (106–7).

Douglas may have wanted to make a distinction between personal property, which was not to be touched, and commercial or productive property, which was to be at the disposal of the community. This interpretation would be consistent with his defence of the property "in the possession of the individual," although it is by no means clear that this is what he had in mind.

Another point to consider is that the Major believed that Social Credit would make everyone fabulously wealthy "without taking anything away from anybody" (1936, 16). Such huge amounts of wealth would be distributed to all that property rights just wouldn't be an issue in a Social Credit society.[18] In addition, Douglas may have explained away the issue of the violation of bourgeois property rights arising from the community control of production and distribution by assuming that the bourgeoisie would have no objection to his plans. In his scheme of things, the control of business had long since passed from the non-financial bourgeoisie to bankers, so implementing community control of the economy would not take anything away from the former that it had not already lost.

In any case, it is clear that Douglas's stand on property was not such that it precluded community control of production and distribution, which itself violates capitalist market principles and bourgeois property rights:

Natural resources are common property, *and the means for their exploitation should also be common property* ...

It may be said in regard to [this] ... proposition ... that it involves a confiscation of plant, which is clearly an injustice to the present owners. But is it?

A reference to the accounting process already described will make it clear that the community has already bought and paid for many times over the whole of the plant used for manufacturing processes, the purchase price being included in the selling price of the articles produced, and representing, in the ultimate, effort of some sort ... If the community can use the plant it is clearly entitled to it, quite apart from the fact that under proper conditions there is no reason why every reasonable requirement of its present owners

55   The Douglas Social Credit Philosophy

should not be met under changed conditions. (1920, 110–13, emphasis added)

As we shall see in the discussion of Alberta Social Credit, the Albertans either proposed or implemented measures that were both consistent with Douglasism and in violation of bourgeois property rights.

Douglas's Views on Capitalism

Given what has been outlined above regarding Douglas's vision of a Social Credit society, the charge that his ideas were a defence of the bourgeoisie or capitalism itself seems strange indeed. In addition to advocating that capitalists be virtually converted into community employees, Douglas's work is peppered with explicit digs against capitalism. He claimed that the "profit-making system as a whole, and as now operated, is inherently centralising in character" (1920, 30), a development that, as we have seen above, he regarded as a major menace to mankind. Douglas maintained that under the current system there is "a complete divorcement between the worker and the finished product, which is in itself conducive to the feeling that he is part of a machine in the final output of which he is not interested." He also perceived a "connection between militarism and capitalism as vehicles for the expression of the will-to-power" (34–5).

Douglas argued that the "capitalist system is tottering to its fall, but, ... it may carry on for a long while, if its opponents obligingly demonstrate at short intervals their inability to supplant it with something better." He also decried the "insane profit-hunting of the super-productionist" (1921, 74, 78). Douglas admired the position taken by rival monetary reformer Arthur Kitson in so far as it would free manufacturers from the control exercised by finance, but ultimately rejected Kitson's scheme because "it also makes ... [manufacturers] independent of the public, because it leaves ... [them] in control of prices ... The manufacturer would then be absolute lord of the earth, since he would have the whole credit system in his hands." Kitson's proposals, Douglas suggests, would create "the manufacturers' paradise and the consumers' purgatory" (138–40).

Douglas maintained that Italian Fascism "was the capitalists' reply to Communism," and that along with "State Socialism" and "Sovietism," fascism was "a complete inversion" of Social Credit principles (1934, 23, 25). He held that "a life-long plot on the part of one man against the well-being of another man is very rare, but a business or national vendetta is the rule," and regretted that the present system was "so largely directed towards money-making rather than goods-making" (75, 87). And so on.

Douglasism Portrayed as "Petit-Bourgeois Ideology"

The conventional academic accounts of Douglasism are often couched in terms of the alleged class character of the doctrine. A key element in Macpherson's famous explication of English Social Credit is the assertion, made without supporting empirical evidence, that "its primary appeal was to those insecure sections of society, whether independent prairie farm producers or middle class English city dwellers, whose economic position may be defined as *petit-bourgeois*" (1962, 93). Similarly, Stein, following Macpherson, claims that Douglasism had a "special appeal" for the petite bourgeoisie:

> The attraction which social credit had for these people is self-evident. Social credit was a reform which required no radical transformation of the existing economic and social structure. It offered to the small property owner an opportunity to get rid of his excess production by stimulating demand among potential consumers. And it gave him, as a consumer, an opportunity to share in the new rewards. Perhaps the most appealing part of the doctrine, however, was its emphasis on the individual as against the group. This had both a class and a universal attraction. Individualism was central in the thinking of the petit bourgeois who valued his status as an independent property owner and feared submergence in the larger forces of concentration represented by the industrialists and the trade unions. (1973, 32–3)[19]

Stein states in a footnote that "in Britain, the doctrine nevertheless appears to have made little headway among the petit bourgeois class" (32 n 46). He does not provide any evidence for this assertion, nor does he explain how something with "self-evident" appeal to a particular class can make no headway with it.

Commentators like Macpherson and Stein imply that opposition to a "radical transformation" of society was foremost in the minds of the petite bourgeoisie but not the working class. The petite bourgeoisie is portrayed as inherently conservative, a trait that supposedly predisposes it to favour schemes like Social Credit, which would merely "fix" capitalism rather than eradicate it. A corollary to this position is that other classes, in particular the working class, do not have such a stake in capitalism and so would be inclined to favour more drastic measures such as the introduction of socialism.

There are major problems with this line of thinking. One is that empirical evidence has never been presented to support the claim that Douglasite Social Credit was more popular among members of the petite bourgeoisie than members of other classes. Another problem, one that will be discussed in greater depth in our analysis of the Alberta Social Credit doctrine in the next chapter, involves the assumption that the petite bourgeoisie is an inherently conservative class. Although the petit-bourgeois conservatism thesis is a popular idea in the social sciences, its veracity has never been adequately demonstrated.[20] The corollary regarding the working class, that it is inherently or potentially a radical class, is also questionable. It is contradicted by the fact that in advanced capitalist societies, working-class politics typically revolve around trade unionism and social democracy, activities that seek to "fix" capitalism rather than eradicate it.

Another very important point in this regard is that the petit-bourgeois argument assumes that the Social Credit philosophy does not advocate a "radical transformation" of society. But, as the preceding discussion has shown, this is a serious misreading of the doctrine. Community control of production and distribution through a command economy *would* involve a radical transformation of the existing system.

A related issue is that those making the petit-bourgeois argument claim that a desire for economic independence led the petite bourgeoisie to support Douglasism. Yet their independence would *diminish* if the plan were implemented. This is not to say that the petite bourgeoisie would necessarily reject the doctrine, but that the reasoning usually given for its acceptance is questionable. Conversely, the idea that Social Credit would have only limited appeal to other classes is suspect.

Ironically, the idea that Social Credit doctrine should have special appeal for the petite bourgeoisie would have been repugnant to Douglas had he ever learned of it. Douglas believed in the main assumptions of the centrist theory of the lower middle class, the theoretical basis of the claim that Social Credit received especially strong support from the petite bourgeoisie. For Douglas,

The first point to notice in regard to this deification of Bigness, is that it is accompanied by the Lower Middle Class Revolution. I recognise the unpleasant impression that such a phrase may convey, but the French equivalent, *petit bourgeois*, which has been largely used in this connection, does not appear to be more descriptive.

... the real cleavage in the world to-day is a cultural, not an economic cleavage, although the two may not be wholly distinct. The Lower Middle Class is a warped cultural class ... One characteristic of the class is blatancy, quite often joined with qualities much more admirable, and it appears to be specially and no doubt unconsciously, amenable to outside influence.

... The backbone of Socialism in every country (which is not to say its inspiration) is the Lower Middle Class, the type which yearns to have power without respectability and looks to exchange its unenviable situation for a "safe government job." It was the Lower Middle Class who were the tools of revolution in Russia, it is the lower middle class who are the most enthusiastic supporters of National Socialism in Germany ... The coming revolution in Japan will be of the same nature. (1942, 25–6)

It is quite clear, then, that Douglas did not see himself as the saviour of the petite bourgeoisie.

The issue of class support for the Douglas doctrine is ultimately an empirical question that can only be answered by empirical means. Unfortunately, the necessary data are almost completely non-existent with regard to the British movement, unlike the Albertan. Some clues to class support can be gained, however, by examining the organizations that expressed an interest in Social Credit.

Douglas initially believed that his scheme stood the greatest chance of succeeding through acceptance by organized labour (Finlay 1972, 122). The first political organization to consider Douglas's proposals was the British National Guilds League, which was endeavouring to bring about a decentralized form of socialism. Social Credit was hotly debated in the organization in 1919 and 1920, but ultimately rejected. Its rejection, however, caused a split in the guild socialist movement, with several factions breaking away to form Social Credit groups.

Similarly, in 1921 the Scottish Labour Advisory Committee requested that the British Labour Party investigate A.R. Orage and Douglas's "Draught Scheme" for the mining industry (reprinted in Douglas 1920, 145–51). The Labour Advisory Committee stated, "Some of us are not prepared to endorse all Major Douglas's views; but we are convinced that bank credits are one of the main constituents – if not indeed the main constituent – of selling prices; and no final solution of the problem is possible that does not bring the issue of credit and the fixing of selling prices under the community's control" (quoted in Douglas 1922b, 20–1).

Douglas refused an invitation to give evidence before a special Labour Party committee struck to consider Social Credit, citing several reasons,[21] including his objection that the committee would take "certain orthodox financial propositions as manifestations of natural law; a position only contestable to persons familiar with their origins" (1922b, 39). The committee met anyway, and rejected Social Credit.[22]

59   The Douglas Social Credit Philosophy

Also to be considered are the Green Shirts, the most militant Social Credit group in Britain. They were led by John Hargrave, who had earlier headed a naturalist organization called the Kibbo Kift. The Green Shirts were formed in 1933 through the merging of the Kibbo Kift and the Coventry Crusader Legion. The latter organization was formed by mobilizing the local unemployed, which again is indicative of some proletarian support for Douglasism. Similarly, in New Zealand the Labour Party won the 1935 election on a largely Douglasite platform (Paddock 1936).

It is also important to consider that Social Credit started as a movement of intellectuals associated with the *New Age*. One would expect that a movement of intellectuals would have a preponderance of members from middle-class or higher social positions, so it is quite likely that some of the support for Douglas Social Credit came from these strata.

CONCLUSIONS

This chapter has provided an account of the Douglas Social Credit philosophy that examines aspects of it that have been largely ignored by other researchers. In so doing, it challenges conventional interpretations of Douglasism by maintaining that the implementation of a Social Credit system would bring about fundamental changes to the way wealth is created and distributed. Douglas proposed that a command economy be introduced wherein the community, rather than the state or the market, determined what is to be produced, while the wealth created was to be distributed equally to all members of the community. This interpretation of Douglasism as very radical runs contrary to earlier accounts that portray Douglasism as an ultimately conservative doctrine that merely proposes to "tinker" with or prop up capitalism.

This chapter also questions the orthodox view of Douglasism as "petit-bourgeois ideology" for a number of reasons: this view is not substantiated with empirical evidence of disproportionate petit-rgeois support; it assumes that the petite bourgeoisie is an especially conservative class; and it seriously misconstrues the Social Credit doctrine itself. With regard to the last point, the petit-bourgeois thesis maintains that this class creates or looks favourably upon doctrines such as Douglasism because such systems of ideas stand to improve the petite bourgeoisie's position in capitalism without threatening the existence of capitalism itself. But this argument is quite misguided because Douglasism, if implemented, would eradicate capitalism as we know it, including the so-called "independence" of the petite bourgeoisie. Also, the assumption that the petite bourgeoisie has a special desire to maintain the capitalist system that is not shared by other classes low in the stratification system, in particular the working class, is questionable.

The greatest support for Social Credit came in Alberta. It is to the Alberta movement's adaptation of the Douglas doctrine that we now turn.

5 The Alberta Social Credit Philosophy

THE ALBERTA SOCIAL CREDIT DOCTRINE

William Aberhart and his followers were very successful in promulgating the Douglas Social Credit philosophy in Alberta, but they evidently misunderstood some aspects of it and also presented various themes and ideas under the Social Credit rubric that were foreign to Major Douglas. In addition, although Aberhart's adoption of the Social Credit cause was sudden and dramatic (see Irving 1959, 48–9), his knowledge and interpretation of the doctrine changed over the course of the eleven years in which he was at the forefront of the Alberta movement. Hence it makes sense to consider the Alberta Social Credit philosophy not as a fixed group of principles but as a malleable set of ideas that were frequently altered in reaction to criticism and events.

The malleability of the doctrine may be indicative of the Aberhart's ambivalence about the feasibility of the scheme as well as his lack of confidence in his grasp of Douglasism. Before he was elected he claimed that he was merely trying to generate interest in Social Credit and that the first step he would take if given the chance to implement the plan would be to put Major Douglas in charge (Alberta 1934, 11, 73). In making his case for the Social Credit system before a provincial government committee in 1934, Aberhart stated, "To be frank with you, I feel somewhat like a young man getting married for the first time. I want to go on with it but I hardly know where it will land me" (11).

62   Social Classes and Social Credit in Alberta

The Alberta Social Crediters followed Douglas in arguing that poverty does not stem from an inability to *produce* an abundance of goods but from a faulty monetary system that deprives consumers of the purchasing power necessary to buy all the goods available. Their goal was to eliminate "poverty in the midst of plenty," a catch-phrase that was used to great effect in the province and one that aptly summarized Douglas's view that material abundance had been achieved but was not being properly distributed. The Albertans used the nomenclature popularized by Douglas to explain the apparent paradox of poverty in the midst of plenty, and promised to introduce both the just price and social credit dividends to remedy the situation. The latter, which were to provide each adult in Alberta with twenty-five dollars per month, irrespective of other income, caused a sensation and received more attention than any other feature of their program. The movement also advocated that Social Credit experts control all wages, salaries, and profits in the province in the public interest. Moreover, there was talk of replacing the taking of profits with the granting of a "commission on turnover." The Alberta Social Crediters also adopted Douglas's views on the powers of the banks, including his mistaken view of how the banks create money.

The Shortage of Purchasing Power

The A + B theorem, in its original form, was offered as an explanation of the deficiency in consumer purchasing power. Generally, however, when the theorem came under attack, little effort was made to revise it, unlike the tack taken by Douglas and his followers in Britain. At first the criticism was simply ignored, but eventually movement activists gave the theorem a much less prominent place in the organization's propaganda.

The technical deficiencies of the A + B theorem presented no problem for the Alberta Social Crediters, as it took little effort to convince Albertans in the 1930s that they lacked adequate purchasing power. The high level of both public and private debt made the argument that financiers ultimately controlled the province a relatively easy sell as well.

Social Credit Dividends

While it was not difficult to convince Albertans that they lacked adequate purchasing power, there was considerable controversy surrounding the feasibility of paying a dividend of twenty-five dollars per month. The most common question asked of the Alberta Social

63 The Alberta Social Credit Philosophy

Crediters was "Where's the money for the dividend going to come from?" Aberhart's answer was that the dividends were to be paid in the form of "credit," not money. The credit was to be issued "much in the same way that the banks issue many of their loans" (Aberhart 1935, 23). However, as the dividends were not to be paid back, they would certainly have been money, albeit deposit money. As will become apparent as we proceed, the Albertans often failed to distinguish between the granting of conventional bank credit and the creation of social credit.

True to the founder's approach, Aberhart suggested that in order to issue social credit, the "state shall be viewed by its citizens as a gigantic joint-stock company with the resources of the province behind its credit" (1935, 19). In accord with Douglasism, Alberta Social Crediters maintained that they simply wanted to "monetize" existing wealth – that is, make the amount of money in the hands of consumers equal to the value of the material wealth already existing in the province. Thus Aberhart's statement that the "credit issued will be a charge against the Natural Resources of the Province" (1935, 27) is in keeping with Douglas's idea that "real credit" should be based on the community's ability to deliver goods and services.

In explaining how the dividend was to be subsidized, Aberhart ventured away from the Douglas doctrine, although the vague and contradictory nature of his proposals makes it difficult to determine just how far he had strayed from Douglas. Aberhart claimed that "there is an enormous spread in price between the producer's cost and the consumer's price. It is the intention under the Social Credit system to reduce this spread" (1935, 27).[1] The increased flow of funds through the issuing of social credit to consumers and producers would produce an "increased turn-over," enabling the producer and distributor to "carry on their business with a closer margin of profit or commission on turnover. Thus the province will be able to collect a levy that will provide the basic dividends to distribute to the various citizens" (29). Aberhart then gave an example wherein a bushel of wheat with a just price of 60 cents would be charged a 5-cent levy (he avoided the word "tax"), flour worth $1.10 would have 10 cents excised, and a loaf of bread costing 7 cents would have a levy of 1 cent. With somewhat questionable logic, he also claimed that his plan would *reduce* the level of taxation because it would no longer be necessary for the province to borrow money, the distribution of social credit and the resulting increase in commercial activity more than compensating for the levies introduced. Aberhart's confusion about the nature of the dividend is evident in a question he repeatedly asked in the presence of English Green Shirt leader John Hargrave some sixteen months after the 1935 election: "If I issue a dividend, how do I get the money back?" (Social Credit Party of Great Britain and Northern Ireland 1937, 2). Moreover, Aberhart did not enhance his credibility by occasionally denying that taxation would pay for the dividend (see Alberta 1934, 23, 66).

The idea of taxing producers and consumers to pay for the social credit issued runs contrary to Douglasism, as Aberhart's critics were quick to point out. Douglas believed that the modern industrial system, if accompanied by a proper monetary system, was capable of providing an extraordinarily high standard of living for all without relying on taxation.[2] The claim that there is usually a huge difference between the capitalist's costs and the market price (i.e., that the taking of exorbitant profits is a widespread, fundamental problem in capitalist economies) is not to be found in Douglas's thought, although the Major would not permit excessive profits to be made in his system. This difference in assessing economic problems is indicative of a social democratic bent in Aberhart that was absent in the inventor of Social Credit, as the Alberta leader's position implies that the economic crisis was at least partially attributable to the taking of excessive profits as opposed to a flaw in the monetary system.

Other elements of the Alberta Social Credit philosophy also suggest a belief, contrary to Douglasism, that many are poor because a few rich people, including those who are not financiers, refuse to share their wealth. Aberhart claimed that "no one should be allowed to have an income that is greater than he himself and his loved ones can possibly enjoy, to the privation of his fellow citizens" (1935, 55). For Douglas, one need not worry about a few rich people, since with Social Credit all will enjoy a high standard of living. Aberhart also tended to downplay Douglas's vision of the vast riches possible under a Social Credit system, claiming instead that the dividend would be used primarily for the "bare necessities" of food, clothing, and shelter.

The quasi–social democratic deviations from Douglasism were not viewed by Aberhartite Social Crediters as errors to be corrected. According to Ernest Manning they were positive contributions to the doctrine. Manning claimed that the Alberta plan to distribute excessive profits to consumers in the form of dividends would belie "the common hearsay abroad today that Social Credit simply means the socialization of financial credit advocated by various progressive reformers of our day" (*Alberta Social Credit Chronicle*, 10 August 1934, 1, 5). These deviations from Douglasism are important to acknowledge because they suggest that in supporting the Social Credit Party, people were in favour of much more than simple monetary reform.

65   The Alberta Social Credit Philosophy

Just Price

The Alberta movement's rationale for the introduction of the just price reflected the non-Douglasite belief in the harmful effect of price spreads mentioned earlier. Ernest Manning, as minister of Trade and Commerce in the first Aberhart administration, explained that "no group of consumers should be exploited by anyone having possession of goods, to charge prices that are unfair and excessive." For Douglas, prices for consumer goods were definitely too high, not because producers or merchants were exploiting consumers, though, but because the existing monetary system did not put enough money into circulation. The Albertans claimed that the just price would also solve the opposite problem, namely the inability of producers to earn a sufficient or fair amount of profit. As Manning explained it, the producer "must be protected from having to produce articles and place them on the market at so low a price that he cannot secure the cost of production, plus something to them for their work" (1936).

"Alberta Credit" To Be the Main Medium of Exchange
in Alberta

In the system proposed by William Aberhart, "Alberta credit," the social credit issued by the province, would replace Canadian currency as the most common medium of exchange. All wages and salaries were to be paid "as now, but in credit, not money" (1935, 21). An exception would be made for the employees of firms based outside the province, such as those working for the post office or the Canadian Pacific Railway, who would continue to be paid in Canadian funds. Aberhart did not address the issue of the value of Alberta credit relative to the Canadian dollar.

Wage Rates To Be Fixed by Experts

The Alberta Social Credit leader explained that "experts would fix the minimum and maximum wage just the same as they could fix the price of goods. It is understood, however, that wages must not be reduced on account of the issuance of the basic dividends" (1935, 43). The control of all wages in the public interest and their payment in the form of Alberta credit is consistent with the Douglasite notion that production is communal in nature and that distribution should be communal as well. The Albertans believed that their system would be fair to consumers, producers, and wage earners alike. The

66   Social Classes and Social Credit in Alberta

Lethbridge Social Credit organization, for instance, campaigned with the slogan "Vote for Social Credit and justice for the worker and producer" (*Lethbridge Herald*, 13 August 1935, 3).

The Albertans' ultimate reliance on experts to fix wages and prices was another departure from Douglasism. Many of the decisions to be made by the "community" in Douglas's scheme were to be made by "experts" in the Alberta plan.

"Controlled" Individual Ownership of Productive Enterprises

In addition to granting dividends, introducing the just price, and controlling all wages and profits, the province was to issue all "producers" "temporary, supervised credit to enable them to serve the citizenship in the best possible way" (Aberhart 1935, 23). The idea of "supervised" credit designed to meet public needs, although not elaborated upon, implies a measure of control over what is to be produced. The Albertans declared that they stood for "*controlled* individual ownership*" of business (57, emphasis added), which is consistent with Major Douglas's view that the public should determine economic policy, while the formal ownership and day-to-day administration of business must remain private. Like Douglas, Aberhart also advocated the production of "useful" goods rather than those produced by an unregulated market. He claimed that "direction should be given from time to time as to the products most needed" (57), and he attacked unscrupulous advertisers. However, he did not explain how the province's economic needs were to be determined.

In order to clarify what the implications were for the relationship between the individual and the state under a Social Credit system, a questioner at the provincial Social Credit hearings of 1934 remarked to Aberhart, "I gather from you the credit loans would not be fixed on any flat basis at all but be according to the requirements of the producer." To this Aberhart replied, "The requirements of the *country or state*. The producer might say I am going to produce this but your control of policy is the same as that of the banks today. They control production by the amount of loans they are willing to give" (Alberta 1934, 74, emphasis added). Aberhart's remarks are consistent with the Douglasite notion that the economy is to be controlled through public control of credit, although Douglas would have taken issue with the idea of meeting the requirements of the state. After asking further questions in an attempt to clarify Aberhart's position on the relationship between the individual and the state, the questioner asked, "Then we have to be the dictators as to the amount of credit any one man must have?" To this Aberhart replied, "I think that is about the same position. You have to come to the place where you say what will you produce? Wheat? Did you ever raise wheat? We do not give loans to risky borrowers." The questioner's retort to this was, "Then that is the same as Soviet Russia. To work out your plan then we have to put the state in a position where it is controlling the individual initiative of the man?" Aberhart answered, "I would not so control the position of the individual man as much as the banks should do it today. The state should be a better adviser" (74–5).

Some people raised concerns that regulating wages, prices, and profits and otherwise "controlling" production would lead to excessive state bureaucracy. In his opening remarks at the provincial hearings of 1934 Aberhart stated that he had been asked whether an "army of clerks" would be needed to implement his scheme. "There would be no more clerks needed than now," he explained, "for there would be less duplication. Think of the number of banks scattered all over the province often duplicating the need of clerks." He added, in good Douglasite fashion, "Besides this there are machines to do the work." He then read a brief quotation from British Social Crediter Maurice Colbourne's *Economic Nationalism* (1934), which stated that "a [new] machine of four feet high like a mammoth typewriter with levers instead of keys" could perform the work of sixty bank clerks. "I do not think we need to fear having an army of clerks," Aberhart concluded (Alberta 1934, 16).

The Role of the Banks

The Alberta movement shared Douglas's views on how the banks create money. In a pamphlet entitled "Tax the Banks – It Costs Them Nothing!" (ca 1935) it is explained that the total value of bank notes in Canada in 1933 was $141 million, yet the value of all bank deposits was $2.26 billion. The difference between the two, about $2.12 billion, was "created out of nothing" and therefore "could have been used to eliminate taxes ... thus giving a higher standard of living to the present generation." Social Crediters in Alberta, like Douglas, claimed that money flows from the end of a banker's fountain pen and wanted this money to be a community resource. Not surprisingly, they held that the modern banking system "was established by deceit and trickery,"[3] since this fantastic system of money creation had been kept secret. We shall see in chapter 7 that the Social Credit legislation passed in the party's first term of office was consistent with these views of the banks.

However, it is not clear that Aberhart himself understood Douglas's position on how the banks create money. When Douglas suggested

68 Social Classes and Social Credit in Alberta

that the newly elected Social Credit administration ask the banks for an outright grant of $5 million on the grounds that money simply flows from the end of a banker's pen, Aberhart assumed that he was referring to a loan and dismissed the suggestion as a "matter of detail" (Douglas 1937, 137). This prompted Douglas to reply that "the nature of the transaction which is involved is quite fundamental and vital" and that the transaction was to be a granting of social credit, not a loan (144–7).

Members of the Alberta movement, like Douglas, also believed that bankers wield a tremendous amount of power both nationally and internationally. Every social issue, according to Aberhart (1940, 6), "is centred in a conflict between the People and the Money power." Financiers were held responsible for wars, were considered to be in control of the media of communication, ruled the various political parties, and so on. The heavy hand of finance was even felt in everyday life. The Lethbridge Social Credit organization asked, "Do the big shots who control our very lives care how you or your family suffer? They manipulate the price of all we receive, be it wheat or wages, as well as all we buy" (*Lethbridge Herald*, 13 August 1935, 3).

Views on Maintaining the Existing Economic System

Contrary to the impression given in many accounts of the movement, the Alberta Social Crediters were not wary of upsetting the existing order of things.[4] In a Social Credit pamphlet the claim was made that "Adam Smith was the first great political economist. Since his day there have been only two others, Karl Marx and Major Douglas. All the rest have been and are economists without political sense or vision."[5]

Movement supporters did not have it in their minds that they were "saving capitalism." As in the work of Major Douglas, there are numerous anti-capitalist references in the Alberta Social Credit ideology. Aberhart, for example, argued against the "old, feudal, capitalistic opinion that work is the only way to give purchasing power."[6] The *Alberta Social Credit Chronicle* claimed that "the system of Social Credit can be traced back many thousands of years, but was unfortunately crushed by the capitalistic system" (27 July 1934, 3). Under the headline "Capitalists Attack Social Credit" the *Chronicle* warned that "extreme fright almost amounting to panic has at last seized the Moguls of Capitalism, all their forces are being marshalled to combat the possibility of the people of Alberta at last obtaining a fair opportunity of acquiring an equitable share of the blessing so amply provided by Providence" (16 August 1935, 3). "Prior to elections," according to the *Chronicle*, "the silver-tongued orators of the capitalist party flood our platforms, and with subtle tongues tell us of the wonderful days in store for the people ... but they don't tell you that it will only be until the day following the election, and then they find it best to revert back to the old order of things" (3 August 1934, 4).

Social Crediters maintained that "Social Credit Science proposes the removal of all profit in its generally accepted sense and the granting of commission on turnover as a substitute" (Social Credit League of Alberta 1935, 7). The replacement of profit with a "commission on turnover" is a very important part of the Social Credit program because *commissions, unlike profits, accrue to those who do not enjoy the prerogatives normally associated with ownership*. Those earning commissions do not have the power to set wages or prices for the company as a whole and do not have a claim on the surplus wealth generated by the enterprise as a whole. Under the Social Credit "commissions" scheme, capitalists would essentially be converted into employees. The commission policy, in conjunction with state regulation of wages and prices, the issuing of a communally generated dividend, and state control over what is to be produced, illustrates that the Social Credit movement was not in favour of maintaining a capitalist, market-oriented economy. This observation will be seen as especially significant in our discussion of the popular interpretation of Social Credit as an economically conservative movement.

Rather than conservative, the Alberta movement was in fact something of a millenarian movement, as it claimed that Social Credit would not only end the Depression but "lead the world into a new Social Order," as the Lethbridge Social Credit organization put it (*Lethbridge Herald*, 8 August 1935, 3). Alberta was to be the location of the first great breakthrough for Douglasism; it was to signal the beginning of the world-wide Social Credit epoch in which the human condition would be forever changed.[7]

Social Crediters in Alberta, however, like Douglas, may have deluded themselves with regard to the social disruption that the implementation of a Social Credit plan would bring about. Aberhart described his plan as "wondrously simple," stating that Social Credit principles "can be introduced into our present system without a very great upheaval of Social, Commercial or Political interests, but they will effectively *change the whole system* in a very short space of time" (1933, 2, emphasis added).[8] Here the Alberta leader appears to share with Douglas the view that the Social Credit plan could be implemented without taking anything away from anyone (except bankers), and hence without any social disorder. Aberhart was even innocent of any inkling of how the banks would react to the scheme he was proposing. When asked at the provincial government inquiry in 1934 "Would this [Social Credit] scheme be looked upon favourably or not by private banks?" he replied, "I have no idea. I have spoken to some bank managers and they have told me it is a splendid scheme, but I cannot tell you what headquarters of finance will say" (Alberta 1934, 28).

Critics, however, contended that if the plan were implemented it would cause severe disruption. In addition to the economic chaos feared by various chambers of commerce, discussed below, it was pointed out that issuing the dividend would cost about $120 million per year, which was approximately eight times the amount of the 1934 provincial government revenues, before expenditures. Added to this would be the cost of subsidizing the just price. Another problem was that much of what was produced in the province was bought by people outside Alberta, while many of the goods sold in Alberta were brought in from outside the province. This meant that Alberta firms would have to convert Alberta credit into Canadian or foreign funds, which would be problematic as it would in effect create two currencies in Canada, one of which would rest on highly questionable economic foundations.

Property Rights

For a movement that supposedly "would not do anything which would undermine the sanctity of property rights" (Macpherson 1962, 220), the Social Credit movement in Alberta gave a rather tepid official endorsement of these rights. The "property rights of the individual," Aberhart wrote, "would be respected, and supported *where possible*" (1933, 8, emphasis added).

Like the founder of the movement, Aberhart did not elaborate on his theory of property. But since the movement maintained that social credit would derive from the existing resources of the province; that wages, prices, and profits (in effect, the distribution of wealth) should be controlled by experts in the public interest; and that conventional profits should be replaced with "commissions on turnover," it is clear that the movement did not have a strong philosophical commitment to conventional bourgeois property rights. As chapter 7 will reveal, while the movement did not advocate the abolition of private property, when in power it tried to implement several measures that would have severely restricted property rights.

That the movement was viewed by some as a threat to property rights is suggested by the position taken by the Edmonton Chamber of Commerce, which strongly condemned Social Credit because "it threatens the ultimate mortgaging or confiscation of all private property."[9] The Calgary Board of Trade also feared that Social Credit intervention in economic affairs would be disastrous for its members, claiming that "any attempt to fix just prices can only result in incredible confusion and paralysis of business ... The Social Credit proposals will isolate Alberta and render it impossible for either the farmer or businessman to buy or sell to advantage."[10]

Views on Socialism

In spite of their collectivist sentiments and condemnation of the existing system, the Alberta movement, like Douglas himself, was anti-socialist. It is significant, however, that anti-socialism was not a prominent feature of the Alberta program until the mid-1940s, when a surge in CCF popularity swept across Canada. The absence of anti-socialist attitudes in the early movement was reflected in the fact that in the 1930s Social Crediters entered into formal and informal electoral alliances with Alberta socialists and communists in a few ridings (Finkel 1989, 50–1). Also, there was sentiment among rank and file members of Social Credit and the CCF in favour of merging the two movements, especially in Saskatchewan (Lipset 1971, 134–46). Some ideological overlap occurred. Parts of the CCF's Regina Manifesto have a distinctly Douglasite ring to them, and many of the policies advocated by Social Credit in its early years were social democratic rather than Douglasite in nature.

The problem with socialism, according to Alberta Social Crediters, is that it creates a society in which "the state is supreme," whereas under a Social Credit regime, "the individual is supreme." In condemning socialism, however, the Albertans still put considerable distance between themselves and the existing order. A Social Credit pamphlet, for instance, states that people should be even "more suspicious of our probable fate at the hands of [socialist] political planners than the risks we run from money-grubbing commercialism." "Monetization" and "controllership" rather than "socialization" and "ownership" was their goal (Alberta Social Credit Women's Auxiliaries 1944, 2).

Support for Large-Scale Industry

Like Douglas, members of the Alberta movement were not endeavouring to return their society to a bygone paradise of small, independent entrepreneurs, although one sometimes gets this impression from reading academic accounts of the movement.[11] The Alberta movement was not against large-scale industry, and in fact promised to expand it in the province. Members of Alberta study groups were taught that "the abundant production made possible by modern power driven machinery combined with the discoveries of science and improved methods of organization, ensures that economic security and freedom for all could be made available."[12] Social Crediters claimed that as well as supporting agriculture,

a vote for Social Credit is a vote for the mining industry.

We have a cement industry that can also be greatly increased to the benefit of the people of Alberta ... Alberta needs many industries that will use our raw products, burn our coal and use our power. (*Lethbridge Herald*, 8 August 1935, 3)

Anti-Semitism

Neither Aberhart nor his successor Ernest Manning shared Douglas's anti-Semitism (Hiller 1977, 70; Palmer 1982, 151–8), and anti-Semitism was never a feature of any Alberta Social Credit electoral platform. Anti-Semitism did manifest itself in the party in the 1940s, however, when the government's Social Credit Board began to propagate Douglas's Jewish conspiracy theories. These theories received some support among Social Credit MLAS. Manning, who had become premier following Aberhart's death in 1943, would have nothing to do with the anti-Semitic elements in the party and unceremoniously put an end to the Social Credit Board. He also expelled from the party two MLAS, including a Cabinet minister, who were sympathetic to it. (See Barr 1974, 127–30.) In 1982 Manning received the National Humanitarian Award from B'nai B'rith.

Addenda to Douglasism

The Alberta Social Crediters went beyond nascent social democratic themes in putting their distinctive signature on the Social Credit philosophy. Aberhart also had the idea that the provincial government's debt could be liquidated by having those with funds in bank accounts, trust companies, or life insurance policies withdraw their investments and purchase government bonds, which would be redeemed in Alberta credit (1933, 2–3). This would, according to Aberhart, "transfer our external debt to an internal matter to be handled by social credit" (Alberta 1934, 19).

The owners of real estate, industries, retail stores, and other enterprises were encouraged to sell their property or business to the future Social Credit government in exchange for bonds payable in Alberta credit. Those holding farm or home mortgages were advised to allow the Social Credit government to take over their mortgages and make their payments to the government in Alberta credit. These measures would facilitate private debt reduction and contribute to a functioning social credit system.

However, the movement gave these proposals very little prominence in the months before the 1935 election, probably because concern was raised about the possibility that a Social Credit government might confiscate private wealth. On the eve of the election the *Alberta Social Credit Chronicle* declared in large, bold type that the party would not "interfere with" pensions, savings, or insurance policies (16 August 1935, 5).

A well-known addition to the Douglas doctrine was the religious themes and overtones introduced by the Alberta movement. An active lay preacher and radio evangelist, Aberhart would often infuse his political statements with religious themes and biblical allusions. He often pondered the idea that Social Credit was a solution sent to him by God to solve the problems of the Depression. Some Social Crediters called their movement "applied Christianity," while the *Chronicle* maintained that "one of the finest and greatest exponents of Social Credit was Jesus Christ himself" (5 October 1935, 2, quoted in Hiller 1972, 306). The ritual of a Social Credit Women's Auxiliary included the following prayer: "Almighty God, our Father in Heaven, we do acknowledge Thy goodness and mercy to us. Thou hast provided an abundance for Thy creatures, but mankind in its selfishness has been unable to distribute Thy bounty."[13]

Another uniquely Albertan element in the movement's philosophy was a direct appeal for women's rights. Aberhart claimed that "economic security is the right of every citizen, male or female. Women were never intended to be slaves, but helpmates. There would, no doubt, be more wholesome marriages consummated [under Social Credit]. They would not have to marry for a meal ticket" (1935, 51). In their study groups Social Crediters were taught that "under the present system the position of most women is devoid of any real measure of economic freedom," while under a Social Credit regime, "at long last, every woman would have the economic security which would give her the standing in the community that has hitherto been denied women."[14] The mobilization of women appears to have been especially successful in Calgary, where more women voted than men,

74   Social Classes and Social Credit in Alberta

although there were more men on the voters' list. Fully 83 per cent of eligible women voted in Calgary in that election, compared to only 70 per cent of the men.[15] The Alberta Social Credit movement had several very capable female leaders, including Edith Rogers and Edith Gostick, both of whom were elected to the legislature in 1935.[16]

ACADEMIC INTERPRETATIONS OF THE ALBERTA SOCIAL CREDIT IDEOLOGY

Two key themes in the academic interpretation of the Alberta Social Credit doctrine concern us here, both of which have had a major influence on the leading assessments of the Alberta Social Credit movement. One is that the ideology was, like Douglasism proper, "petit-bourgeois" in nature. The other is that it was largely a reaction against central Canadian "imperialism" or the national policy.

Alberta Social Credit Portrayed as "Petit-Bourgeois Ideology"

According to the petit-bourgeois thesis, the Alberta Social Credit ideology derives from or is compatible with the Alberta petite bourgeoisie's position in the capitalist class structure. C.B. Macpherson claims that Social Credit's program for monetary reform and its conception of democracy are the "products of the same assumptions" and are "equally false solutions of the *petit-bourgeois* predicament" (1962, 234). He maintains that the "*petit-bourgeois* concept of society, which had impaired the U.F.A. theory, was now carried to its extreme [by Social Credit]" (160). The movement had, in brief, a "small-producer ideology" (216). Likewise, Finkel makes reference to the "Social Credit petit bourgeois philosophy" (1984, 123), and Conway maintains that Social Credit (and the CCF) "reflected a protest and critique of capitalism, and proposed developmental alternatives, articulated from the point-of-view of the agrarian *petit-bourgeoisie*" (1979, 78–9).

Macpherson's famous interpretation holds that since Alberta was primarily a province of independent or petit-bourgeois producers, serious radicalism was out of the question. In keeping with the centrist theory of the lower middle class discussed in chapter 1, he suggests that the petite bourgeoisie, unlike the working class or bourgeoisie, is incapable of comprehending its real class position in capitalist society. Macpherson writes that "historically, while working class and bourgeoisie have both displayed this awareness [of class relations] at crucial periods, the *petite-bourgeoisie* has typically not done so" (1962, 225). Macpherson provides no evidence in support

75   The Alberta Social Credit Philosophy

of this claim, nor does he spell out what true consciousness would be for any class, although he does intimate that the best course history could take would involve the abolition of capitalism and private property.

As we saw in chapter 1, Macpherson argues that members of the petite bourgeoisie have a "delusive understanding of the nature of society, of the economy, and of their own place in it" (1962, 226). The petite bourgeoisie will never do anything to undermine the capitalist system, the argument goes, because it is itself a class of small capitalists. It is maintained that the best the petite bourgeoisie can do in times of crisis is endeavour to alter the terms of capitalist trade in its favour. But this is said to result in little significant change, given the power of the bourgeoisie in advanced capitalism. Similarly, this class supposedly cherishes its independence, however illusory that independence may be. The received interpretation of Alberta Social Credit holds that, as with Douglasism elsewhere, the petite bourgeoisie in Alberta was especially attracted to Social Credit because the movement promised to solve this class's problems without disrupting the capitalist system.[17]

The same points of objection may be raised concerning the argument that the Alberta Social Credit movement had a petit-bourgeois ideology as were raised in the previous chapter with regard to the notion that Douglasism was petit-bourgeois. First of all, as discussed in chapter 3, the petit-bourgeois thesis is not supported by empirical data. Those who claim that the doctrine was a reflection of the petit-bourgeois world-view do not provide evidence that this class embraced it in proportionately greater numbers than members of other classes. The fact that Macpherson's own analysis indicates that only 38 per cent of Alberta's work-force in 1931 was made up of the agrarian petite bourgeoisie and 7 per cent the non-agrarian petite bourgeoisie is relevant as well, as the petit-bourgeois thesis says virtually nothing about how the non-petit-bourgeois majority would react to the Social Credit doctrine.

Secondly, this interpretation takes for granted what Macpherson calls "the classic pattern of the *petit-bourgeois* class" (1962, 224), namely that the petite bourgeoisie is inherently conservative relative to other classes. However, it is worth repeating that the popularity of the petit-bourgeois conservatism thesis is not commensurate with the state of the evidence advanced in support of it. According to A.J.P. Taylor,

all experience shows that revolutions come from those who are economically independent, not from factory workers. Very few revolutionary leaders have done manual work, and those who did soon abandoned it for political activities. The factory worker wants higher wages and better conditions, not a revolution. It is the man on his own who wants to remake society, and moreover he can happily defy those in power without economic risk. In old England the village cobbler was always the radical and the Dissenter. After all, the lord of the manor had to have his boots made and mended, whatever the cobbler's political opinions. The independent craftsman, like the intellectual, cannot be dismissed from his job. His skill protects him from the penalties which society imposes on the non-conformist. (1967, 20–1)[18]

While Taylor's statement does not constitute a refutation of the petit-bourgeois conservatism idea, it does provide some reasonable grounds for doubt. Taking the case at hand, we may wonder whether the prairie agrarian petite bourgeoisie really was as conservative as Macpherson contends. In reviewing the larger corpus of Macpherson's writings on democracy, K.R. Minogue weighs Macpherson's view that the defence of private property has been a persistent problem for thinkers throughout the modern era. Minogue finds this view to be considerably exaggerated, and suggests that "Macpherson tends to project this exaggeration back through the centuries. *His* problem [property] is everybody's problem" (1976, 388). One wonders whether in *Democracy in Alberta* Macpherson's problem is projected on to the petite bourgeoisie. Were property rights, especially those of central Canadian bankers and industrialists, really an overriding concern for the agrarian petite bourgeoisie at this time? Would the violation of bourgeois property really have been perceived as a threat to the petite bourgeoisie's very existence, as Macpherson suggests?

Contrary to the position taken in *Democracy in Alberta*, it is not self-evident that the agrarian petite bourgeoisie would have an unshakable faith in "the basic tenets of capitalist enterprise," especially during a prolonged depression. As one writer put it,

"Why should *we* worry about property rights?" the farmers ask when you suggest that they are striking at the fundamental economic structure ...

When your farm is covered with mortgages, your cattle tied up with a barnyard loan, your machinery attached by a chattel mortgage, your previous year's taxes unpaid, and your coming crop covered by a seed lien – and then you get no crop – you fail to see just what it is you may lose with the collapse of capitalism. (D.C. Smith 1934, 205; quoted in Lipset 1971, 155).

A cursory review of the history of the Canadian prairies in the period in question casts doubt on the petit-bourgeois conservatism thesis. Aberhartite Social Credit would have radically altered the way wealth was created and distributed. In so far as the petite bourgeoisie supported the movement, an issue that is examined using empirical methods in the next chapter, its support is hardly indicative of an inherent conservatism.

A more obvious illustration of agrarian petit-bourgeois radicalism can be found in the history of the CCF. The popularity of this ostensibly socialist movement, a movement that formed the government in Saskatchewan in 1944 and achieved considerable popular support in Alberta as well,[19] is definitely at odds with the petit-bourgeois conservatism thesis. While no claim is made here that CCF support was predominantly or disproportionately petit-bourgeois, there is little doubt that it received substantial support from the agrarian segment of this class, especially in Saskatchewan.

The stock answer to this dilemma is that the CCF was not socialist and was not perceived to be socialist. While there is no consensus concerning the definition of the word "socialism," it is a fact that in the 1930s and 1940s the CCF advocated the socialization of large sections of Canadian industry and finance and proposed that "planning" replace the largely unregulated market as the driving force of the economy. This would make the CCF at least "as socialist" as, say, the British Labour Party. There is a striking incongruence, therefore, between agrarian petit-bourgeois support for the CCF and the portrayal of this class as inherently conservative or reactionary.

One may wish to argue in opposition to this view that the petite bourgeoisie's support for the CCF did not entail a desire to see capitalism torn asunder. But this argument can be made with equal force for the working class's endorsement of the party, or for workers' support for social democratic parties the world over. The idea that the working class is a revolutionary or potentially revolutionary class, while the petite bourgeoisie is irretrievably reactionary, is not buttressed by a history of Marxist-socialist militancy on the part of a substantial proportion of the working class in capitalist societies. The Canadian working class in the 1930s and 1940s, for example, was not throwing its weight behind a "real" socialist party when a substantial proportion of the prairie agrarian petite bourgeoisie was settling for the CCF. Similarly, the argument sometimes put forward that the petite bourgeoisie is a vacillating class, that it swings back and forth from progressive to reactionary causes without making a firm commitment to either kind, may be equally true of the working class and other classes. Other classes too do not have a history of unambiguous and enduring support for all "progressive" movements and rejection of all "reactionary" ones.

A further problem with the contention that the Alberta Social Credit philosophy is "petit-bourgeois" ideology is that the Alberta program is not consistent with what centrist theorists purport to be the typical ideology of this class. For one thing, as the foregoing discussion suggests, it is not conservative. Embracing a scheme that would involve controlling all prices, profits, and wages in the public interest, in effect altering the existing relations of production so that the power to distribute wealth would be placed in the hands of experts acting at the behest of the public; allowing the government to control economic activity through its ability to issue social credit; and replacing the taking of profits with "commissions on turnover" – all these radical initiatives hardly seem like the way to preserve capitalism as we know it. Nor is social credit a scheme that would protect the economic independence that the petite bourgeoisie is said to cherish.

We must consider as well the Alberta movement's explicit support for the development of large-scale industry. This too runs contrary to the depiction of the world-view of the petite bourgoisie provided by centrist theorists of the lower middle class. These theorists maintain that the small-business proprietor fears being crushed by big business on one side and big labour on the other, and so has feelings of animosity towards both groups. The centrist theory also holds that in the mind of the petit-bourgeois, large enterprises do not embody the many virtues of small businesses, such as an ethos of rugged individualism, hard work, and fair competition. Hence the Alberta movement's advocacy of the development of large enterprises is also not in accord with the centrist notion of how the petite bourgeoisie thinks.

In sum, the proposition that the Social Credit program was "petit-bourgeois ideology" is questionable on a number of counts: those making the claim do not provide evidence of disproportionate support among members of this class; the claim is based on the unfounded thesis that the petite bourgeoisie is an inherently conservative class; and the radicalism of the Social Credit ideology and the movement's desire to develop large-scale industry are inconsistent with the centrist account of the petit-bourgeois world-view.

It must be emphasized that the position taken in this book is not that the petite bourgeoisie would necessarily reject Social Credit but that the reasons given by centrist theorists for its purported support are suspect. The issue of which classes actually supported Social Credit in Alberta and why is taken up in chapters 6, 8, and 9.

Alberta Social Credit Portrayed as Anti-Imperialist

In addition to its alleged petit-bourgeois nature, the Social Credit philosophy is said to have been anti-imperialist. Macpherson's view that Social Credit was "in rebellion against eastern imperialism" is shared by many other commentators.

79   The Alberta Social Credit Philosophy

Since the notion of central Canadian imperialism is a broad and sometimes vague concept, for analytical purposes it will be divided into three elements. The first, which we may refer to as economic imperialism, involves the idea that a significant portion of the wealth created in western Canada in the period in question was expropriated by central Canadian interests through protective tariffs, discriminatory freight rates, and other federal measures that operated to the detriment of western Canada. This position also maintains that such policies restricted the economic development of the west by discouraging investment. The policies in question are considered to be part of the national policy of economic development in Canada, a general policy having its origins in Macdonald's National Policy of 1879. The plan involved the fostering of secondary industry in central Canada through import tariffs on manufactured goods, the building of transcontinental railways, and the agrarian development and settlement of the west. These measures were designed to create a truly national economy characterized by an east-west flow of trade.

The second component of central-Canadian imperialism, which is closely related to the first, is of a politico-legal nature. It results from the federal government's ability to introduce measures detrimental to the west by virtue of the fact that a majority of the seats in the House of Commons are held by Ontario and Quebec. Having no countervailing body by which the prairie provinces can check the power of the Commons is said to make the region a political colony of central Canada.

Macpherson appears to have these two facets of colonialism in mind when he makes reference to the "quasi-colonial" position of the three prairie provinces. He writes that it is a "commonplace of Canadian economic history that the main economic policies of the central government toward the Canadian west ever since Confederation, and even before, have been designed in the interests of eastern capital" (1962, 6–10, 220). He further suggests that the "protective tariff has been the fundamental federal imposition by which [western farmers] ... have seen themselves victimized" (6,9).[20] Mallory makes a similar argument, claiming that "the formation of a Social Credit government under the premiership of William Aberhart in 1935 symbolized a rejection of the National Policy and of the subordinate role which the West played in that policy" (1954, 54). Comparable arguments are made by Lipset (1971, 154–8), Conway (1978, 100, 118–124), and Palmer and Palmer (1990, 287).

Those making the economic-imperialism argument sometimes link it to the petit-bourgeois thesis discussed in the previous section. Macpherson (1962, 220–30), for instance, implies that since the petite bourgeoisie is incapable of comprehending its real position in

80   Social Classes and Social Credit in Alberta

capitalist economies, and since it would never dream of changing capitalism in any fundamental way, its only recourse is to challenge the terms of trade that affect its position in the capitalist marketplace. Such terms of trade include tariffs, railway policies, and other aspects of national economic policy.

The third element of imperialism that analysts of Social Credit sometimes claim was part of the Alberta movement's ethos involves the division of legislative powers between the federal and provincial governments. According to S.D. Clark,

An examination of developments in Alberta from 1935 to 1942 indicates very clearly that Aberhart's attempts to introduce Social Credit were directed primarily towards the object of strengthening the political position of the province in its relations with the federal government. Monetary reform was thus a means to an end ... In seeking the increased separation of Alberta from the Canadian federal system, Aberhart was prepared to go to very great lengths. In this respect he was a true radical; crying war upon the powers of Ottawa, he could remain faithful to his chosen role of a prophet who had led his followers out of the corrupt, eastern-dominated churches and was now called upon to lead them out of the equally corrupt, eastern-dominated federal state.   (1954, viii).

Social Credit as Anti-Imperialist: An Assessment

Before discussing further the role of central Canadian imperialism in the Social Credit movement, it should be made clear that the existence of such colonialism is not at issue in this study. At issue is what Social Crediters themselves were actually objecting to, and what they were endeavouring to do about it.

Tellingly, although those making the argument that Social Credit was an attempt to resist regional economic exploitation often cite academic viewpoints on the west's position in Canadian capitalism, they do not provide statements from William Aberhart or any other Social Crediter indicating that Social Credit supporters believed that the desperate conditions in the province were ultimately a result of the national policy. There is good reason for this, for unlike the Progressives before them, who put forth a "New National Policy," the Social Credit movement had little to say about the protective tariff, free trade, freight rates, or western exploitation in general.[21] In the Farmers' Platform of 1921, the Progressives' political agenda, almost half the text is devoted to the issue of the protective tariff.[22] In Social Credit proclamations one occasionally finds passing references to issues such as tariffs or freight rates, but these are not presented in the context of an argument decrying regional exploitation. In the

81   The Alberta Social Credit Philosophy

vast majority of Social Credit publications, including the widely cir-
culated "Blue Manual" (Aberhart 1935), tariffs, freight rates, and the
like are not mentioned at all. Aberhart even went so far as to say
that "in no way should the introduction of this system [of Social
Credit] be allowed to interfere with the relationship between Alberta
and Canada or any of the other provinces" and that "Alberta cannot
ask Ontario or Saskatchewan or Quebec to provide for her people.
That would be unreasonable. They have all they can do to provide
for their own" (5). William Aberhart was not a subtle man. If he
could, as is alleged, call his political opponents "grafters, crooks,
scheming politicians," and accuse them of "fornication, graft and
hypocrisy" (Irving 1959, 302), surely he could explain that Alberta's
problems stemmed primarily from an internal colonialism whereby
conventional national economic policies are formulated to the detriment of western Canada.

The contention that regional grievances per se were Social Credit's
raison d'être overlooks the fact that the party's ideology maintained
that there were fundamental problems with the economic system as
a whole and that the implementation of the scheme would, as Aberhart put it, "change the whole system." Social Credit was offered as
a policy that would ultimately solve the *world's* economic problems,
not one that would merely alter conventional regional trading and
development policies in favour of western Canada.

For Alberta Social Crediters the heart of the issue was not central
Canadian control of federal economic policy, or the fact that the
province's debts were owed to banks with head offices in Toronto
and Montreal. The problems were larger than that – they were
believed to be inherent in the nature of the existing economic system,
and it was assumed that they would still exist even if issues like
protective tariffs and freight rates were resolved to the satisfaction
of westerners and if the owners and operators of the banks were
located in Alberta. The Alberta Social Crediters knew that the problems of poverty and unemployment were not restricted to the province or to western Canada. They knew they were living in a period
of world-wide depression in which metropolitan as well as hinterland
areas were suffering. There is no suggestion in their election propaganda that they believed that regional exploitation was responsible
for conditions in the province or the world at large. Free trade, better
freight rates, even national independence for Alberta would not in
themselves bring about the Social Credit system that was to "lead
the world into a new Social Order."[23]

Furthermore, although Aberhart was not very active in politics
prior to the Depression, he was nominally a Conservative and was
an acquaintance of R.B. Bennett. Hence he had supported a party

82   Social Classes and Social Credit in Alberta

that at the time was associated with high tariffs and other elements of the national policy. In addition, his career as a teacher and principal in urban schools had kept him several steps removed from issues associated with agrarian politics, such as tariffs and freight rates.

It is worth noting as well that regionalism is not a part of the Douglas philosophy. Douglas himself lived in an international financial metropolis, London, but still claimed that there were fundamental problems with the existing economic system.

The regional-grievance argument also tends to overlook the fact that the west's position in Confederation changed appreciably in the Progressive era. The restoration of the Crow's Nest Pass freight rates in the early 1920s, the transfer of jurisdiction over natural resources from the federal government to prairie provincial governments in 1930, the increased presence of western representatives in the federal cabinet, and greater sensitivity to western grievances on the part of the federal government did much to ameliorate the colonial subordination of the west in Confederation (Morton 1950, 157, 293–4). Hence there are some awkward historical facts that would have to be bent to accommodate the anti-economic-imperialism thesis. For example, although Macpherson claims that the protective tariff was "the fundamental federal imposition," he quotes Fowke to the effect that

agrarian opposition [to the National Policy of protective tariffs] reached peaks of strength from 1907 to 1911, and again in the early nineteen-twenties ... The National Policy came to an end by 1930 ... The transfer of the natural resources of the western provinces in 1930 signified that the "national" policy out of which Confederation grew in 1867, and of which Macdonald's National Policy of tariffs was but a part, had been fulfilled.   (Fowke 1947, 270; quoted in Macpherson 1962, 9).

As Fowke's statement reveals, opposition to tariffs had waned some ten years before Social Credit came on the scene. Fowke's contribution to the Social Science Research Council's series on the background and development of Social Credit in Alberta, *The National Policy and the Wheat Economy* (1957), does not contain an analysis of the Social Credit movement. This suggests that the movement and the national policy were not intimately connected. Furthermore, a segment of the movement's prospective followers, organized labour, *favoured* protectionist policies (Craven and Traves 1979, 37).

A systematic presentation of conventional western economic grievances by the Aberhart forces did not appear until *The Case for Alberta* (Alberta 1938) was published three years after the movement had taken power, and after the Alberta government had become embit-

83 The Alberta Social Credit Philosophy

tered by the federal government's disallowance of its social credit legislation. *The Case for Alberta* is discussed in chapter 7, where the movement's first term of office is considered.

As for the third kind of imputed anti-imperialism, the interpretation of Social Credit as a movement bent on increasing the authority of the provincial government, Aberhart initially contended, unlike his critics, that the introduction of a social-credit plan would not contravene any provision of the British North America Act. Albertans were even led to believe by Mackenzie King, who was campaigning to replace R.B. Bennett as prime minister of Canada, that if his Liberals were elected in the federal election of 1935, King would not interfere with the implementation of social credit in Alberta. The Liberal leader even made statements that appeared to mean that he would welcome the plan. King stated,

If Social Credit ever gets a chance to prove itself it will be in Alberta. Mr. Aberhart has the whole province in his hands and if a Liberal Government is returned to power at Ottawa he will be given the fullest opportunity to work out his plan. But until it has proved itself let us confine it to Alberta. [Mr. Aberhart] ... promised to do certain definite things in a certain time. If he does them you won't need a Social Credit party to carry those ideas across the Dominion. They will spread to the whole world. This thing of $25 or $75 a month is just what the world had been looking for for hundreds and thousands of years.   (*Montreal Gazette*, 23 September 1935, 1)

King's Liberals won the 1935 federal election, but his promises concerning Social Credit in Alberta turned out to be hollow. None the less, it is notable that King describes social credit as an economic program that could spread "across the Dominion" and "to the whole world," not as some kind of hinterland or anti-federalist revolt. Further, as will be explained in more detail in chapter 7, it was only after the movement came to power, following the disallowance of social-credit legislation by federal instititions, that animosity towards the federal government came to the fore among Social Credit supporters, and even then the movement did not advocate sweeping changes to the existing division of powers.

Also to be considered in assessing the role of anti-imperialism in the Alberta Social Credit movement is an account of Social Credit that is not in agreement with the anti-imperialist interpretations. W.L. Morton, in a passage that seems to have been ignored by most Social Credit analysts, writes:

The rise of the Social Credit movement and the Cooperative Commonwealth Federation marked the beginning of a new phase of Canadian political development, a phase of *class rather than sectional politics*, of urban rather than rural dominance. The period 1910 to 1935 was one of transition in Canada from an agrarian to an industrial society; with the Progressive movement passed the Canadian, and the North American, agricultural frontier. Social Credit and the c.c.f. were the successors of the Progressive movement rather than continuations of it. (1950, 287).

Morton's inclusion of the CCF in this statement is entirely appropriate. Both the Social Credit and the CCF movements came into being at roughly the same time, in the early years of the Depression, and offered solutions for the same problems. Like Social Crediters, CCF followers did not see regional issues as being at the heart of the 1930s dilemma. The CCF's Regina Manifesto of 1932 states that although the "strangling of our export trade by insane protectionist policies must be brought to an end," the "old controversies between free traders and protectionists *are now largely obsolete*" (section 5, emphasis added). With the onset of the Depression, write Craven and Traves, "divisions between free traders and protectionists were subordinated to the struggle between socialism and capitalism" (1979, 36). Thus it seems that the CCF, like Social Credit, believed that the ultimate cause of the crisis was not the national policy or some part thereof but something much more fundamental and universal.

The foregoing discussion of the role of anti-imperialism in the Social Credit movement should not be construed to mean that anti-central Canadian feelings were absent in Alberta in the 1930s. Such feelings had by this time already developed deep historical roots. Every time Aberhart used the word "bankers," such animosity was triggered in some people. In addition, although the Liberals and Conservatives together received a respectable 30 per cent of the popular vote in the 1935 Alberta election, the historical perception that these parties were ultimately controlled by central Canadian interests probably made it easier for some voters to support a non-traditional party like Social Credit. None the less, the hypothesis advanced here is that the movement did not see the west's relationship with central Canada as the root cause of the Depression crisis. As explained above, the Social Credit ideology identifies fundamental shortcomings in all capitalist economies; it was these shortcomings, rather than regional exploitation, that Social Crediters saw as the crux of the problem. The proposed view thus maintains that there were important differences that are often overlooked between the Progressive movement of the 1920s and the Depression-inspired movements of the 1930s such as Social Credit and the Co-operative Commonwealth Federation.

85   The Alberta Social Credit Philosophy

CONCLUSIONS

We have seen that the adoption of Douglasism by Aberhartite Social Crediters involved some innovation and emendation. The general idea of poverty amidst plenty caused by a faulty monetary system remained intact, but non-Douglasite social democratic criticisms of super profits or "price spreads" and the policy of economic amelioration through taxation also found their way into the Alberta doctrine. The Douglasite belief that the "community" should control production and distribution was replaced by the notion that "experts," acting in the public interest, ought to exercise this prerogative. In Alberta experts were to control wage levels, prices, and incomes accruing to the owners of enterprises – in effect, the distribution of wealth. Public control of production was also to be achieved through the granting of social credit to enterprises deemed worthy by the state. In addition, profits were to be replaced by "commissions on turnover." Thus the Alberta Social Credit program, if implemented, would have involved a fundamental restructuring of the economic system.

This chapter challenges some widely accepted academic portrayals of the Social Credit doctrine. The thesis that Social Credit ideas are "petit-bourgeois ideology" is rejected on the grounds that this position is not substantiated by empirical evidence of disproportionate petit-bourgeois support, that it is based on a highly questionable general theory of this class, and that the Social Credit doctrine itself does not match the alleged petit-bourgeois world-view. The received notion that the Social Credit ideology is a manifestation of anti–central Canadian imperialism is also placed in doubt, as anti-imperialist claims are largely absent from the movement's body of ideas. Social Credit stood for a fundamental restructuring of the economy, as opposed to the reform of tariff and transportation policies or a shift in the division of federal-provincial powers.

Now that an account of both Douglasism proper and Aberhartite Social Credit has been presented, it is possible to go beyond theories and assertions regarding the class basis of the Alberta mass movement and analyse some data. This is the topic of the next chapter.

6 The 1935 Election:
Cities, Towns, and Countryside

THE CITIES

Voting data for Edmonton by polling subdivision (the area within a constituency covered by a single polling place) are not available.[1] For this reason Edmonton must be excluded from the within-cities analysis of the vote for 1935. This is especially unfortunate because Edmonton was the only city having a comparatively low Social Credit vote;[2] an analysis of the results there might have provided clues to why this was the case. None the less, such data are available for Calgary, Lethbridge, and Medicine Hat.

Census data could not be used in the analysis that follows, as provincial constituency and polling subdivision boundaries do not correspond with census districts or census tracts, the latter being the census areas within the major cities. Also, data by census tract were only first compiled in 1946 and have never been gathered in this form for the smaller cities of Lethbridge and Medicine Hat.

To overcome the difficulties with the census, it was decided to divide each city's polling subdivisions into a small number of groups according to an assessment of the social class of the subdivision residents at the time of the election. Their social class was estimated using information given by local informants and by consulting the literature available on each city.[3]

In ecological studies there is often a lack of uniformity within the boundaries of the districts being compared. This is true of certain districts in the present study, since few if any cities contain neighbourhoods having a preponderance of petit-bourgeois or lower-middle-class residents. This problem is compounded by the fact that members of these classes, in particular the independent petite bourgeoisie, made up only a small proportion of the urban populace. Without survey data it is very difficult to determine how this small minority of a city's population voted.

The ecological method used here is not ideal for determining patterns of class voting, but given the limitations of the existing data, there is no better method. All a researcher can do in such a situation is acknowledge the shortcomings of the method used and interpret the findings accordingly.[4] Also, it should be remembered that most accounts of popular support for Social Credit base their claims on no empirical evidence whatever, and that those advancing the petit-bourgeois thesis use the crudest of all ecological possibilities: the province as a whole.

The issue of the definition of the various class categories must also receive attention at this point. "Petite bourgeoisie" is defined as the class comprising self-employed individuals who hire few if any employees apart from family members. This definition implies that members of this class have marginal or unsteady incomes. The definition was chosen to keep the usage of the term consistent with that of the leading proponent of the petit-bourgeois position, C.B. Macpherson. Although few writers in this school besides Macpherson provide an explicit definition of "petite bourgeoisie," it would appear from usage and context that most writers on Social Credit in Alberta would concur with this definition.

We have seen that some writers use the term "lower middle class" to describe the class basis of Social Credit support. They do not define this term. One can only assume that their definition is in agreement with that found in other works using this designation. The term is generally used to describe what I have defined here as the petite bourgeoisie, plus the lesser-paid, non-manual employees. Examples of the latter include clerks, secretaries, lower-level management personnel, etc. I shall use this definition of the lower middle class as well.

The term "lower middle class" implies an upper middle class, but rarely does one find explicit instructions on how to differentiate between the two categories. Again, one can only go by usage and context; in this case a key differentia is income – those in the upper middle class make more money than those in the lower. The dividing line between the two is then somewhat arbitrary, although one may assume that the latter constitute a larger proportion of the workforce than the former. Examples of upper-middle-class occupations

88   Social Classes and Social Credit in Alberta

include upper-level civil servants, high management officials, and well-paid professionals.

To complete my depiction of the class structure, all employees doing manual work will be defined as working class and the owners of the major non-agricultural means of production, the bourgeoisie, as upper class. The latter is defined such that it represents only 1 to 2 per cent of the non-farm work-force.

A final methodological issue that should be considered involves the electoral system in use in Alberta when Social Credit came to power. From 1935 to 1959 all constituencies except Edmonton and Calgary were single-member ridings using the "transferable ballot" system of electing candidates. Under this system voters were instructed to mark their ballots by placing a 1 opposite the name of the candidate they would most like to see elected, a 2 opposite their second choice, and so on. Thus, if there were six candidates in a particular constituency, a voter could place numbers 1 through 6 opposite the candidates' names according to his or her preference. If no candidate received an absolute majority of first choices after the first count, the one with the fewest 1s would be declared a loser. The ballots of this candidate would then be examined for second choices, which would be reallocated to the appropriate remaining candidates. This process would be repeated until one candidate received a majority of the votes.

Calgary and Edmonton were multi-member constituencies at this time, each electing several members from the city at large; it was not until 1959 that each city was divided up into separate ridings. The electoral system used in these two cities was called "proportional representation," which was similar in principle to the system used in other ridings, but somewhat more complicated since it involved the election of more than one candidate per consituency. In Calgary in 1935, for instance, six candidates were to be elected from the twenty running. As elsewhere in the province, electors were instructed to indicate their first choice by placing a 1 opposite the appropriate candidate's name, their second by putting a 2, etc., thus placing numbers 1 through 20 opposite the names on the ballot. With six candidates to be elected, a candidate was declared elected if he or she received one vote more than one-seventh of the total vote. If after the first count no candidate had a sufficient number of first choices to be elected, the one with the fewest votes would be declared a loser; those voting for this candidate would then have their votes reallocated according to their second choice. What normally happened, however, was that a small number of candidates had more than enough votes to be elected on the first count. In this situation those elected had their surplus votes (i.e., the votes exceeding one more than one-seventh of the total vote) reallocated according to the second choices indicated. The process was repeated until no candidate had surplus votes, at which time the candidate with the fewest votes was eliminated. The reallocation of a losing candidate's votes and of surplus votes continued until six candidates were declared elected. The counting of the vote in Calgary and Edmonton sometimes took days, as numerous reallocations or "counts" had to be made. In Calgary in 1935, for example, the sixth winning candidate was declared elected after the eighteenth count; in Edmonton, twenty-three counts were required.[5]

In the ecological analysis that follows, the results reported are for first choices. After election officials counted and recorded first choices for each polling subdivision, they pooled the ballots from all subdivisions in the city to permit the transfer of votes. Thus results by polling subdivision are available for first choices only. This presents no problem, however, as an analysis of first choices is equivalent to an analysis based on conventional election procedures.

Calgary

A HISTORICAL SKETCH

Fort Calgary was established as an outpost of the North-West Mounted Police in 1875 and soon became a local trading centre and way station. Its role was greatly expanded with the arrival of the railway in 1883. As cattle were brought into the region, it became the centre of the livestock industry, being the site of slaughterhouses, tanning facilities, and ranching-goods stores. Soon lumber mills, soapworks, and breweries appeared. After the turn of the century, farming overtook ranching as the principal economic activity in southern Alberta, which further diversified Calgary's economic activity. Flour mills, grain elevators, ironworks, and a booming construction industry appeared before the First World War. The city's economy received a major boost with the construction of the CPR's Ogden Shops in 1912–13, which established Calgary as a major prairie railway city. The construction of the Ogden Shops employed about 1,500 people (Foran 1978, 82), and in 1930 about 2,000 regular employees worked there (Hannant 1985, 99).

The discovery of oil in 1914 in Turner Valley, thirty miles to the southwest, touched off Calgary's first oil boom. Although Turner Valley did not fulfil the dreams of all the speculators and oilmen in

90 Social Classes and Social Credit in Alberta

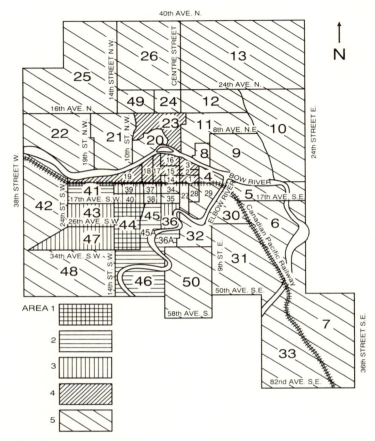

Map 6.1
Calgary Provincial Polling Subdivisions, 1935

the province, it was Canada's largest oil producer until the Leduc, Alberta, find of 1947. It also aided the city's general economic growth. In 1931 Calgary had a population of 83,761.

THE 1935 PROVINCIAL ELECTION
The city's 52 polling subdivisions were divided into five areas according to an assessment of the class level of the residents who lived there in 1935. Map 6.1 illustrates the location of the five areas.

The first area is the predominantly upper-class section, which contained only one polling subdivision, number 44, and which accounted for only 3 per cent of the votes recorded in the city in 1935.

It was completely within the boundaries of the Mount Royal neighbourhood, the wealthiest and most exclusive district in Calgary.

The second area, most of which is adjacent to Mount Royal, was predominantly upper middle class, with a small upper-class and lower-middle-class minority. It consists of the Glencoe, Rideau, Roxborough Place, Elbow Park, and Scarborough neighbourhoods, as well as a small portion of Mount Royal. This area provided 13 per cent of the city's vote.

The third area was an upper-middle/lower-middle-class mixed area containing upper- and working-class minorities. Voters here constituted 14 per cent of Calgary's 1935 total. Included in it is the Beltline district, which was the location of the Lougheed and Hull mansions, as well as the elite Ranchmen's Club. Interspersed throughout the Beltline, however, were some not-so-elite dwellings and institutions. Also in this sector are the Bankview, Knob Hill, and Rouleauville neighbourhoods, containing single-family detached homes of little or no ostentation.

Neighbourhoods containing an approximately even mix of middle- and working-class residents made up a fourth area, which provided 18 per cent of Calgary's 1935 voters. Judging by the type of housing in this area, most of the middle-class residents were lower middle class. Polling subdivisions 1 and 2 were in this area; parts of these subdivisions were located in the downtown area, while the remainder of 1 and 2 contained the Calgary Iron Works and some machine shops. The area due west of downtown, also in this area, was mainly residential in 1935, containing some fashionable housing, some ordinary housing, and many rooming-houses. Polling subdivision 23 was also placed in this category because it contained a small strip of upper-middle-class dwellings along Crescent Road overlooking the Bow River from the north, but a majority of its housing was of the type affordable to persons in the lower middle and working classes. Polling subdivision 3, which encapsulated virtually all of Calgary's Chinatown and little else, was placed in this area as well.

The fifth and final area of the city included all districts that were predominantly working-class. Just over half (52 per cent) of Calgary's 1935 vote was recorded here. It comprised all of the city north of the Bow River except for polling subdivision 23, contained in area four. On the south side it included polling subdivisions 42 and 48, which formed Calgary's southwestern outskirts. It also contained the industrial sector of the city located in the southeast. The Victoria Park, Ogden, Highfield, Manchester, Connaught, and Inglewood neighbourhoods are found here. The CPR's Ogden Shops are found in the

92 Social Classes and Social Credit in Alberta

southeast; numerous mills, meat-packing plants, and ironworks were also located here. The British American and Imperial Oil companies had oil refineries in southeast Calgary; Dominion Bridge and the Canada Cement Company also had operations in the area. The Canadian National Railway's freightyards were in the vicinity as well.

To sum up our description of the five areas of Calgary: area one is the upper-class district; area two, upper middle class; area three, an approximately even mix of upper middle and lower middle classes; the fourth area, a roughly even mix of lower middle and working classes; and the fifth area predominantly working class.

The results of the 1935 election in each of the five areas are listed in Table 6.1. The results for the previous provincial election, which took place in 1930, are given in Table 6.2.[6] The cardinal finding is that support for Social Credit in Calgary in 1935 varied inversely with class level, ranging from a low of 20 per cent in upper-class Mount Royal to a high of 68 per cent in the working-class sector.

The opposite pattern of support is evident for the Liberal and Conservative parties. Their support appears to have varied positively with class level in both elections. Labor support was consistently low in all classes in 1935, never rising above 5 per cent in any district. In 1930 the Labor vote, like the Social Credit vote five years later, varied inversely with class level, ranging from 30 per cent in the working-class districts to 3 per cent in Mount Royal.[7]

It is useful to consider the working-class vote in 1935 in some detail. In the working-class area, Labor Party support was all but wiped out by Social Credit, falling from 30 per cent in 1930 to 5 per cent in 1935. Labor support also decreased in absolute terms in the working-class districts, falling from 3,503 votes to 993, despite a 65 per cent increase in the number of people voting in this area. The Liberal and Conservative parties, which together had garnered a majority of the vote in the working-class districts in 1930, also declined both relatively and absolutely there. The Liberals dropped from 25 per cent to 14 per cent in this area, their votes received declining from 2,942 to 2,633. The Conservative Party was a bigger loser, sliding from 39 per cent to 10 per cent in its share of the popular vote and from 4,512 to 1,834 in votes received.

An examination of the most heavily industrialized area of Calgary, the southeast, is also instructive. This area, all of which is included in the working-class districts, contained polling subdivisions 5, 6, 7, 30, 31, 32, 33, and 50. These eight subdivisions together had a Social Credit vote of 75 per cent (N = 4,072), 7 percentage points higher than the working-class area as a whole and 17 points above the city-wide mark. Polling subdivision 7, which contained the CPR Ogden

93 The 1935 Election

Table 6.1
Vote in Calgary in the 1935 Provincial Election, by Area[a]

	%					
	Social Credit	Liberal	Conservative	Labor	Other	N
AREA						
1) Upper class	20	38	35	4	3	1,094
2) Upper middle class	34	35	25	3	3	4,618
3) Upper middle/ lower middle class	52	24	18	4	2	5,295
4) Lower middle/ working class	59	18	14	5	4	6,662
5) Working class	68	14	10	5	3	19,085
CITY	58	20	15	5	3	38,443[b]

Source: Calgary Herald, 23 August 1935, 20.

[a] Rows do not total 100 in some cases due to rounding.

[b] Includes advance poll and hospital vote.

Table 6.2
Vote in Calgary in the 1930 Provincial Election, by Area[a]

	%				
	Liberal	Conservative	Labor	Other	N
AREA					
1) Upper class	44	51	3	2	694
2) Upper middle class	41	48	6	4	3,080
3) Upper middle/ lower middle class	36	45	14	5	4,285
4) Lower middle/ working class	29	48	16	7	3,379
5) Working class	25	39	30	7	11,713
CITY	30	43	21	6	23,652[b]

Source: Statement of Vote for the 1930 election, Provincial Archives of Alberta.

[a] Rows do not total 100 in some cases due to rounding.

[b] Includes advance poll and hospital vote.

Shops, had the highest Social Credit vote in the entire city, with 87 per cent (N = 173) in favour. Irving describes the Ogden Shops themselves as a "strong Social Credit centre" (1959, 78). Hannant (1985, 113) reports that William Aberhart gave a speech there. The small Ogden suburb of Ceepeear (named after the ubiquitous railway company), which in 1935 was just outside the city limits, voted 93 per cent (N = 153) Social Credit.

94 Social Classes and Social Credit in Alberta

It is difficult to determine how the petite bourgeoisie voted in the cities since it composed only approximately 11 per cent of the work-force there and did not congregate in a district of its own. Given this situation, no valid measure of urban petit-bourgeois support exists, and the level of support for Social Credit among members of the urban petite bourgeoisie must remain one of the mysteries of Canadian social science.[8]

Some indication of the level of support among the salaried lower middle class is provided by the results in area three, the upper-middle/lower-middle-class area, and area four, the lower-middle/working-class sector. Table 6.1 indicates that residents in the former district voted 52 per cent Social Credit, in the latter, 59 per cent. Thus Social Credit support in these areas, although substantial, was lower than that in the predominantly working-class neighbourhoods.

Although the party's support was strongest in the working-class sector, its success in the upper-middle and upper-class districts should not be ignored. The 34 per cent Social Credit earned in the upper-middle-class region allowed the party to finish second in this area, only 1 percentage point behind the Liberals and 9 points ahead of the Conservatives. That one in five voters in the upper-class poll voted Social Credit is also something of a revelation, given the conventional wisdom on the class basis of the movement. It would appear that as far as Calgary is concerned, existing accounts of the movement have underestimated the support for Social Credit in the upper and upper-middle classes, especially in the latter.[9]

Previous non-voters may have had a significant impact on the election, as the number of eligible voters increased by 21 per cent over 1930 in the constituency of Calgary, while the number of people actually voting increased by 68 per cent. Voter turnout in the constituency was 58 per cent in 1930, 80 per cent in 1935.[10] If, as Hamilton (1972, 293) suggests, voter participation normally varies directly with class level, those who were first-time voters in this rather unusual election may have come disproportionately from the lower classes, which would also mean that the increased turnout benefited the Social Credit Party. However, without survey data it is impossible to know for sure how this increased participation influenced the election.[11]

In sum, the data presented indicate that support for Social Credit in Calgary in 1935 varied inversely with class level, with the highest level of support coming from the working-class districts. The opposite pattern of support is evident for the Liberal and Conservative parties, while support for Labor all but disappeared in this election.

95   The 1935 Election

Lethbridge

A HISTORICAL SKETCH
Lethbridge originated as a coal-mining centre in the early 1880s, having a population of about one thousand by 1886 (Johnston and den Otter 1985, 230). By the first decade of the twentieth century a foundry, ironworks, a brewery, grain elevators, grain mills, and other small manufacturing industries were located in the city. With the expansion of agriculture in the surrounding southern Alberta region, Lethbridge came to see itself as "the coal city in the wheat country" (78). Its economy diversified as farming flourished in the area and it became a regional service and distribution centre. Lethbridge had a population of 13,489 in 1931.

THE 1935 PROVINCIAL ELECTION
In 1935 there were fourteen polling subdivisions in the Lethbridge constituency, nine of which were located in the city itself. The city polls accounted for 87 per cent of the Lethbridge riding vote and had a Social Credit tally of 53 per cent.

The most pronounced boundary in the city of Lethbridge is formed by the CPR tracks, which divide the city into its north and south sides (see Map 6.2). The class composition of south Lethbridge in 1935 may be described as a middle-class mix with a substantial working-class minority; the latter class made up about one third of its population. The London Road neighbourhood, the wealthiest residential area of Lethbridge, is located on the south side. London Road was primarily an upper-middle-class district with a small upper-class minority.[12] The south provided 65 per cent of the city vote in 1935. North Lethbridge in 1935 was predominantly working class, home to many coal miners and CPR workers. The CPR shops, brickyards, and a coal-mine were located in or near north Lethbridge. The results for Lethbridge by area for the provincial election of 1935 are shown in Table 6.3; the locations of the polls are shown in Map 6.2. The results for the election of 1930 are given in Table 6.4.

North Lethbridge, the working-class area, was covered by three polling subdivisions, numbers 6, 7, and 8, which accounted for 35 per cent of the city total. These three together had a Social Credit vote of 73 per cent. The highest Social Credit vote in the city was recorded at poll 6, with 81 per cent in favour. Labor support in the north fell from 69 per cent in 1930 to 11 per cent.

South Lethbridge was covered by six polling subdivisions, numbers 9, 10, 11, 12, 13, and 14, which together recorded a Social Credit

96 Social Classes and Social Credit in Alberta

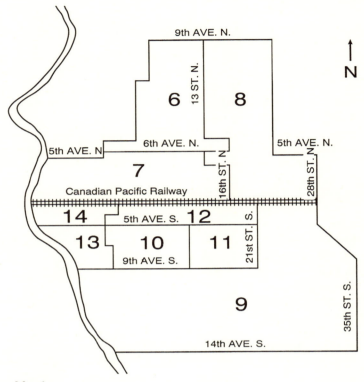

Map 6.2
Lethbridge Provincial Polling Subdivisions, 1935

vote of 42 per cent (N = 3,631). The salaried lower middle class in Lethbridge was located primarily in the south, excluding the London Road area. The south minus London Road, then, contained a middle-class mix that was mainly lower-middle-class, along with a sizable working-class minority. Poll 10 covered about half of London Road; no other poll had a greater proportion of voters from this neighbourhood. The south minus poll 10, the region that appears as the lower-middle/working-class area in Table 6.3, voted 43 per cent Social Credit. Poll 10, which comprises the upper-middle-class area in the table, had a Social Credit vote of 39 per cent.

Considering Social Credit support in the south, the three southern polls with the highest levels of Social Credit voting in 1935 also had the highest levels of Labor voting in 1930. Polls 14, 9, and 13 had Labor votes of 42, 37, and 29 per cent in 1930, while the Social Credit vote in these polls in 1935 was 62, 56, and 50 per cent respectively.

97   The 1935 Election

Table 6.3
Vote in Lethbridge in the 1935 Provincial Election, by Area[a]

	%				
	Social Credit	Liberal	Conservative	Labor	N
SOUTH					
Upper middle class	39	43	8	9	957
Lower middle/					
working class	43	41	7	9	2,674
NORTH					
Working class	73	13	2	11	1,948
CITY	53	32	5	10	5,798[b]

Source: Statement of Vote for the 1935 election, Provincial Archives of Alberta.

[a] Rows do not total 100 in some cases due to rounding.

[b] Includes advance poll and hospital vote.

Table 6.4
Vote in Lethbridge in the 1930 Provincial Election, by Area[a]

	%			
	Barrowman (Independent)	Hardie (Independent)	Labor	N
SOUTH				
Upper middle class	31	49	20	641
Lower middle/				
working class	28	43	29	1,892
NORTH				
Working class	10	21	69	1,405
CITY	22	36	42	4,006[a]

Source: General Statement by Returning Officer for the 1930 election, Provincial Archives of Alberta.

[a] Includes advance poll.

Thus we have reason to believe that the comparatively high Social Credit vote in these south-side polls resulted from the presence of a relatively high proportion of working-class voters. This does not, of course, rule out a high lower-middle-class vote for the party in these areas.

Support for the Liberals and Conservatives in the city of Lethbridge was again the opposite of that for Social Credit, varying positively with class level, although Conservative voting was low in all areas.

98   Social Classes and Social Credit in Alberta

As in Calgary, previous non-voters may have had a significant impact on the vote, as voter turnout increased from 67 per cent in 1930 to 82 per cent in 1935 for the Lethbridge constituency.[13] But, to reiterate, without survey data it is impossible to determine how this affected the vote. In sum these results indicate that in Lethbridge as in Calgary, support for Social Credit varied inversely with class level, with the highest support found in the working-class districts.

Medicine Hat

A HISTORICAL SKETCH

Medicine Hat began as a railway centre in the early 1880s. It was a divisional point of the CPR's main line and later the eastern terminus of the Crowsnest Pass branch line. The CPR built maintenance shops, a roundhouse, stock- and freightyards, and railway bridges at Medicine Hat. Fifty men were employed in the first shops; about the same number worked to maintain the tracks, and another sixty-six formed the train crew, which was based at the local depot (Gould 1981, 27). At about the same time ranching developed in the surrounding region, with Medicine Hat becoming a local service centre.

The accidental discovery of natural gas by a CPR water-well crew in 1883 led to the use of the gas in small-scale manufacturing plants in the city. Brick factories operated as early as 1888 in Medicine Hat, as did pottery plants before the First World War. The rapid migration of farmers into Alberta enhanced the city's role as a regional commercial centre. Flour mills, a brewery, and a greenhouse industry also operated in Medicine Hat, the latter using natural gas. The city had a population of 9,634 in 1921, which increased to 10,300 in 1931.

THE 1935 PROVINCIAL ELECTION

The wealthiest residential area in Medicine Hat in 1935 comprised First and Second Streets NW, east of Fifth Avenue (see Map 6.3). Local informants mentioned the "Club 400" in connection with this neighbourhood, the "400" being the first residents of Medicine Hat. As in other western cities, in Medicine Hat great pride is taken in being a long-time resident.[14] The residents of this neighbourhood were classified as upper middle class; their wealth was generated largely from ranching and real estate.

A neighbourhood called "the Hill" is the second wealthiest district and is also predominantly upper middle class. It is located just west of the railway tracks, south of Fourth Street. Many CPR management personnel lived in this area. To the west of the Hill is a mixed lower-middle/working-class area called the "West Hill." North of the South

99 The 1935 Election

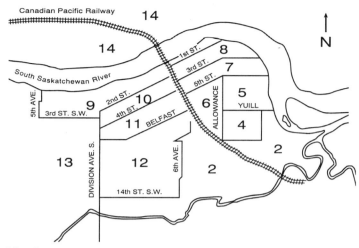

Map 6.3
Medicine Hat Provincial Polling Subdivisions, 1935

Saskatchewan River, which divides the city into its north and south sides, is the Riverside area, which in 1935 was also a lower-middle/working-class area. Adjacent to Riverside to its north is Crescent Heights, which had a similar class composition.

East of the railway tracks, immediately south of the river, was a small neighbourhood that contained a mixture of upper-middle and lower-middle-class residents. On this side of the tracks, the farther south one went, the greater the proportion of working-class residents; the area south of Third Street South was predominantly working class. The latter part of Medicine Hat is called "Moccasin Flats" (or simply "the Flats"), so named because in the early days of the city it was the location of an Indian encampment. Workers employed in the potteries, brickplant, foundry, crayon factory, and CPR works lived in the Flats. The area due south of the Flats, east of Sixth Avenue SE, was also predominantly working class.

The results of the 1935 election are shown in Table 6.5 and those for the 1930 election in Table 6.6. The locations of the polling subdivisions are indicated on Map 6.3.

Five polls were located in the working-class districts, polls 2, 4, 5, 6, and 7, which together had a 76 per cent Social Credit vote. Poll 2, however, in addition to covering a large area of the city, also covered a portion of the countryside. (The other four working-class polls were completely enclosed in the city.) Unfortunately, it is impossible to determine what proportion of poll 2 was rural. Poll 16, a completely

100   Social Classes and Social Credit in Alberta

Table 6.5
Vote in Medicine Hat in the 1935 Provincial Election, by Area[a]

| | % | | | |
	Social Credit	Liberal	Conservative	N
Upper middle class	38	38	23	749
Upper middle/ lower middle class	53	30	17	1,190
Lower middle/ working class[b]	63	25	12	457
Working class[b]	76	19	5	1,674
CITY	62	25	12	4,582[c]

Source: Statement of Vote for the 1935 election, Provincial Archives of Alberta.

[a] Rows do not total 100 in some cases due to rounding.

[b] Includes some rural voters. See pp 99–101.

[c] Includes advance poll.

Table 6.6
Vote in Medicine Hat in the 1930 Provincial Election, by Area[a]

| | % | | | |
	Liberal	Conservative	Independent	N
Upper middle class	38	38	24	667
Upper middle/ lower middle class	49	29	21	972
Lower middle/ working class[b]	39	31	30	336
Working class[b]	51	21	28	1,250
CITY	46	28	26	3,346[c]

Source: General Statement by Returning Officer for the 1930 election, Provincial Archives of Alberta.

[a] Rows do not total 100 in some cases due to rounding.

[b] Includes some rural voters. See pp 99–101.

[c] Includes advance poll.

rural poll in the riding but slightly larger in size, contained only 19 voters; poll 3, another rural poll of about the same size, had 195 voters. As poll 2 received 477 votes, in all likelihood a majority of these were urban. (The polling place itself was located in the city proper.)

The lower-middle/working-class mixed areas were covered by polls 13 and 14. These polls covered portions of the countryside, but again it is impossible to determine the number of rural voters in them.

101   The 1935 Election

(The actual polling places were urban.) Polls 13 and 14 together voted 63 per cent Social Credit.

Polls 8, 10, and 12 contained about an even mix of upper-middle-class and lower-middle-class voters, and recorded a 53 per cent Social Credit vote. Polls 9 and 11, which covered the two upper-middle-class areas, together recorded a 38 per cent Social Credit vote. All urban polls combined, including the three that contained some rural voters, registered a 62 per cent Social Credit vote.

As in Calgary and Lethbridge, support for the Liberal and Conservative parties varied positively with class level. Similarly, previous non-voters may have been a significant factor in Medicine Hat, since voter turnout increased from 74 to 83 per cent in the constituency.[15]

In summary, in Medicine Hat a similar pattern to that observed for Calgary and Lethbridge is evident, whereby the support for Social Credit varied inversely with class level, with the greatest support found in the working-class districts. The opposite pattern is again evident for the Liberals and Conservatives.

The observed pattern of support for Social Credit in Alberta's cities in 1935 may be compared with that reported by Maurice Pinard for a later Social Credit movement in Quebec. Data taken from Pinard's Table 6.1 (1975, 93) are shown in Table 6.7, with some modification.[16] The data are from a survey taken shortly after the 1962 federal election, in which the Social Credit Party, led in Quebec by Réal Caouette, catured 26 of 75 seats in the province and obtained 25.9 per cent of the popular vote (4).

Pinard's results indicate that the non-farm Social Credit vote varied inversely with class level, with the highest support found among members of the working class. Of special interest to our study is the fact that workers gave greater support to Social Credit than did small businessmen, 27 per cent as against 20 per cent. The table also indicates, however, that farmers showed the highest level of support for Social Credit of any occupational category.

Pinard also found that among workers,[17] those with a working-class identification were more likely to support Social Credit than those without such an identification, and that members of unions, as opposed to non-members, were more supportive (1975, chaps. 8 and 11). Significantly, he also found that support for Social Credit in Quebec was not associated with conservative attitudes (chap. 12).[18] These findings are in keeping with the discussion of the Social Credit philosophy in previous chapters, where it is suggested that the Social Credit ideology was not conservative.

102   Social Classes and Social Credit in Alberta

Table 6.7
Quebec Federal Social Credit Vote, 1962, by Class

	Social Class				
	Upper middle[a]	Salaried lower middle[b]	Small businessmen[c]	Working class[d]	Farmers[e]
% Social Credit	9	11	20	27	32
n = 601	(94)	(79)	(56)	(299)	(73)

Source: Pinard 1971, 93.
[a] Professional, technical and kindred occupations, managers and officials, and non-farm proprietors with annual net incomes exceeding $4,000.
[b] Clerical and sales workers.
[c] Self-employed proprietors with annual net incomes of $4,000 or less, or if income was unknown, with eight years of education or less. Includes self-employed manuals.
[d] Manual wage-earners.
[e] Farmers, farm managers, labourers, and foremen.

THE SMALL TOWNS

In chapter 3 we saw that despite Social Credit's reputation as a small-town movement, only 11 of the 27 small towns in the province had a Social Credit vote greater than the provincial average. In Table 6.8 the results in the small towns for all parties are given. Social Credit received 52 per cent of the vote in all small towns combined, two percentage points *below* the provincial average.

The contention that the small towns provided high levels of support for the movement is often made on the assumption that these communities were disproportionately petit-bourgeois. Unfortunately, as with the cities, problems arise in attempting to isolate the petit-bourgeois vote in the small towns, making a rigorous test of the received hypothesis impossible.

THE COUNTRYSIDE

In order to get a measure of the farm vote, the results from all urban areas with a population of 1,000 or more were subtracted from all constituencies; the remainder constituted 65 per cent of all votes cast in the provincial election of 1935. The Social Credit vote with the cities and towns removed in this way was 57 per cent (N = 195,840), which, although high, was only 3 percentage points above the province-wide mark.

103   The 1935 Election

Table 6.8
Vote in the 1935 Provincial Election, for Urban Areas with Populations from 1,000 to 5,000[a]

	Social Credit	UFA	Liberal	Conservative	Labor	Other	N
Blairmore	45	—	—	13	—	41	864
Camrose	46	19	36	—	—	—	1,307
Cardston	69	8	22	—	—	—	794
Claresholm	54	8	25	13	—	—	475
Coleman	63	—	24	—	—	13	1,187
Drumheller	55	—	11	—	—	35	1,540
Edson	35	—	34	—	32	—	748
Fort Saskatchewan	31	35	24	10	—	—	367
Grande Prairie	30	10	47	13	—	—	798
Hanna	78	7	15	—	—	—	627
High River	50	17	27	6	—	—	930
Innisfail	50	3	32	15	—	—	946
Lacombe	39	4	31	25	—	—	832
Lloydminster	45	22	19	8	—	6	436
Macleod	56	28	17	—	—	—	752
Magrath	55	31	14	—	—	—	456
Olds	49	18	28	4	—	—	869
Pincher Creek	46	8	22	23	—	—	577
Raymond	66	27	6	—	—	1	832
Redcliff	66	—	16	18	—	—	493
Red Deer	49	—	20	20	—	12	1,089
Stettler	56	5	28	10	—	—	783
Taber	70	13	17	—	—	—	825
Vegreville	45	13	40	2	—	—	1,036
Vermillion	53	12	26	7	—	2	653
Wainright	35	17	42	6	—	—	683
Wetaskiwin	60	5	28	7	—	1	1,092
ALL SMALL TOWNS	52	10	24	7	1	6	21,451
PROVINCE	54	11	23	6	2	3	301,752

Source: Statement of Vote for the 1935 election, Provincial Archives of Alberta.

[a] Excluding Beverly, for which data are not available. Rows do not total 100 in some cases due to rounding.

REGIONAL VARIATION

A more meaningful comparison among the cities, towns, and countryside, in particular between farmer and working-class support, may be gained by controlling for region of the province. It is sometimes noted that Social Credit was more popular in southern Alberta,

104 Social Classes and Social Credit in Alberta

although rarely does one find a writer willing to provide an explicit dividing line. If we take as our dividing line the boundary drawn on Map 6.4 (which uses the northern boundary of the Red Deer constituency as the dividing line), the north had a Social Credit vote of 49 per cent (N = 160,226), the south 61 per cent (N = 141,526). This line allows a comparison of the three cities for which polling subdivision data are available (all of which are in the south) with the surrounding southern countryside.

The rural south voted 63 per cent Social Credit (N = 77,824), whereas the vote for the party in the working-class districts of Calgary, Lethbridge, and Medicine Hat was 68, 73, and 76 per cent respectively; the working-class areas of the three cities combined had a 69 per cent Social Credit vote (N = 22,363). Thus we have reason to believe that working-class support in the three southern cities was somewhat higher than southern farmer support, although, to be sure, support was high among both groups. We may also note that support for the movement in the working-class districts of the southern cities exceeded southern small-town support, as the 17 southern small towns taken together had a 57 per cent Social Credit vote (N = 13,589). Northern rural areas voted 53 per cent Social Credit (N = 115,007), the 10 northern small towns 43 per cent (N = 7,952). Thus not only Edmonton but the entire northern region had lower levels of Social Credit support than did the south.

CONCLUSIONS

Some general conclusions are warranted from the findings discussed here. One is that popular support for Social Credit was much more diffuse than is commonly believed. The statistics indicate that support for Social Credit was certainly not restricted to any single class nor to agrarian regions and small towns, as some previous studies have suggested. However, even though support for the movement was not as concentrated as many commentators have contended, a pattern of polarization is evident whereby workers and farmers provided very high levels of support, with those levels decreasing as class level increased.

We will never know for sure whether working-class support exceeded petit-bourgeois support in the cities or in the province as a whole, but we can now be certain that workers backed the movement in very large numbers in Calgary, Lethbridge, and Medicine Hat. Also, since support for Social Credit in these cities was lower in the middle-class areas than in the working-class districts, we have reason to believe that Social Credit was not a characteris-

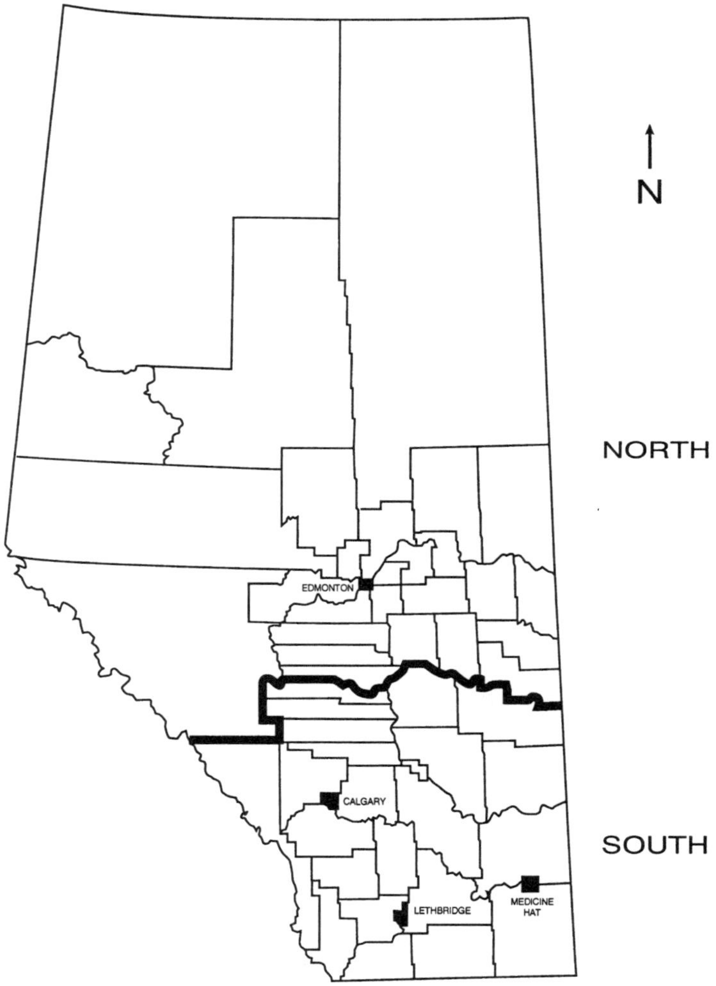

105   The 1935 Election

Map 6.4
Alberta Electoral Divisions 1935, Showing North–South Boundary

tically *middle-class* phenomenon, contrary to what some accounts suggest.

A final conclusion is that the evidence indicating a very high level of working-class support is inconsistent with the claim that support for Social Credit was rooted in petit-bourgeois false consciousness, in particular that arising from the petite bourgeoisie's lack of exposure to the relations of production between labour and capital. It will be suggested in chapter 9 that *shared* experiences, such as economic hardship and a lack of more promising alternatives, may have led both classes to support the movement. This rather straightforward explanation may take us farther in understanding Social Credit than the elaborate notions contained in the petit-bourgeois theory.

7 Social Credit in Power

Social Credit in power is often portrayed as a conservative, even reactionary party bent on freeing Alberta from the forces of imperialism.[1] It is often suggested that since it was a petit-bourgeois movement, as a government it was a priori conservative and incapable of any truly radical action. This approach is taken by Macpherson, who supports this theoretical position with the assertion that "Aberhart, from his first day in office, preferred to placate the established outside interests ... his economic radicalism was very limited ... nothing he did was in conflict with a basic acceptance of the established order" (1962, 219–20). Similarly, Irving writes that "Aberhart was an arch-conservative in education, religion and politics" (1959, 345). A comparable assessment has been made by S.D. Clark (1954, vii-ix).

But do such accounts provide an accurate description of Social Credit's policy and behaviour in office? Perhaps the best way to address this question is to review what actually happened in Alberta once the movement formed the government. Once this has been done, we will be in a better position to assess the conventional interpretations.

SOCIAL CREDIT IN OFFICE

Legend has it that when William Aberhart received a Canadian Press telegram on the evening of 22 August 1935 stating that Social Credit had just won the provincial election,[2] he blanched and fell against his pulpit in the Prophetic Bible Institute (Irving 1959, 333). The crowd of supporters present sustained him by singing "O God Our Help in Ages Past," the Social Credit anthem. Although shocked at the news, Aberhart's recovery was swift.[3]

In London the Green Shirts, the pro–Social Credit organization led by the charismatic John Hargrave, celebrated the victory by triumphantly marching seven times around the Bank of England. With much fanfare, Hargrave announced that the Alberta party's win marked the beginning of the end of the old economic order.

Also in England, Major Douglas received what became a famous telegram. It read simply, "Victorious when could you come? – ABERHART" (Douglas 1937, 125).[4] Douglas appeared to be eager to join forces with Aberhart, cabling back, "If necessary could sail middle September" (125), and later writing, "I take this opportunity of assuring you that you have a solid body of many millions all over the world behind you, and that anything I can do to bring these forces to bear to insure your success will be done" (127).

At the time of the 1935 election Douglas was under contract as the "principal reconstruction adviser" to the UFA government. Shortly before the election, he submitted to the government his "First Interim Report on the Possibilities of the Application of Social Credit Principles to the Province of Alberta."[5] His contract extended beyond the date of the election and so required him to work with Aberhart. The contract did not stipulate that he had to remain in the province, however, and by the time the election was held he had returned to England.

During the election campaign Aberhart had stated that it would take at least eighteen months to implement a Social Credit program. This gave him some breathing room immediately after the party's victory, but there was a tremendous sense of anticipation and, in some circles, fear as soon as the results were announced.

Shortly after the election the Social Credit Party learned the sorry details of the province's financial situation. The Treasury was so depleted that there was some doubt that civil servants' salaries could be paid, while teachers' salaries were already in arrears (Hooke 1971, 108–9).

Bigger problems loomed in the near future. A bond maturity of $5.2 million, interest charges of $2.8 million, bank debts of $6 million, and other assorted financial obligations were due by 31 March 1936. The magnitude of these obligations may be appreciated if it is realized that the Alberta government's revenues totalled only $16 million per annum at the time, which was not sufficient to pay for the routine expenses involved in running the province (Hooke 1971, 108–9).

109   Social Credit in Power

Aberhart's immediate response to the government's financial crisis did not involve any radical measures.[6] He travelled to Ottawa to ask Prime Minister R.B. Bennett, whom Aberhart had known in Calgary, for a loan of $18,389,000. He was granted $2,250,000 (Mallory 1954, 126). Bennett told him that he could only authorize funds to cover the period up to the next federal election (Elliott and Miller 1987, 210), which was eventually held in October 1935 and won by Mackenzie King's Liberals.

During his Ottawa trip Aberhart decided to hire Robert J. Magor as a financial consultant. Magor, a well-to-do Montreal economic adviser and philanthropist, had previously been in the employ of the Newfoundland government, where he used conventional but effective cost-cutting measures to streamline the Crown colony's administration.

The appointment of Magor piqued Douglas, who believed that *he* was to be in charge of the province's financial affairs. Douglas came to see Magor's presence as a plot by finance to destroy Social Credit in Alberta. He believed that the whole episode had been orchestrated by Montagu Norman, governor of the Bank of England, who had visited Canada in August 1935 to meet with Graham Tower, governor of the recently formed Bank of Canada (Hooke 1971, 120). Douglas wrote to Aberhart, "A policy which apparently aims at defeating the banks with the assistance of the banks themselves, under the supervision of an agent of the banks, seems to be so dangerous that I do not feel it has a reasonable chance of success" (1937, 149). In the same letter he also suggested that his contract with the Alberta government be "terminated by mutual consent."

Relations between Douglas and Aberhart had always been delicate, and were at times hostile. Before the election the UFA government, as well as the Liberal and Conservative parties and the major Alberta newspapers, did their utmost to play up any disagreement between the two men. Those opposed to Aberhart claimed that he grossly misinterpreted Douglas's theories, while Aberhart himself claimed to be a true disciple.

The relationship between the two had been further complicated by the existence in Alberta of Douglasite organizations such as the New Age Club and the Open Mind Club, which took issue with Aberhart's leadership of the movement and openly attacked his interpretation of the Douglas doctrine. During the Major's visits to Alberta the anti-Aberhart Douglasites had tried to get the master to denounce Aberhart, but Douglas was reluctant to do this, knowing that the vast majority of Social Crediters in the province were loyal to Aberhart and that only he could generate such mass enthusiasm for Social Credit.

For his part, Aberhart had claimed that there was little friction between himself and Major Douglas, but this posture became difficult to maintain after the election. He was torn between his conventional role as premier, which involved government leadership and responsibility, and his adherence to the Social Credit philosophy, which states that it is the government's duty to bring in "experts" (like Douglas) to implement the will of the people. Both men intensely disliked the thought of taking orders from the other; it seems that they both wanted to be in control of the Alberta project. Aberhart answered Douglas's letter criticizing Magor's appointment by stating that "nothing can be gained by your assuming the position of dictation rather than advice" (Douglas 1937, 155).

The strain between the two men continued to be aggravated by the anti-Aberhart Douglasites, who regularly reported their displeasure with the premier to Douglas. The means of communication between Alberta and London also caused frustration, as letters took over two weeks to travel the distance,[7] while telegrams between the two men, although much faster, were rarely longer than a sentence or two. Although transatlantic telephone service was available, it seems that the two men were reluctant to use it. Another problem was that the financial position of the Alberta government in the first few months following the election was so poor that the province simply could not afford to pay Douglas's expenses for another trip to Alberta (Douglas 1937, 152).

The long-distance advice that Douglas had to offer the Alberta Social Credit government was puzzling to Premier Aberhart. In chapter 4 we saw that the Major had recommended that the premier simply approach the banks and ask for a gift of $5 million. Should this ploy fail, Aberhart was to "organize either a bank under the Dominion Bank Charter Act, or devise, with the aid of your legal advisors, some method by which an institution can be organized outside the Dominion Bank Charter Act, not issuing notes, but creating and granting credits to the Goverment as may be required and issuing cheques along familiar lines, so that no unnecessay difficulties may arise between the boundaries of Alberta and the rest of Canada" (Douglas 1937, 146). The government was to devise a "mechanism to enable it to create its own credit upon its own terms" (146). Once such a mechanism was in place, Douglas would be glad to offer further help. Aberhart's difficulty with this sort of advice was summed up neatly in a sentence contained in a letter of reply to Douglas: "Be more specific" (Douglas 1937, 156).

111 Social Credit in Power

The two men exchanged a series of letters and telegrams for several months, which typically involved Aberhart asking for concrete instructions on how to implement Social Credit and Douglas answering with vague suggestions, such as that the Alberta government should gain "access to the Public Credit," make "inroads upon the monopoly of credit," "secure the control of Social Credit," or "challenge Financial Dictatorship" (Douglas 1937, 145, 149, 159, 193). Douglas maintained that he would have nothing further to contribute until these oracular demands were met, suggesting that an unwillingness to fulfil them was tantamount to a commitment to financial orthodoxy. Aberhart continued to plead for details on how to implement these directives, but Douglas offered nothing of substance.

Douglas did have a few specific suggestions, however, that he thought would be of assistance in defending the province from the inevitable counter-offensives of finance. The government was to build up a store of Dominion and foreign currency, a rather exacting proposal since the province did not even have the funds to meet its day-to-day expenses. A government news service was to be created to combat anti–Social Credit propaganda; this recommendation Aberhart tried to fulfil by having the Social Credit League buy the *Calgary Albertan* and a radio station owned by the paper, but the deal ultimately failed. Douglas also recommended that the province create its own police force; this proposal was met with little enthusiasm.

While the negotiations between Douglas and Aberhart were going on, the premier announced that due to the severity of the financial crisis in the province, it would be necessary for him to stabilize the situation using conventional means. He promised to create a system of social credit once the province's finances were on a sound footing. In addition to getting federal government loans, he merged departments and generally tried to make the province's administration as cost-effective as possible.

The first legislative session of the Social Credit government witnessed the passing of the Social Credit Measures Act, which was largely a statement of purpose for the new administration. Authorization was granted to adopt a program that would "bring about the equation of consumption to production and thus ensure to the people of the Province the full benefit of the increment arising from their association" (Alberta 1936a, 26). Just what this meant was not explained.

The new Social Credit minister of Trade and Industry, Ernest Manning, went about creating a new industrial code for the province that would systematize the provincial regulation of labour, commerce, and natural-resource development. The young Manning met with

112   Social Classes and Social Credit in Alberta

both labour leaders and business people to lay the groundwork for the new social legislation. In 1936 the Male Minimum Wage Act created minimum wages for all but farm and domestic labour. The Hours of Work Act established maximum working times and guaranteed one day of rest per week. The Tradesmen's Qualification Act regulated the skilled trades, protecting tradesmen from unqualified competition and the public from inferior workmanship. In 1938 the Industrial Conciliation and Arbitration Act provided labour with collective bargaining rights, while the Industrial Wages Security Act guaranteed the payment of wages to coal miners (Hooke 1971, 128). While these measures may not appear terribly bold to present-day observers, they were controversial at the time, and the Alberta Manufacturers' Association was quick to condemn them (Barr 1974, 91).

The new Social Credit administration also raised provincial taxes. A Social Services Tax was brought in, with the funds used to eliminate charges the municipalities paid towards Mothers' Allowances and tuberculosis care; the latter from then on was provided without charge at the provincial sanatorium.[8] A 2 per cent sales tax was introduced, along with an assortment of other taxes pertaining to motor vehicles and fuel oil. Liquor prices went up, as did land taxes and taxes on personal and corporate income.

On 1 April 1936 Alberta defaulted on a provincial bond issue of $3.2 million. In addition to the funds borrowed from the Bennett administration, Aberhart had received loans of $1 million and $3 million from the King government. He requested a further loan to cover the bond issue but was refused. Aberhart had the option of participating in a federal-provincial loan council that was designed to cover such bond issues and other debts, but declined because, in participating, the Alberta government would have had to gain the consent of the federal minister of Finance and the governor of the Bank of Canada to borrow any more money, a condition the premier would not accept.

Two months after the default, the Social Credit government unilaterally reduced the interest owing on Alberta government bonds such that bondholders would suffer a loss of 50 per cent on their interest income. Shortly thereafter, Alberta bonds were barred from the London Stock Exchange (Barr 1974, 95). Alf Hooke, who was a Social Credit MLA from 1935 to 1971, writes that after the interest reduction was enacted, "the cry went up that the Aberhart administration did not recognize the sanctity of contracts and that as a result of government action thousands of widows and orphans in many parts of the world would suffer the consequences of government action" (1971, 113). One could also add that the interest reduction and default violated property rights, which contradicts several accounts of the movement's views on property. As will become even more apparent, it was really *opponents* of Social Credit who held property rights to be inviolable, not Social Crediters themselves.

In the summer of 1936 the Social Credit administration announced its plan to issue "Prosperity Certificates." These certificates also came to be known as provincial "script," and, to some, as "funny money." The certificates were issued to government employees as partial payment for services rendered, in particular to road crews building provincial highways. Issued in one-dollar denominations (the bills had "One Dollar" printed on the front), the bearer had to affix a one-cent stamp, sold by the province, to the back of the certificate each week for a total of 104 weeks. This made it a form of depreciating currency in that, if the bearer did not spend the certificate, he or she would have to keep buying stamps for it. It was hoped that this would encourage a rapid turnover of the bills, which would then stimulate economic activity. In Social Credit jargon, the certificates were designed to enhance the "circulation of credit." A total of $359,788 worth of prosperity certificates were issued (Whalen 1952, 507, n 33).

The script system met with little success, as many businesses and individuals, including some Social Credit MLAS, refused to accept them as money. They were also not accepted as payment for provincial fines or taxes (except sales taxes at prescribed times) or for liquor purchases. The government fulfilled its promise to redeem each bill, but several thousand were never returned, kept by Albertans as curiosity pieces.

Although the issuing of script was a novel idea, Albertans realized that it was not the same thing as the distribution of social credit dividends. Almost a year had gone by since the party had been elected, yet there was still no sign that a real social credit system was in the works. The growing restlessness was met by the government's distribution of "Registration Covenants." The covenants were essentially contracts stating that if the Alberta resident co-operated with the government, he or she would be entitled to the benefits of the social credit system.

Four types of covenants were issued. The "Citizens'" covenant stated that registrants must co-operate with the provincial government and their fellow Albertans "in providing food, clothing and shelter for every one of us." Registrants agreed to accept their remuneration in "Alberta Credit," which for the time being could not be used to pay for "provincial taxes, licences, royalties, fines, etc." For its part the government agreed to establish and maintain "a just rate of wages with reasonable hours of labour." Interest-free loans in Alberta credit were to be issued for home building, or for businesses if the latter were "conducive to the economic requirements of the Province." The government also promised to issue "monthly dividends," although no amount was specified (*Alberta Gazette*, 15 August 1936, 819).

The covenant for "Manufacturers and Processors" required that such people "co-operate with the Alberta Government in planning the supply of goods and produce required for the Province," and sell at least 50 per cent of their output within Alberta for Alberta credit so long as the selling price was at least equal to the general market price. In return the government promised to issue Alberta credit, "primarily for use in purchasing Alberta-made goods and services," and to establish just prices for such goods and services. Government-established prices would assure manufacturers and processors "a fair commission on the turn-over." A "compensating discount" on goods would be arranged "when an accelerated sale is desired." Interest-free loans were also promised, as were "bonuses" to sell "surplus goods" on the world market. Comparable covenants were arranged for retailers and "Farmers and Producers" (*Alberta Gazette*, 15 August 1936, 821–6).

The covenants are an important part of the Alberta movement's history, as they clearly illustrate that in a social credit system, production and distribution are to be communal matters regulated by the government. They show again how great a departure from the existing system was envisaged and the extent to which the movement's radicalism has been underestimated.

Unlike the script program, the registration drive won the eager participation of Albertans. When it was finished, more people had signed up than had voted Social Credit in the provincial election. But not everyone was happy with the covenants, and some people even described them as fascist (see Elliott and Miller 1987, 243). An Edmonton bookstore owner formed a "League of Freedom" that opposed the registration, which claimed a membership of 13,000 (Hooke 1971, 123).

Shortly after the covenants were introduced, the government passed the Alberta Credit House Act, which stated that Alberta credit was to be issued to all covenanted Albertans. The act also allowed for the taking of a "levy representing the unearned increment included in the price of commodities and services" (Alberta 1936b, 17). A few days later the Debt Adjustment Act and the Reduction and Settlement of Debts Act were introduced. The former allowed the Debt Adjustment Board to pass decisions that could not be overturned in the courts and to declare a debt moratorium. The latter bill declared that for private loans made before 1 July 1932, interest was cancelled as of that date, with all payments made on such loans after this time to be applied to principal. It also stipulated that the maximum interest payable on any private debt was to be 5 per cent, regardless of the initial terms (McGoun 1936, 523).

The legislation made a big media splash. The *Financial Post* declared that Alberta Social Credit was a "Thin Disguise for Communism" and that the debt legislation "is the most radical ever passed by a government in Canada." It also claimed that "recent debt legislation is akin to confiscation of private property. It strikes at the very roots of commerce, business and finance in a way which characterized the early stages of the Russian Revolution" (19 September 1936, 1). The government's actions demonstrate once more that Social Crediters did not have the property fetish commonly attributed to them.

The Fuel Oil Licensing Act of 1936 gave the province the right to enter into the business of distributing fuel oil as either a retail or wholesale dealer. An amendment to the Department of Trade and Industry Act assented to that year established the Price Spreads Board, which was given the authority to prescribe maximum and minimum prices for a wide array of goods and services. That same year the introduction of the Licensing of Trades and Businesses Act required that virtually all employers and employees register with and be licensed by the government. The act stated that it was created to force compliance with other acts such as the Minimum Wage Act, 1925, and the Industrial Standards Act. According to Dr W.W. Cross, who served as minister of Health and minister of Trade and Industry in the first Aberhart administration, the Licensing Act as well as the Department of Trade and Industry Act were designed "to try and keep business honest so that the farmer and laborer and the small businessman would not be kicked out on the street and enter the relief ranks ... Now, what's the use of a government going to the expense and the trouble of bringing industries into the province if all that they do is exploit the people after they come in?" (*Edmonton Journal*, 30 March 1937, 7).

By the fall of 1936 it seemed that the government was poised and ready to implement its eagerly awaited social credit system. The registration drive was well under way, and Manning had announced that preliminary steps had been taken to permit the payment of basic dividends. In September, Aberhart promised that the payment of dividends would begin in three months (Barr 1974, 99).

A special committee to formulate a social credit bill was struck in December following the unsolicited arrival of John Hargrave, the man who had led his Green Shirts in the noisy march around the Bank

116   Social Classes and Social Credit in Alberta

of England. The committee, aided by Hargrave, produced a plan involving price discounts, a monthly dividend of five dollars in Alberta credit, and government regulation of the export of goods from the province. Hargrave was impressed by the fact that the value of goods exported from Alberta anually exceeded the value of imports by $55 million. He recommended that the provincial government buy with Alberta credit all goods to be exported, sell them for cash, use a portion of this cash to purchase all imports, and use the $55 million difference to subsidize a social credit system. His plan also involved an embargo on money leaving Alberta except for the cash payments made by the province for imports; creditors outside Alberta were to be paid in goods instead of currency (Social Credit Party of Great Britain and Northern Ireland 1937, 15–17). According to W.W. Cross, "It was a good plan." Cross stated that the plan "was presented to the caucus and it was accepted almost unanimously" (*Edmonton Journal*, 30 March 1937, 7).

However, the Cabinet disapproved of the scheme. In a tempestuous caucus meeting attended by Hargrave, Attorney General John Hugill asked the English Social Crediter, "You realize, Mr. Hargrave, that this scheme you are putting forward would not be legal?" Hugill knew that the BNA Act stipulated that the issuing of currency, regulation of the banks, and interprovincial trade fell under federal jurisdiction. "What would you do if your legislation was disallowed and your parliament dissolved?" Hargrave replied that the only way the government could be removed would be to call in the troops, which he claimed the federal government would never be willing to do (Elliott and Miller 1987, 253).

Hargrave's patience quickly ran out, and he left Alberta in a huff at the end of January 1937. He believed that nothing would be done to implement the committee's recommendations, declaring in a written statement given to the press before he left that the Aberhart administration had merely "groped its way like a man stumbling along on a pitch black night" and that the Alberta government was "a mere vacillating machine which operates in starts, stops and reversals" (*Edmonton Bulletin*, 25 January 1937, 1, 2). Hargrave also mentioned in his statement that

the committee drafted the final report, containing ten points, with the help of Mr. Aberhart himself and this report was signed ... by the committee members and myself.

On January 9, Mr. Aberhart brought the final report before his cabinet who, however, did not pass on it. This was the first time that the full cabinet had official information regarding the committee or its report. (*Edmonton Bulletin*, 25 January 1937, 2)

The premier's involvement in producing the proposed social credit measures is considered again below.

The speech from the throne opening the next session of the Alberta legislature, which convened in February, contained only scant mention of social credit. Government backbenchers were extremely disappointed that it included no measures to implement a system of social credit, with some stating so on the floor of the House. The eighteen-month period needed to fulfil the government's promises was at an end, yet it appeared that the Aberhart administration was not going to take the final steps to realize the plan. When the government introduced its budget two weeks later, again no social credit measures were included. This prompted an organized rebellion of dissident backbenchers, whom the press referred to as the "insurgents," a term used to designate one faction in the Spanish Civil War, which was then raging. Likewise, Aberhart's supporters, including the entire Cabinet and another group of backbenchers, were described as "loyalists."

The insurgents were determined to prevent the budget from being passed unless it included measures to implement social credit. They became numerous enough that the life of the government was clearly in jeopardy; some called for Aberhart's resignation. The insurgents decided to engage in a filibuster during the budget debate, which resulted in Aberhart's invoking a motion of closure against members of his own party. It was defeated.

An impasse had been reached, as neither faction wanted an election, yet there was no consensus on how to proceed. After a series of heated meetings and confrontations, a compromise was worked out whereby the insurgents agreed to allow a three-month supply bill to pass in the legislature in return for Aberhart's introduction of the Social Credit Measures Amendment Act. The act stipulated that a board composed of private members would be formed that would have the power to appoint a small commission of experts who would oversee the implementation of a social credit plan.

Although the supply bill was passed, the insurgents were not happy with the Social Credit Measures Amendment Act, which was then withdrawn and replaced by the Alberta Social Credit Act. This was much broader in scope, calling for the creation of Alberta credit, the setting up of credit houses to distribute the credit, and the provision of subsidies to businesses in order to lower prices. The latter were to be calculated by determining the "percentage which unused productive capacity bears to total productive capacity" (Alberta 1937, 58). The act also called for the creation of a Social Credit Board, which was to consist of five private members of the assembly. The board would be responsible for appointing a small

118   Social Classes and Social Credit in Alberta

commission of experts to implement social credit and for ensuring that adequate legislation was introduced to do this.

Many observers thought it strange, even a dereliction of duty, that a government would transfer its sovereign right to control such an important issue to a five-member board, which itself would share some of its power with a group of outsiders, the expert commission. It was also believed that the creation of the Social Credit Board represented a complete victory for the insurgents. Aberhart justified the move by claiming that it was best to leave the implementation of Social Credit to experts, as this would remove it from political influence. In taking this position he appeared to be acting in accordance with the Social Credit political philosophy, which states that politicians should step aside and allow experts to realize mass demand.

The Cabinet tried to distance itself from the Alberta Social Credit Act, claiming that it was drawn up by insurgents. A committee of ten, including four insurgents, "helped draught the bill" (Schultz 1960, 13), but the insurgents later disagreed among themselves over whether the Cabinet had altered it prior to its introduction in the legislature. In any event, it appears that the Cabinet did not want to have the board's powers for itself, as Cabinet members helped to defeat an amendment calling for the board's functions to be transferred to the Cabinet (14–15).

Some analysts of the movement have questioned the Cabinet's stated reasons for assenting to the act creating the Social Credit Board. Macpherson, for example, claims that it "served the strategic purpose of dividing and defeating the insurgency, and it was not long before the bulk of the social credit legislative party was again united behind the cabinet" (1962, 174). Macpherson also argues that the Cabinet did not abdicate its powers to the extent believed at the time, suggesting that many of the methods to be used to implement social credit were outlined in the act, and so were not to be decided upon by the expert commission; that the responsibility for the administration of the plan was split among the experts, the Social Credit Board, and the government; and that the supplementary legislation needed to carry out the scheme had to be passed by the government (174). This interpretation implies that Aberhart and his Cabinet did not agree in principle with what the board was set up to do but assented to its creation in order to save their political lives. Also, in stating that the bill served the "strategic purpose" of defeating the insurgency, Macpherson goes full circle by implying a complete victory for the Cabinet.

Schultz (1960, 15, 18), whose account of the insurgency is partially based on Macpherson's presentation, takes a similar view. S.D. Clark makes a comparable, although much more explicit argument, claiming that

Mr. Aberhart's thunderings in 1935 did create the general impression that he would balk at nothing to put into effect a programme of monetary reform, but, once he was elected to office, it quickly became evident that he was as much frightened by the radical as bored by the administrative implications of such a programme. Had his back-benchers been content, he would thus have happily forgotten the election promises he had so recklessly made ... As it turned out, Mr. Aberhart had to play at the game of introducing Social Credit for a few years ...

... the successful implementation of his monetary reform legislation would have been acutely embarrassing to Mr. Aberhart. (1954, vii-viii).

Barr, however, is reluctant to come to any firm conclusions. He claims:

It is difficult to unscramble Aberhart's motives in agreeing to the compromise. From one standpoint, it did represent a capitulation to the insurgent's demands – or seemed to. It took the final step necessary for the implementation of the party's promises. On the other hand, the Social Credit Board was a queer hybrid: it was fully responsible for the implementation of Social Credit, yet it was still under the cabinet. *If it failed, the cabinet could absolve itself of any blame.* Moreover, the board ... was staffed primarily by insurgents.[9] If the board failed, the insurgents could be pinned with the blame. Finally, the cabinet was left with power to supplement or alter the provisions of the Alberta Social Credit Act, and to keep reign [sic] on the board. Very strange indeed. (1974, 103, emphasis added)

It is indeed difficult to unscramble Aberhart's motives in this complex and secretive affair, but his subsequent relations with his Cabinet and the Social Credit Board give some indication of where he stood.

Shortly after the Alberta Social Credit Act was passed, G.L. MacLachlan, former insurgent and now chairman of the Social Credit Board, went to England in an effort to convince Major Douglas to return to Alberta. MacLachlan told Douglas he would be granted a "free hand to direct operations and choose colleagues" (Elliott and Miller 1987, 262), but the Major declined the offer. Douglas suggested that two of his associates, G.F. Powell and L.D. Byrne, go to Edmonton; if they found the situation to be satisfactory, Douglas would come.

Powell and Byrne left England on short notice and were soon in Edmonton planning new Social Credit strategy. On the eve of the next legislative session Aberhart announced over the radio, "I believe in the session of August 3 [1937], history will begin to be written" (Barr 1974, 107). Within days, radical legislation was introduced that, according to Barr, "struck at the powers of the banks in a way more profound than any legislation ever drafted in a free nation" (107). The Credit of Alberta Regulation Act stipulated that every bank in the province be controlled by a local directorate, a majority of which was to be appointed by the Social Credit Board. It also required that all bankers and bank employees be licensed by the Social Credit Commission. The banks and their employees were prevented from taking court action against these measures by another new bill, the Bank Employees Civil Rights Act. A third bill, the Judicature Act Amendment Act, placed restrictions on any attempt to challenge the constitutional validity of provincial legislation.

As one might expect from his reaction to John Hargrave's proposals, Attorney General Hugill was taken aback by the new legislation. Like many other Albertans, Hugill believed the three bills to be unconstitutional. Lieutenant Governor John Bowen was soon under pressure to refuse assent. Among other influences, Bowen had received a telegram from the Lethbridge Board of Trade claiming that the legislation violated the BNA Act (Elliott and Miller 1987, 267).

The following passage from Elliott and Miller illustrates the bind Bowen was in, and also provides an indication of how Aberhart viewed the matter.

In the office of the lieutenant-governor a strange little drama ensued ... when the lieutenant-governor asked Hugill for his opinion of the bills, Aberhart was waiting for him to approve, glowering ominously over the conversation. Hugill was embarrassed by the presence of Aberhart, but unintimidated he said that in his opinion the bills were unconstitutional. Aberhart could see the Social Credit legislation stumbling at the first hurdle and, without waiting for Hugill to advise the lieutenant-governor to withhold his assent, Aberhart insisted that Bowen sign the bills. He would, he said, take the responsibility himself. The lieutenant-governor signed, and in this bizarre manner the controversial bills became law. (1987, 267–8).

The bills did not remain law for long, however, for within two weeks the federal government disallowed all three. Nor did Hugill last as attorney general; he resigned shortly after the incident described above took place.

Mallory provides what appears to be the most plausible account of the Cabinet's, and in particular Aberhart's, role in the party's first two years in office. He claims that at least three of the eight Cabinet members were moderates having no firm belief in the Social Credit doctrine. These were C.C. Ross, minister of Lands and Mines; Charles Cockroft, Provincial Treasurer; and Hugill (1954, 74). Ross resigned in December 1936 and Cockroft in January 1937. Mallory maintains that Hugill's resignation "marked a turning point in the history of the Social Credit regime. He was the last of the moderates in cabinet and with his departure the policy of the administration headed into a direct challenge to Dominion authority" (76).

It may be the case, then, that Aberhart sincerely favoured the implementation of a social credit scheme but could not come up with a plan that would not violate the constitution, and thus be acceptable to his Cabinet. John Hargrave's statement that Aberhart had assisted in drawing up radical social credit measures only to have them rejected by the Cabinet is in keeping with this assessment. Also consistent with this interpretation is Cabinet member W.W. Cross's statement that "the caucus went away satisfied [with the Hargrave plan]. We were satisfied, but we took it up with every constitutional authority that we could find in this province, with everyone we could contact and they told us 100 per cent that this province had no authority to interfere with exports and that ended it. We could not go any further" (*Edmonton Journal*, 27 March 1937, 7).

After the disallowance of the three radical bills, the Alberta government tried to persuade Albertans to send telegrams of protest to the federal government. Some groups, such as the Edmonton Chamber of Commerce, signed telegrams stating that they were opposed to the Aberhart government (Barr 1974, 197).

In September 1937 the Alberta government introduced several bills that reenacted the ones disallowed by Ottawa. It also brought forth the Bank Taxation Act, which increased the provincial tax payable by the banks by 2,883 per cent (Mallory 1954, 86). The banks argued that the tax was discriminatory and coercive. Other enterprises also faced large tax hikes, although these were small by comparison: life insurance companies were hit with a 50 per cent tax increase, finance companies a 100 per cent increase, power companies a 90 per cent increase, and other companies an increase of 25 per cent (86). The bill appeared to satisfy Douglas's directive that the banks be induced to comply with the implementation of a social credit system. It also dovetailed with the Social Credit belief that money flows from the end of a banker's pen. In addition, it helped to fulfil the administration's plan to shift the burden of taxation from individuals to institutions.

Another bill introduced at this time was the Accurate News and Information Act, which was soon dubbed the "press gag bill." The press in Alberta and across Canada had directed searing criticism at the Social Credit movement before the election and continued its negative treatment of the party after Social Credit took power. Under the bill, newspapers were to have been required to publish a statement from the chairman of the Social Credit Board if the latter felt that there had been inaccuracies in any story pertaining to the governing of the provice. The chairman's statement would have had to be published with a layout similar to that of the offending article. Newspapers would also have been required to inform the board of the source of any information and the name of the author of any article. Any refusal to comply with the act would have led to the suspension of the newspaper or author in question.

Needless to say, opposition to the press bill was immediate and thoroughgoing. A group of Alberta newspapers won a Pulitzer Prize in 1938 for their campaign against it. The legislation itself, along with the Bank Taxation Act and the bills re-enacting the previous social credit legislation, were reserved by the lieutenant governor. In 1938 the Supreme Court of Canada struck down all the acts reserved by the lieutenant governor.

The Alberta government received a major setback when Social Credit Party whip Joe Unwin and G.F. Powell, one of the "experts" sent over from England on Douglas's recommendation, were charged with seditious libel, defamatory libel, and counselling to murder. The charges stemmed from publication of a one-page pamphlet listing several prominent Albertans, including the leader of the provincial Conservative Party, as "Bankers' Toadies." After the list of names, the pamphlet stated: "EXTERMINATE THEM / And to Prevent all Evasion, Demand the Result You Want / $25 A MONTH and a Lower Cost to Live."[10] The other side of the sheet read:

Bankers' Toadies

My child, you should NEVER say hard or unkind things about Bankers' Toadies. God made Bankers' Toadies, just as He made snakes, slugs, snails and other creepy-crawly, treacherous and poisonous things. NEVER, therefore, abuse them – just exterminate them!

AND TO PREVENT ALL EVASION
Demand the *Result* you want
$25.00 a month
and a lower cost to live.

Unwin and Powell were found guilty of defamatory libel; the other charges were dropped. Unwin was sentenced to three months at hard labour, Powell to six plus deportation upon release. Before his departure for England the Alberta government gave Powell four thousand dollars by order-in-council (Mallory 1954, 83).

The granting of funds to Powell upon his release appears to have been indicative of Aberhart's relationship with the Social Credit Board. Alf Hooke, who himself was a member of the board from 1938 to 1943, writes that "Mr. Aberhart worked in close cooperation with the Social Credit Board from its inception and especially after the Powell-Unwin episode and the return of Mr. Powell to Great Britain. He worked very closely with Mr. L.D. Byrne, in whom he had the greatest confidence" (1971, 144). Here again is evidence that Aberhart was not merely pretending "to play at the game of introducing Social Credit for a few years."

The year 1937 was indeed a devastating one for the government. In addition to the insurgency and the criminal convictions, that year saw the Supreme Court rule that the government's action reducing the interest paid on provincial bonds was unconstitutional; the court rendered an identical decision with regard to the government's debt legislation. In response to these decisions, Aberhart signed a six-month debt moratorium, pending an appeal (Barr 1974, 101).

A further humiliation came that year when the government repealed a Recall Act passed in 1936, which had stated that any member of the legislature must resign if 66.6 per cent or more of the electors in his or her riding signed a recall petition. Such a petition was organized against Premier Aberhart and the requisite signatures apparently secured, but the act was repealed in time to save the premier's seat. The government claimed that there were irregularities in acquiring the signatures, but it suffered a serious loss of face none the less. Before the year was out the government had also fought and lost a by-election in Lethbridge, a riding it had won easily in 1935.

The government found itself in the unenviable position of having antagonized the established interests in the province without having any tangible benefit to show for it. Another problem for the government was the growing unity of the political parties in opposition to it. The provincial Liberals and Conservatives, as well as some UFA activists, agreed to work together to defeat the Aberhart government. The coalition, known variously as the People's League, Unity Party, Citizen's Committee, and most commonly as the Independents, was encouraged by the fact that its strategy had worked in the Lethbridge by-election.

Apparently undaunted, the government launched into 1938 by re-enacting much of the debt legislation that had been disallowed the previous year. It also maintained that it would not pay the full value of the interest on the provincial government's own debts. By August 1939 it had avoided $3.4 million in interest charges and had defaulted on $12 million worth of payments (Barr 1974, 113). Once again the issue of property rights came to the fore, and once again it was not the Social Credit Party that was defending them. The *Montreal Gazette* wrote that Aberhart's movement "has now run amok through a field of radical legislation that is without precedent in any country, civilized or savage. It has legalized theft. Having attempted to exploit the banks, to muzzle the press and to tie the hands of the courts, and having been frustrated in these efforts, it has proceeded to the enactment of laws which are equally if not more vicious ... Alberta debtors may avail themselves of the opportunities to steal the money of others as afforded under these acts" (12 May 1938, 8).

Try as they might, the Social Crediters could not escape the fact that federal institutions could and would veto virtually every piece of legislation that strayed from orthodox methods of financial management. In an effort to regroup, the government embarked on what it optimistically called the "Interim Program." It involved the creation of "Treasury Branches," which accepted deposits and offered loans much as did credit unions, except that depositors were encouraged to use non-negotiable "transfer vouchers" rather than legal tender in their transactions. The Treasury Branch system was designed to create a bookkeeping network that would eventually cover every transaction in the province, eliminate the use of standard currency and the chartered banks, and thereby allow the government to introduce a social credit system. The Treasury Branches initially provided a 3 per cent bonus to customers who used transfer vouchers in purchases in which Alberta-produced goods formed at least one-third of the value of the transaction; subsequently, a 2 per cent bonus was paid on the purchase of any goods. However, the transfer vouchers met the same fate the Prosperity Certificates had two years earlier: many people were reluctant to accept them as money. The Treasury Branches attracted only a small percentage of all deposits in Alberta and posed no serious challenge to the existence of the chartered banks in the province.

A final bit of legislation that characterized the first Social Credit administration's economic policy was the Alberta Marketing Act, passed in 1939. Remarkably, the legislation not only allowed the government to control the marketing of a wide variety of products; it permitted the government itself to get involved in the business of buying and selling virtually any product. It also enabled the government to engage in the business of manufacturing or producing any product, and to purchase any land or property necessary to do so.

125   Social Credit in Power

The Alberta government's first term of office also helped to clarify its view of federal-provincial relations and regional grievances. In 1937 the federal government appointed a royal commission on Dominion-provincial relations to examine the troubled economic foundation of Confederation as well as the distribution of legislative powers. Embittered by the federal disallowance of its social credit legislation, Aberhart's government refused to assist the committee in any way, claiming that any changes to the constitution would be wrought to the advantage of finance. Douglas had always warned Aberhart that such bodies were the work of finance, and in this case he told the Social Credit Board that the royal commission was designed to promote the hegemony of the Bank of Canada over the provinces (Mallory 1954, 141).

Rather than give evidence before the committee,[11] the government submitted *The Case for Alberta* (Alberta, 1938) to outline its position on Dominion-provincial relations. Before reviewing this position, it may be useful to consider S.D. Clark's (1954) view of Aberhart's designs on this matter, as his analysis illustrates one element of the thesis holding that Social Credit was inspired by opposition to central Canadian "imperialism." As noted in chapter 5, Clark maintains that "Aberhart's attempts to introduce Social Credit were directed primarily towards the object of strengthening the political position of the province in its relations with the federal government. Monetary reform thus was a means to an end ... In seeking the increased separation of Alberta from the Canadian federal system, Aberhart was prepared to go to very great lengths" (viii).

The Case for Alberta tells another story. It states:

The Government of Alberta does not concur in the view that the constitutional structure so carefully planned by the Fathers of Confederation has materially failed, that is in so far as the distribution of legislative powers is concerned. Neither does it share the view taken by some that in order to meet adequately the problems of the day there is any need for a wide transference of powers and legislative authority from the Provinces to the Dominion or from the Dominion to the Provinces.   (Alberta 1938, pt I, 9)

The Case for Alberta is also relevant to the first element of the anti-imperialist thesis, namely that the movement's efforts were concentrated on redressing conventional regional economic grievances. The document is divided into two parts. Part I addresses a number of provincial economic concerns, with recommendations that could be enacted under the existing financial system – that is, without the implementation of social credit. These issues include some traditional prairie grievances, such as the detrimental effects of freight rates and import tariffs on Alberta, issues that did not figure in the 1935 or 1940 election campaigns. The report makes it clear that the adoption of the recommendations of part I "would do no more than tide over the national situation until definite economic reconstruction along the lines recommended in Part II [which advocates the implementation of social credit] has been put into effect ... These recommendations [in part I] are made within the limitations of the present defective monetary system and its adaptation to meet the transition period to a new economic order. *The fundamental issues involved are dealt with fully in Part II of this brief"* (Alberta 1938, pt. I, 377, emphasis added). It is no wonder that the recommendations of part I are presented as temporary expedients, since part II argues that the introduction of social credit measures would result in an eightfold increase in the standard of living in Alberta (5)! In part II the government "unreservedly offers to test the soundness of the economic proposals submitted in this chapter ... Is it too much to ask that our Province be afforded the privilege of leading the way out of the present chaos of poverty, debt and crushing taxation in a land of abundance and promise?" (55)

It is evident, then, that the standard western economic grievances were not the centrepiece of the philosophy and activity of the first Social Credit government. They were invoked in a government document after the movement's accession to power and after its plan for a "new economic order" had been nullifed by the federal government. It seems likely that the enumeration of these grievances was an attempt to achieve something – anything – for the people of Alberta, even if the measures recommended fell far short of what was believed to be possible and even if it would leave the root cause of the malaise untouched. For this reason it is argued here that the main impetus and *raison d'être* of the Social Credit movement was not the elimination of unfair conventional national economic policies nor an expansion of provincial jurisdiction but the rectification of what it saw as fundamental shortcomings in all capitalist economies.

Before the government's first term of office came to an end, war had broken out in Europe, with Canada embarking on a full mobilization. The war effort tended to lessen demands for bold moves on the part of the provinces and generally contributed to a spirit of co-operation with the federal government.

Aberhart wanted to conduct his first re-election campaign at the same time as a forthcoming federal campaign in order to embarrass the erstwhile Liberal and Conservative activists now presenting themselves as "Independents." He reasoned that in a federal election contest they would have to show their real party colours (Schultz 1962, 17). Mackenzie King called an election for 26 March 1940. The Alberta premier called his for 21 March.

Always a thorough and energetic organizer, the premier saw to it that the party was ready to wage the campaign in every constituency. Actually, Aberhart had never stopped the campaigning he had begun before the 1935 election. In his weekly radio broadcasts he would discuss whatever government business was before him, using his oratorical skills to great effect in presenting the government's case.

The party also benefited from the tireless work of the Social Credit Board. The board was not a passive unit that merely sought out "experts" to carry out Social Credit policy but was actively engaged in promoting government initiatives and defending the administration's reputation. Members of the board would travel into all regions of the province, holding public meetings at least five days a week.

Board members used considerable ingenuity in getting their message across. Floyd Baker, for example, mounted a generator on the back of his automobile, which enabled him to show lantern slides in rural areas, many of which still had no electricity. He later added motion pictures and comic strips to attract a general audience. In many areas those attending Baker's meetings saw not only motion pictures but also electric lights for the first time (Hooke 1971, 149).

Aberhart stepped up his usual anti-finance rhetoric for the campaign, but there was no promise to bring in a social credit system or to issue dividends. He preferred to talk about the Social Credit debt legislation rather than dividends, stating in a Grande Prairie speech: "Never mind dividends, let them go. After getting 95 per cent, are you going to pluck me on that?" (Schultz 1962, 20). As for the debt legislation, many farmers came to believe that their choice was between "Aberhart or the sheriff" (23). The Social Credit Party focused its campaign on what it described as its record of good government and the provision of social services.

The Independents, being a coalition party, were reluctant to propose any initiatives that smacked of the Liberal or Conservative parties' programs for fear of alienating opposing factions in the coalition. The same reasoning prevented them from naming a party leader or establishing a campaign headquarters. They were united mainly in their opposition to the Social Credit government and their desire to take office. This meant that although they were against Aberhart, it was difficult for the voters to determine what they were *for*. The Independents reminded the public of the government's broken promises and provided harsh (possibly too harsh for their own purposes) criticism of Social Credit's record, exhorting voters to "FREE YOURSELVES FROM SOCIAL CREDIT'S POCKET HITLERISMS" (Schultz 1962, 22).

CONCLUSIONS

The foregoing indicates that the Social Credit movement's first term of office involved an attempt to implement a philosophy that was one part Douglasism and one part social democracy. The Douglasism was evident in the attempt to put into operation the still inchoate plan to issue dividends, control wages and prices, regulate production and distribution, and use "fountain pen" money to serve public ends. These measures represented a clear departure from the existing way of organizing the economy and producing and distributing wealth. The labour, debt, and social legislation enacted by the government, as well as its raising of taxes, did not have its origins in the Douglas philosophy and was similar in principle to measures introduced by other reform movements.

This chapter also suggests that the idea conveyed in some accounts that Mr Aberhart was insincere in his advocacy of Social Credit is unfounded. As for the Social Credit movement's allegedly fervent war against imperialism, the history reviewed above suggests that a provincial campaign to redress conventional regional economic grievances and expand the jurisdiction of the province was not the driving force behind the movement. The driving force was the movement's economic radicalism. In the final chapter of this study, the argument is made that for the most part, Social Credit has been mistakenly interpreted as a slightly modified version of the Progressive movement, a movement that did fight regional injustice. But before discussing any general conclusions it is advantageous to examine the pattern of class voting in the 1940 provincial election, which is the topic of the next chapter.

8 The 1940 Election: Cities, Towns, and Countryside

In the 1940 election the popular vote for Social Credit dropped from 54 per cent to 43 per cent, the lowest point it would reach until the party's defeat in 1971. None the less, Social Credit retained its majority in the legislature, taking 36 of 57 seats. The Independents, a coalition of Liberals, Conservatives, and UFA supporters, were a close second, earning 42 per cent of the popular vote and 19 seats (Alberta 1983, 13). Voter turnout was high at 75 per cent, but not as high as the 82 per cent recorded in 1935 (53, 59).

THE CITIES

Unfortunately, missing data once again prevent an analysis of the election results in Edmonton. Ironically, for the 1935 election the location of the polls as well as the polling subdivision boundaries are available for Edmonton, but not the results by polling subdivision. For the 1940 election the results by polling subdivision are available from the provincial archives, but not the location of the polls and their boundaries are not.[1] For the record, in the constituency of Edmonton the Independents received 54 per cent of the vote (N = 43,743), Social Credit 33 per cent and the CCF 10 per cent (Alberta 1983, 56).[2]

Calgary

Support for Social Credit in the city of Calgary decreased considerably, dropping from 58 per cent in 1935 to 37 per cent in 1940. The

130   Social Classes and Social Credit in Alberta

Table 8.1
Vote in Calgary in the 1940 Provincial Election, by Area

	%				
	Social Credit	CCF	Independents	Other	N
AREA					
1) Upper class	11	3	85	1	1,332
2) Upper middle class	17	4	78	1	5,197
3) Upper middle/ lower middle class	29	7	63	1	8,121
4) Lower middle/ working class	36	10	53	1	7,693
5) Working class	47	11	41	1	20,070
CITY	37	9	53	1	43,848[a]

Source: Statement of Vote for the 1940 election, Provincial Archives of Alberta

[a] Includes advance poll, hospital, and soldiers' vote.

party ran only four candidates in Calgary, even though the riding was a five-member constituency; two of the four Social Credit candidates, including William Aberhart, were elected. The Independent slate elected the other three members. The results for Calgary in 1940 by area are contained in Table 8.1.[3]

It should be noted that Aberhart ran successfully in the *city* of Calgary, Manning in the city of Edmonton. Manning continued to run in Edmonton as premier until his retirement in 1968, winning by a large margin each time. These observations are not in keeping with the popular academic characterization of Social Credit as an *agrarian* movement.

Once again the data indicate that support for Social Credit varied inversely with class level, ranging from 11 per cent in the upper-class area to 47 per cent in the working-class districts. Support for the Independents was of the opposite pattern, going from 85 per cent in the upper-class neighbourhood to 41 per cent in the working-class areas. CCF support varied in the same "direction" as that for Social Credit, ranging from 3 per cent in the first area to 11 per cent in the working-class neighbourhoods. This suggests that part of the reason for the failure of the CCF in Calgary (and possibly in Alberta as a whole, as we shall see) was that it competed with Social Credit for the same type of voter.

In working-class areas Social Credit support decreased by 21 percentage points. The Independents received a level of support here that was 17 percentage points higher than the total for the Liberals and Conservatives in these areas in 1935. The CCF figure was 6 percentage points above the Labor result in these areas for 1935. It would appear, then, that almost three-quarters of the losses incurred by Social Credit in the working-class districts were picked up by the Independents, although survey data would be necessary to substantiate this.[4] None the less, it is a reasonable hypothesis that the threat to Social Credit dominance among the working class in Calgary in 1940 came from the non-socialist Independents rather than the CCF. At only 11 per cent, CCF support in Calgary's working-class neighbourhoods in 1940 was still well below the 30 per cent earned by Labor in 1930.

Support for Social Credit in the most heavily industrialized part of the city, the southeast, was again higher than in the working-class areas as a whole: 54 per cent (N = 2267) as compared to 46 per cent for the entire area. Surprisingly, CCF support was 1 percentage point lower in the southeast (10 per cent) than in the working-class districts as a whole. In 1930 Labor support in the southeast was 35 per cent, compared to 30 per cent in these areas as a whole.

The results in area 4, the lower-middle/working-class area, and area 3, the upper-middle/lower-middle-class region, are also important in assessing the pattern of class voting in the city. In area 4 Social Credit support fell by 23 percentage points to 36 per cent; in area 3 it also decreased by 23 points, to 29 per cent. In upper-middle-class area 2, the party's support dropped by 17 percentage points to 17 per cent. In area 1 the decrease was 9 points to 11 per cent.

These results may be more meaningful if we consider the *relative* decrease in Social Credit support in each area. Social Credit's 47 per cent showing in the working-class area is a decrease of 31 per cent from the 68 per cent figure achieved in 1935. Its performance in area 4 showed a 39 per cent decrease, in area 3 a 44 per cent decrease, area 2 a 50 per cent decrease, and area 1 a 45 per cent decrease. From this it may be inferred that not only did the working-class area exhibit the highest level of Social Credit voting, but voters in this area were also the most "loyal" to the party. The data suggest that those in the middle classes who voted Social Credit in 1935 were more likely to desert the party in 1940 than those in the working class, and of middle-class voters, those in the upper middle class were more likely to desert than those in the lower. Hence, as the levels of support for the party in the 1935 election indicated, the 1940 results again suggest that Social Credit was not a characteristically middle-class phenomenon, contrary to what many academic accounts maintain.

To sum up, although Social Credit support declined markedly in 1940 in Calgary, it still varied inversely with class level, with the highest support coming from the working-class districts. Once again

132   Social Classes and Social Credit in Alberta

the heavily industrialized southeast had a higher level of Social Credit support than the working-class districts as a whole. The Independent coalition benefited most from the decline in Social Credit voting, apparently capturing a solid majority of those deserting the party. The data also suggest that of those who voted Social Credit in Calgary in 1935, voters in the working-class neighbourhoods were the most loyal to the party.

Lethbridge

In the general election of 1940 Social Credit failed to regain the seat lost in the 1937 by-election in Lethbridge, taking only 39 per cent of the vote. Independent candidate Dr P.M. Campbell, the only other candidate in the race, took the other 61 per cent.

Missing information presents some complications for the interpretation of the Lethbridge vote. The number of polls in the riding declined from 14 in 1935 to 10 in 1940. The geographical size of the constituency was reduced by approximately one-half; all the areas reassigned to other ridings were rural. Of the 10 1940 polls, 9 were located within the city limits; there were also 9 in the city limits in 1935, which were analysed in chapter 6 as Lethbridge's urban polls. Of the 9 1940 urban polls, 7 were in exactly the same place as the 1935 polls;[5] the other 2 were near the 2 remaining 1935 urban polls and fell within the corresponding 1935 subdivision boundaries. No statement of the 1940 polling subdivision boundaries could be found. The analysis below assumes that the polling subdivision boundaries were the same in 1935 and 1940 for the 9 urban polls.[6]

The results recorded in Table 8.2 indicate that support for Social Credit again varied inversely with class level in Lethbridge, with the greatest support found in the working-class neighbourhoods. Support for the Independent candidate varied positively with class level. The three polls (71, 72, 73) in North Lethbridge, the working-class area, together had a 61 per cent Social Credit vote, down by 12 percentage points from 1935. Poll 71 had the highest Social Credit vote in the city, with 73 per cent (N = 820) in favour. South Lethbridge, which contained a middle-class mix with a sizable working-class minority, voted 27 per cent Social Credit (N = 4449), down by 15 percentage points.

To get an indication of the extent of lower-middle-class support for the party in Lethbridge, the south side minus the upper-middle-class London Road poll was once again examined. (The south without London Road contained a middle-class mix that was mainly lower middle class, as well as a substantial working-class minority.) The

Table 8.2
Vote in Lethbridge in the 1940 Provincial Election, by Area

	%		
	Social Credit	Independent	N
SOUTH			
Upper middle class	24	76	1,161
Lower middle/			
working class	28	72	3,288
NORTH			
Working class	61	39	2,396
CITY	39	61	7,036[a]

Source: Statement of Vote for the 1940 election, Provincial Archives of Alberta.
[a] Includes advance poll, hospital, and soldiers' vote.

south excluding poll 77, which covered about half of London Road, voted 28 per cent Social Credit. This figure appears in Table 8.2 as the lower-middle/working-class neighbourhood vote. Poll 77, used as a measure of upper-middle-class voting, had a 24 per cent Social Credit tally.

The three southside polls with the highest Social Credit vote in 1940, polls 75, 79, and 76 (47, 37, and 36 per cent Social Credit respectively), also had the highest level of Social Credit voting in 1935 and Labor support in 1930 of all southside polls; they also kept the same ranking on these scores for all three elections. Thus, again, we have reason to believe that the comparatively high level of Social Credit voting in these areas was associated with a relatively high proportion of working-class residents in them. As in 1935, however, these results do not preclude the possibility that in these polls the lower middle class gave a high level of support to the party.

Considering the relative decline in Social Credit voting, the 12-percentage-point drop in the working-class neighbourhoods represents a 16 per cent decrease over the 1935 figure of 73 per cent. In the lower-middle/working-class area, the decline was 35 per cent, and in the London Road poll, 38 per cent. Thus in Lethbridge as in Calgary, the working-class areas were the most loyal to Social Credit, with the desertion rate apparently varying positively with class level. Again the data bring into question the idea that Social Credit was primarily a middle-class movement.

In summary, although Social Credit failed to take the Lethbridge seat, the party's support once more varied inversely with class level,

134   Social Classes and Social Credit in Alberta

with the greatest support found in working-class North Lethbridge. A majority of the voters in this area supported the party. The data also suggest that the desertion rate varied positively with class level. As only the Independent candidate competed with Social Credit for the seat, he received all the votes of those voters who deserted the party. The class basis of his support was the opposite of that for Social Credit.

Medicine Hat

The election was very close in Medicine Hat, with Social Credit incumbent Dr J.L. Robinson winning by only 80 votes out of a total of 5,806. He too was opposed by only one candidate, W.C. Yuill, an Independent. The results in the city polls are shown in Table 8.3.[7]

As in the other cities, the results for Medicine Hat indicate that support for Social Credit continued to vary inversely with class level. All city polls combined registered a 48 per cent Social Credit vote. The five polls covering the working-class districts, numbers 2, 4, 5, 6, and 7, showed the highest level of support for the party with 66 per cent in favour; this represented a 10-percentage-point drop from 1935.

The lower-middle/working-class areas of the city, covered by polls 13 and 14, voted 44 per cent Social Credit, a decline of 19 percentage points. Polls 8, 10, and 12, which contained a roughly even mix of upper-middle and lower-middle-class residents, had a 39 per cent Social Credit vote, down by 13 percentage points. In polls 9 and 11, which were located in upper-middle-class neighbourhoods, Social Credit captured 30 per cent of the vote, a decline of 8 percentage points.

Considering the relative decline in support in the various neighbourhoods, the 10-percentage-point decrease in the working-class areas represents a 13 per cent decline from the 1935 figure of 76 per cent. The lower-middle/working-class areas declined by 30 per cent, the upper-middle/lower-middle-class sections by 25 per cent, and the upper-middle-class neighbourhoods by 21 per cent. Thus, unlike the other cities, the desertion rate in Medicine Hat does not appear to have varied directly with class level, although, as in Calgary and Lethbridge, the working-class districts were the most loyal.

In summary, in 1940 in Medicine Hat support for Social Credit again varied inversely with class level, with the greatest support found in the working-class areas. A large majority of the voters living in these areas continued to support the party, and these districts also showed the highest level of loyalty. As only one candidate opposed

135   The 1940 Election

Table 8.3
Vote in Medicine Hat in the 1940 Provincial Election, by Area

	%		
	Social Credit	Independent	N
Upper middle class	30	70	979
Upper middle/ lower middle class	39	61	1,404
Lower middle/ working class[a]	44	56	512
Working class[a]	66	34	1,879
CITY	48	52	5,023[b]

Source: Statement of Vote for the 1940 election, Provincial Archives of Alberta.
[a] Includes some rural voters. See chap. 6, 99–101.
[b] Includes advance poll, hospital, and soldiers' vote.

Social Credit, an Independent, he received the support of all voters who deserted the party. As in Calgary and Lethbridge, the Independent vote varied positively with class level.

THE SMALL TOWNS

Like the results for the 1935 election, those for 1940 do not support the popular notion that Social Credit received disproportionately high support in the small towns of the province. Looking at the results in the same small towns as were examined in chapter 6, we see in Table 8.4 that the party received 42 per cent of the vote in these 27 towns, 1 percentage point below its province-wide showing. The Independents were actually more popular than Social Credit in the small towns, capturing 47 per cent of the vote there. The Social Credit showing in the small towns in 1940 represented a drop of 10 percentage points from the 1935 figure; the relative decrease was 19 per cent.

THE COUNTRYSIDE

Once again, to get a measure of the farm vote, the results from all urban areas having a population of 1,000 or more were removed from all constituencies. The remaining rural areas accounted for 60 per cent of all votes cast in 1940. Social Credit received 47 per cent of the vote in rural areas (N = 186,228), 4 percentage points more than the party's provincial average. By comparison, the working-class areas

136 Social Classes and Social Credit in Alberta

Table 8.4
Vote in the 1940 Provincial Election, for Urban Areas with Populations from 1,000 to 5,000[a]

	%					
	Social Credit	Independent	Labor	CCF	Other	N
Blairmore	36	28	36	—	—	898
Camrose	26	43	—	31	—	1,468
Cardston	56	44	—	—	—	1,041
Claresholm	37	63	—	—	—	524
Coleman	55	34	12	—	—	1,410
Drumheller	41	50	—	9	—	1,743
Edson	30	—	37	33	—	783
Fort Saskatchewan	28	38	—	33	—	398
Grande Prairie	36	61	—	4	—	962
Hanna	57	43	—	—	—	910
High River	45	55	—	—	—	992
Innisfail	31	56	—	—	13	566
Lacombe	35	61	—	4	—	900
Lloydminster	59	23	—	19	—	350
Macleod	51	49	—	—	—	742
Magrath	44	56	—	—	—	583
Olds	38	60	—	—	2	912
Pincher Creek	34	55	11	—	—	372
Raymond	59	41	—	—	—	1,009
Redcliff	63	37	—	—	—	538
Red Deer	30	58	—	—	11	1,175
Stettler	43	50	—	7	—	888
Taber	40	41	—	18	—	859
Vegreville	35	61	—	5	—	970
Vermillion	30	65	—	5	—	637
Wainright	34	46	—	16	5	617
Wetaskiwin	48	45	—	6	—	1,277
ALL SMALL TOWNS	42	47	3	7	1	23,524
PROVINCE	43	42	1	11	2	308,864

Source: Statement of Vote for the 1940 election, Provincial Archives of Alberta.

[a] Excluding Beverly, for which data are not available. Rows do not total 100 in some cases due to rounding.

of Calgary, Lethbridge, and Medicine Hat combined had a 50 per cent Social Credit vote (N = 24,345). The decline in Social Credit support in the countryside was 10 percentage points, which represents an 18 per cent decrease relative to the 1935 percentage. The Independents won 36 per cent of the rural vote in 1940, and the CCF

13 per cent. The latter result indicates that in rural areas, as in the working-class districts of the three cities for which data are available, the threat to Social Credit dominance came from the Independents rather than the CCF.

REGIONAL VARIATION

In order to determine whether the south again provided greater support for Social Credit than the north, the province was once more divided into two geographical regions (see Map 8.1). Unlike the 1935 election, the 1940 contest did not exhibit a north-south split in Social Credit support. A total of 43 per cent of southern voters supported the party (N = 143,189), the same proportion as in the north (N = 165,675). It may be the case that the north-south difference of 1935 resulted from differential exposure to Social Credit campaigns. Aberhart and Manning had toured more extensively in the south prior to the 1935 election, and the south had been organized by the movement earlier than the north. But once the government had gained power and served a term of office, especially one as tumultuous as Social Credit's first term, it received extensive media and public attention that was not regionally based. If people in northern areas did not know much about Social Credit in 1935, they had surely learned plenty by 1940.

The Independents, by contrast, received 50 per cent of the southern vote but only 36 per cent of the northern. Their relative weakness in the north may have reflected the CCF's popularity there, as the CCF garnered 16 per cent of the vote in the north, compared to only 5 per cent in the south. The CCF ran only 7 of a possible 25 candidates in the south, compared to 29 of a possible 32 in the north.

It is interesting to note that the socialist CCF[8] did better in the predominantly petit-bourgeois countryside than in the cities. The party received 9 per cent of the Calgary city vote and 10 per cent of the Edmonton constituency vote; no CCF candidates entered the Lethbridge or Medicine Hat campaigns. We have seen above that the CCF won 11 per cent of the vote in the working-class districts of Calgary. By comparison, the CCF took 19 per cent of the vote in the rural areas that it contested (N = 130,003). Where the CCF entered candidates in the rural south, it won 15 per cent of the vote (N = 20,800); it took 20 per cent of the vote in the northern rural areas in which it fielded candidates (N = 109,203). These are important findings, as the higher level of support for the CCF in rural areas as compared to urban working-class districts suggests that the agrarian petite bourgeoisie exhibited a higher level of support for socialist-oriented social

Map 8.1
Alberta Electoral Divisions 1940, Showing North–South Boundary

change than did members of the working class, which is contrary to what the petit-bourgeois conservatism thesis would predict.

The rural south and the rural north both had 47 per cent levels of support for Social Credit (N = 72,658 and 113,570 respectively), whereas the working-class areas of the three southern cities had a 50 per cent Social Credit vote. Thus it appears that in 1940 there was little difference between the southern urban working-class vote and the southern farm vote. But once again, the "surprising" finding (with respect to the conventional wisdom) is the high level of working-class support for Social Credit. The rural south and the working-class areas of the three southern cities were also about equal in their loyalty to Social Credit, as the relative decrease in support for the party in the former area was 25 per cent, and in the latter, 28 per cent.

The southern small towns had a level of support for Social Credit 10 percentage points higher than the northern small towns, 45 per cent as against 35 per cent (N = 15,162 and 8,362 respectively). The former score may be compared to the 48 per cent won by the Independents in the southern small towns and to the 50 per cent won by Social Credit in the working-class districts of the three southern cities. Thus, although southern small towns had a level of support for Social Credit that was 2 percentage points above the provincial average, the Independents were even more popular there, and the southern small-town vote was 5 percentage points below that of the working-class districts of the three southern cities.

CONCLUSIONS

In 1940 it was again the case that support for Social Credit varied inversely with class level. In the three cities for which the necessary data are available, the highest level of support was found in the working-class neighbourhoods, with support decreasing as the class composition of the neighbourhoods approached the higher levels. In all these cities the working-class districts were also the most loyal to Social Credit. As for southern rural support as against southern urban working-class support, the latter was only slightly higher, and so indicates that there was little difference between these two groups in their support for Social Credit in 1940. The two groups also had about the same level of loyalty to Social Credit. But once again, the high level of working-class support for the party in Calgary, Lethbridge, and Medicine Hat gives us reason to reconsider the conventional belief that mass support for Social Credit stemmed ultimately from a petit-bourgeois class position, or that Social Credit was a characteristically middle-class phenomenon. The high level of working-class support for Social Credit in 1940 reported here also brings into question the remark made by J.F. Conway in defence of the petit-bourgeois thesis: "Was it accidental that Aberhart, who certainly received large support among the working class and the urban *petite bourgeoisie* in 1935, won the 1940 election in the rural areas?" (1990, 373)

I am now in a position to present an alternative theoretical analysis of the Social Credit movement in Alberta.

9 Social Credit in Alberta:
An Alternative Perspective

In any historical era, a large number of social movements come into being and attempt to change society. Some compete with other movements for public support and political power, while others are more or less on their own, too powerless to be noticed by the larger public and too weak to elicit a response even from those whose interests they oppose.

The vast majority of social movements are of the weaker sort. Most never gain a substantial following, much less embark on a large-scale mobilization. Yet Social Credit was able to do that and more. The movement not only got a large proportion of the populace excited about social credit but seized the reins of government and began to refashion the province according to its principles. Thus, in spite of its failure to implement a plan for social credit, it was in many respects a *successful* social movement. How was this possible? How was it able to achieve such success while others movements could not? Another way of expressing these questions is to ask, What can be learned about social movements *in general* from the Social Credit experience? What *theoretical* lessons can be drawn from this movement?

PREVIOUS EXPLANATIONS

Existing accounts of Social Credit are of two general types. One focuses on social structures or "conditions," in particular Alberta's class structure, the "quasi-colonial" position of the prairie provinces,

141   An Alternative Perspective

and/or the Depression.[1] The other type of study is concerned primarily with discussing the individuals involved in the movement and describing a sequence of specific events in which they took part. The two approaches should be viewed as Weberian ideal types, as no particular work is a pure exemplar of either type. A discussion of the strengths and weaknesses of each kind of study is given below, followed by an interpretation of Social Credit that involves a synthesis of the two methodologies.

Analyses Focusing on Social Structures

Under this heading we find Macpherson's (1962) analysis and those of the writers who follow his general perspective. While an analysis of social structures is useful and necessary, this approach also has serious shortcomings. A problem with explanations that dwell on social structures is that *they lack explicit consideration of human agency and decision-making*. Specifically, they tend not to explain satisfactorily the *mechanisms* by which the structural variables or conditions allegedly produce the outcomes. In the following, each key condition is discussed in light of what previous authors have written about them. The drawbacks to the positions taken are noted as well.

CONDITION 1: THE CLASS STRUCTURE
As chapter 3 revealed, several authors have followed Macpherson in claiming that the rise of Social Credit was possible because Alberta had such a high proportion of petit-bourgeois residents, in particular members of the agrarian petite bourgeoisie. Behind the focus on the class structure is a general theory, the centrist theory of the lower middle class, discussed in chapter 1. A mechanism is posited, namely the Social Credit League, through which the petite bourgeoisie allegedly expressed its disillusionment with the national economy, the Depression, and advanced capitalism itself.

Few writers using this approach have taken pains to establish that it actually was the petite bourgeoisie that was the agent in this case. The pattern of aggregate class support observed in the present study, whereby both workers and farmers provided high levels of support for the movement, militates against the contention that the impetus for the movement was petit-bourgeois alienation and confusion. Also, as Finkel (1989, 210) points out, the identification of the agrarian petite bourgeoisie as the agent in question is at variance with the fact that the movement originated in the *city* of Calgary and only later spread to the agrarian regions. That the early movement included many working-class activists contradicts this view as well.

142 Social Classes and Social Credit in Alberta

This historical reality thus demolishes the assertion that Social Credit was an agrarian party that merely sought working-class support to broaden its electoral base, or that the working class somehow fell under the spell of the agrarian petite bourgeoisie. It should also be borne in mind that many commentators seriously overestimate the relative size of the agrarian petite bourgeoisie in Alberta in the 1930s, which causes them to overstate the political presence and influence of this minority of the work-force. In addition, a key corollary of the general theory of the lower middle class, petit-bourgeois conservatism, lacks empirical substantiation for other times and locales, and so the general theory itself is brought into serious doubt. Another problem with the petit-bourgeois interpretation is that Social Credit philosophy is not congruent with what centrist theorists claim is petit-bourgeois ideology.

The Social Credit movement is sometimes thought to have been conservative or petit-bourgeois simply because it was not socialist. For example, some theorists suggest that the Social Credit administration was petit-bourgeois because it did not do anything that threatened the "fundamental power of capital," a propensity portrayed by many as distinctly petit-bourgeois. But had the plan been implemented, the position of capitalists would have been radically altered, as our discussion of Social Credit philosophy has shown. The petit-bourgeois argument also assumes that the "power of capital" is unambiguous and self-evident, which it is not. In addition, if one follows this line of reasoning, trade unionism must also be deemed petit-bourgeois as it too does not threaten the "fundamental power of capital." Following this logic, unemployment insurance, government health-care schemes, and so forth should all be labelled petit-bourgeois, as they leave the basic capitalist relations of production untouched. But again one could argue that this is an unreasonable approach to the issue, as such non-capital-threatening schemes can and do come out of the heads of those outside the ranks of the petite bourgeoisie and, like Social Credit, one need not be petit-bourgeois or under the spell of its alleged ideology to be in favour of them.

Macpherson was right in paying close attention to the class composition of Alberta in the 1930s, but he was acting on a number of false or at least questionable assumptions. For instance, he assumed that each class has a set of attitudes and beliefs – essentially a world-view – very different from that of the other classes.[2] Yet the similarity of the response of the agrarian petite bourgeoisie and the urban working class observed in this study suggests that these two classes may share many points of *commonality* in both experience and perceptions. Macpherson also assumed that each class's world-view was in keeping with the centrist theory, wherein not only is the petite bourgeoisie portrayed as confused or reactionary and hence susceptible to Social Credit appeals, but the working class is assumed to be potentially revolutionary or at least very interested in fundamental social change along socialist lines, and thus not a natural supporter of Social Credit. This is another questionable set of assertions, as one searches in vain for the necessary empirical and historical substantiation for these generalizations. Macpherson assumed further that there is little differentiation of outlook and behaviour *within* classes,[3] an assumption placed in serious doubt by the findings of this study, in particular those for the 1940 election, in which there was a roughly even split between those harbouring pro– and anti– Social Credit sentiment within both the agrarian petite bourgeoisie and the urban working class.

Rather than focusing on the size of the petite bourgeoisie relative to the working class and other classes, a procedure that follows from Macpherson's questionable assumptions, a better way of looking at Alberta's class structure would be to consider that it had a large "underclass" that comprised the urban working and lower middle classes, the rural working class, and the agrarian petite bourgeoisie.[4] What did the various members of this underclass have in common? Poverty that had come upon them relatively suddenly, as well as powerlessness. They were benefiting least from the existing system and had a limited choice of political alternatives, issues we will examine again below. The data in Table 3.2 show that 90 per cent of Alberta's population were members of this underclass. As those in this category provided the greatest support for Social Credit, its relative size is important.

The mere existence of a large number of people sharing common problems is not, of course, sufficient to cause such people to mobilize and form a social movement to redress their grievances. The additional factors necessary to produce this result are discussed in a subsequent section.

CONDITION 2: CENTRAL CANADIAN IMPERIALISM
Macpherson and others also imply that the Social Credit movement was the mechanism by which Albertans expressed their dissatisfaction with the west's position in Confederation. But again, as with their discussion of the class structure, there is a reluctance on the part of these authors to leave the realm of theory to examine what people actually did and said. To understand what really happened

144 Social Classes and Social Credit in Alberta

in Alberta in the 1930s it is necessary to examine what Albertans themselves, including members of the Social Credit movement, had to say about this issue.

The theme of regional exploitation is not a new one in the west; it dates back at least as far as the Riel uprising of 1870. Several waves of regional protest have occurred since then, but each time the issues have been somewhat different, bringing forth a different configuration of interest groups. The Riel rebellions were, among other things, a clash pitting native and Métis elements against people of European background who wanted to bring a new form of economic and political organization to the region. The rebellions were also a form of ethnic conflict between rival European cultures. The Progressive movement involved both class and regional conflict, with farmers battling against metropolitan railway, manufacturing, and financial interests as well as the two traditional political parties. The struggle over oil policy in the 1970s and early 1980s saw the Alberta government as well as much of the oil industry in conflict with the federal government. All these were pitched battles that left a residue of ill feelings, but they were followed by periods of relative calm in which the issue of regional exploitation did not enter the political picture. The late 1920s were, for the most part, prosperous years on the prairies, a time during which ideas of western exploitation had little political appeal. When the Depression hit, the blame did not fall on central Canada, although there was dissatisfaction with the way the federal Bennett regime was handling the problem. Contrary to what many accounts suggest, not all prairie movements blame every problem in the west on the federal government or regional exploitation. Ironically, Macpherson and others fail to examine in detail the relationship between these two important conditions, the Depression and the "quasi-colonial" relationship.

Macpherson and others tend to view the "quasi-colonial" relationship as a constant, and the "anti-imperialist" reaction as a constant as well. However, the west's relationship with central Canada has changed over time, particularly in the Progressive era. This has caused the relationship between the two regions to be in a state of flux; the strength and immediacy of anti–central Canadian feelings has varied accordingly. Hence it is useful to view anti–central Canadian sentiment as a variable rather than a constant condition.[5]

For Social Crediters the cause of the Depression lay primarily in the financial system; for their socialist rivals it lay in what they described as the inherent contradictions of capitalism. Neither of these two movements blamed Ottawa or central Canada for the

145   An Alternative Perspective

Depression; neither maintained that regional exploitation per se was the root of the problem. How could they, when the whole world was suffering? Both movements envisaged not only nation-wide but world-wide changes of epochal proportions, changes that had little to do with redressing conventional regional grievances.

As the economic and political relationship between central Canada and the prairies did not change markedly in the years immediately preceding the formation of the Social Credit movement, it may be assumed that this relationship was not a sufficient cause of the movement. No new economic policies exacerbating the relationship were introduced; the only new constitutional development of note, the transfer of jurisdiction over natural resources to the prairie provinces, served to *lessen* "imperial" control. Agricultural prices plummeted, unemployment increased, and the level of debt rose, but these were caused by world-wide depression conditions, not the relationship between the two regions. Both the CCF and Social Credit had their own explanation of what was happening, but neither of these listed regional exploitation as a principal cause of the malaise.

That central Canadian imperialism was not viewed by Social Credit as a principal cause of the Depression is also reflected in the pattern of class polarization observed in this study. One would expect that anti–central Canadian feelings would not be restricted to any class or group of classes, yet mass support for Social Credit was strongly related to social class.

By naming anti-imperialism as a definitive feature of Social Credit, many scholars come closer to describing the Progressives than the movement led by William Aberhart. Although the two movements were only about ten years apart, this was a sufficient amount of time for a significant change to occur. (Compare, for example, the student movements of the mid-1950s with those ten years later.) It would appear, then, that Morton's (1950, 287) contention that Social Credit and the CCF represented class rather than sectional conflict better describes what really happened than the accounts that portray these two movements as instruments of regional protest.

CONDITION 3: THE DEPRESSION
Many writers quite rightly cite the Depression as a causal factor in the development of Social Credit in Alberta. Had there been no Depression, there would have been no powerful Social Credit movement in Alberta. After all, William Aberhart organized the movement in an attempt to end the Depression. However, many accounts neglect to explain how it happened that Social Credit rather than some other

146   Social Classes and Social Credit in Alberta

political organization came to control the provincial government. A discussion that aims to explain this issue is provided later in this chapter.

Analyses of Facts and Personages

While an analysis of conditions is important in analysing any social movement, it is also necessary to examine what individuals and small groups did under those conditions. This approach to analysing Social Credit is most commonly adopted by historians. The method referred to is best described as narrative history, an approach that seeks to provide a description of all the relevant facts and participants pertaining to the issue in question. The presentation of these facts is said to constitute an integrated whole that itself illustrates the relevance of the facts presented. This kind of study relies on sufficient rather than necessary causes to explain a sequence of events (Kiser and Hechter 1991, 2). Generalizations or theories are sometimes implicit in such works, but *an explicit and comprehensive theoretical analysis is lacking*.

Writers such as Irving (1959), Schultz (1959, 1960, 1962), Elliott and Miller (1987), and Finkel (1989) provide valuable, and in some cases invaluable accounts of Social Credit using this general approach. In these works various aspects of the movement are described in depth and a variety of explanatory themes make their presence felt, but an explicit and comprehensive theory is not embraced.

In a section below, an interpretation of Social Credit that involves a synthesis of the two general approaches is provided. But before that is done, it is useful to consider how a rather large body of literature has provided an inaccurate account of the ideology, class basis of popular support, and behaviour in office of the Social Credit movement in Alberta. This matter in itself requires some explanation.

A Sociology of Knowledge: Explaining Explanations of Social Credit

One reason so many accounts of the movement are erroneous is that the class heterogeneity of Alberta in the 1930s is usually underestimated. The popular image of the Canadian prairies at this time is of a region inhabited almost exclusively by independent farmers. Macpherson's description of Alberta's class structure as "relatively homogeneous" and Lipset and others' preoccupation with farmers in their works on prairie movements have reinforced this image. If one believes that Alberta was populated almost entirely by independent

147 ˙An Alternative Perspective

farmers, then it follows that any popular movement in the province was a movement of the petite bourgeoisie. But as we saw in chapter 3, Alberta's class structure in the 1930s was far from homogeneous, making the class basis of Social Credit an empirical issue.

Also to be considered is the problem of the "argument from authority." It sometimes happens that intellectuals learn a "fact" from a particular source and then proceed to state that "fact" in their own work, with or without citation. Little concern is shown for the validity of the original statement, as it came from a putative authority. This is the way, I would suggest, the class and anti-imperialist basis of the Social Credit movement has been "learned." The key source was Macpherson (1962), with most scholars uncritically incorporating his ideas into their analyses. The academic learning process is also illustrated by the citing of incorrect dates for both the 1935 breakthrough election and the death of William Aberhart.[6] Barr (1974, 80, 118) appears to have been the first person to present the incorrect dates, which were then used by several other authors. This unreflective repetition of ideas and "facts" suggests that social science can at times take the form of folk wisdom or rumour.

One could argue that given a less than eternal earthly life, it is simply impossible to verify all the statements one encounters or uses in one's work. While this is true enough, those of us specializing in social movements or in the study of social class would do well to concern ourselves with the state of the evidence when key arguments are empirically testable.

Another factor to consider is that we intellectuals, despite our romantic self-images as free and critical thinkers, are conformists to an unrecognized degree. We love to condemn infidels or speak wistfully of our heroes, but there are usually strict group norms limiting whom we may condemn and whom we must praise. As previous chapters have demonstrated, ridiculing Social Credit is a socially acceptable academic pastime.[7]

There are several reasons for this. One is the inordinate amount of scorn that has been heaped upon the petite bourgeoisie since the time of Marx, making it a pariah class among some intellectuals. Although it is no longer intellectually fashionable to consider any race or national group inherently inferior to any other (and rightly so), one may still, with impunity, describe an entire social class – the petite bourgeoisie – as irredeemably confused if not downright dangerous, a priori. Perhaps the crudest act of this sort is the assertion that the lower middle class provided the impetus for the Nazi movement. If any race or ethnic group were given such treatment, there would be an uproar in the academic community. What makes this

148   Social Classes and Social Credit in Alberta

state of affairs all the more remarkable is that the petite bourgeoisie is, by definition, a poor class, and is in most circumstances politically impotent.

By way of contrast, the working class is usually not given such harsh treatment. Although it is occasionally the target of unflattering commentary (e.g., Lipset 1981 [1959], chap. 4), some analysts go out of their way to present the working class in a favourable light – for example, by not discussing its involvement in "unprogressive" social movements. Macpherson portrays the petite bourgeoisie of Depression-era Alberta as a hapless but socially harmful class. What role does the working class or his larger category of "industrial employees" play in his analysis? They are found on his list of dramatis personae, but they never appear on stage, even though in real life they composed about half the work-force and provided very high levels of support for the Social Credit party.

Lipset takes a comparable approach, explaining any undesirable feature of the CCF in Saskatchewan as a failing of farmers. How urban middle-class party leaders or the CCF's working-class leaders and constituency fit into this scenario is never explained. For instance, Lipset writes of the "*characteristic* fumbling of the western farmers" (1971, 141, emphasis added), but the working class emerges from the critique unscathed. My point here is not to cast aspersions on the working class (having grown up in a working-class family) but to expose an intellectual double standard.

The questionable interpretation of the Social Credit ideology should also be considered in this context. Macpherson and others' depiction of the movement's philosophy as conservative or even reactionary made a serious empirical study of the movement's class base seem unnecessary. Who else but the petite bourgeoisie could be responsible for or supportive of such unprogressive and ultimately deleterious ideas?

Part of the general bias against Social Credit may also stem from the fact that some of those who have written about the movement are or were members, in one capacity or another, of rival social movements. It is reasonable to assume, for example, that Macpherson's status as a Marxist and Lipset's as a "young socialist" (1971, ix) coloured the interpretations of Social Credit presented by these authors. Conway's statement that political partisanship "has often contaminated the detachment of many scholars dealing with the [CCF and Social Credit] ... movements" (1990, 373) has considerable validity.[8]

In the literature on the movement there is often the implication that not only is the Social Credit program worthless, but there is a clearly superior route to social change available to anyone willing to listen to reason. That better way frequently involves some hazily sketched variant of democratic socialism. A major lesson in some of the leading works on Social Credit is that the capitalist system as a whole is the real source of the problems the movement sought to resolve. Any program that falls short of advocating capitalism's eradication is often treated as a form of political amateurism. Macpherson, for instance, proclaims that "the modified pattern [of Alberta radicalism] was one of alternate rejection of and reconciliation with outside capital interests; obversely this appears as alternate identification with and distraction from the interests of humanity at large. Each radical movement began with fierce opposition to the outside 'exploiters' (monopolists, manufacturers' association, banks, finance) and gradually came to terms with the system of which they were a part" (1962, 229–30).

When Macpherson makes his renowned claim that Social Credit was "not against the property system," he clearly implies that it should have been. Lipset renders a similar judgment on American populist movements: "The farmers struck out at random at the most visible economic evils that affected them. They opposed the banks, the railroads, the wheat-elevator companies, and the shortage of money, but they saw each evil as an evil in itself, not as part of the total economic system" (1971, 23–4).

The ease with which many of these authors would have their historical actors proceed to implement the favoured solution is illustrated by a statement made by Robert S. Lynd in the foreword to Lipset's *Agrarian Socialism*: "As the cooperating farmer's ideology meets the factory worker and the middle-class businessman, it wavers, blurs, and recedes. An agrarian socialist party becomes a liberal agrarian protest movement, and the programs for the socialization of industry falter. Truly, he who sets out to make significant reforms should never hesitate or compromise!" (1971, 6–7). Taking this position to its logical and inevitable conclusion, the people of Alberta should have demanded that all the means of production be brought under government or social ownership. Had this been achieved, it would have eliminated all economic exploitation, ended all serious social conflict, elevated the material quality of life, and removed all impediments to free cultural development and expression. This is the counter-utopia of some of the leading class analysts of Social Credit.[9]

The discussion above is not intended to condemn or castigate those who have written about Social Credit. Indeed, I do not claim any special immunity from the shortcomings mentioned. The discussion is meant to highlight problems inherent in social scientific research.

SYNTHESIS: MAKING THE MACRO-MICRO LINK

Much recent sociology has been devoted to linking individual or small-group activity and decision-making to society-wide conditions or social structures.[10] An attempt has also been made to merge *theories* of individual or small-group behaviour with those theories that seek to explain the actions of large numbers of people, such as whole societies. In an effort to link the micro with the macro levels of behaviour and analysis, a general theory of social movements and an analysis of the Social Credit rise to power from the perspective of rational-choice theory are provided below.

A General Theory of Social Movements

The general theory of social movements offered here maintains that five factors must be present for a successful movement to develop. If a single factor is not present as specified, no movement or only a very weak one will form. To illustrate the theory, the relevance of each factor for the Social Credit movement will be examined. It must be reiterated that what follows is a theory, not a statement of fact; as such it is subject to logical and empirical assessment.

FACTOR 1: OPPORTUNITY/THREAT/DEPRIVATION
The first two elements of this factor are taken from Tilly (1978, 55). Opportunity refers to a situation in which people have a chance to further their interests but the social action taken does not arise out of a sense of grievance. In such cases people are acting on what Pinard calls "aspirations" (1983a, 55–8), a desire to achieve things that have not been unfairly denied. Threat is straightforward; it refers to a situation in which people believe that something they value is in peril. The notion of deprivation has been added to Tilly's formulation to acknowledge that social movements may develop in situations where people have lost or been deprived of something they value. In such situations, movement participants act out of a sense of grievance. Grievances are an important aspect of many theories of social movements, including those of Smelser (1963) and Pinard (1983a, 1983b), but tend to be downplayed among resource-mobilization theorists (e.g., Tilly 1978, McCarthy and Zald 1973).

The theory proposed here maintains that social movements are formed to pursue group "interests," whether this be to to further, keep, or recapture them. It assumes a Weberian conflict perspective, wherein there is a virtually limitless number of potentially conflicting groups in society who seek to further their interests, often at the expense of other groups. Interests as discussed here include material interests, but they also include non-material things such as values. For example, one may have no material interest whatever in promoting one's views on abortion yet be very active in a movement endeavouring to uphold those values.

The focus on interests does not involve an assumption that all movement participants have the same motivation for participating. Members may not have an equal stake in the outcome of the movement and may not contribute the same personal resources, receive the same rewards for their participation, or share the same beliefs regarding the importance of group goals. Likewise, participants may be entirely self-interested or altruistic, or, more commonly, may combine self-interest with altruism in varying proportions.

An important aspect of opportunity/threat/deprivation involves the *perception* of the state of the group's interests, as opposed to the actual position thereof. As the collective-behaviour perspective suggests (Turner and Killian 1987, 7–8, 25–6, 40–1), people must come to define their situation as problematic before social action is taken, and often those who appear to be in the worst objective conditions do not see themselves as victims. Similarly, the opportunity/threat/deprivation need not be real nor properly understood; it need merely be *perceived* as such. Hitler, for example, erroneously blamed many of Germany's problems on the allegedly deleterious effect of the presence of Jews in Europe. Prohibitionists in North America believed that banning the sale of alcohol would solve a wide array of social problems. The Social Credit movement believed that restructuring the financial system along Douglasite lines would bring prosperity to all. This is not to say that all social movements are based on delusion. Far from it. The point is simply that any social movement must *perceive* that a certain group is in a condition of opportunity/threat/deprivation, regardless of whether that perception is accurate or complete.

In furthering its interests, a social movement must somehow unite in the movement categories of people who would otherwise have conflicting interests. In other words, it must make actual or potential sources of conflict among members secondary or irrelevant. For instance, Social Credit's accession to power was facilitated by the fact that it did not limit its attempts to gain support to any single class in society. The only occupational group to which it expressed hostility was composed of bankers and other "financiers" who made up only a minuscule proportion of the populace and who in any case were primarily an absentee group.

152   Social Classes and Social Credit in Alberta

There has long been a debate among social activists of the left over whether a movement seeking fundamental social change should limit itself to championing the cause of a single class, usually the working class, or offer a program that would serve the interests of a broad coalition of classes against the bourgeoisie. The lack of success of movements seeking broad social change in the name of the working class only, at least in democratic polities, suggests that cross-class appeals stand a greater chance of succeeding. Also, those opposed to class coalitions often share questionable assumptions about the working class, in particular a belief that this class has a natural attraction to "socialism," a concept that is often left undefined.

Those advocating change in the interests of a single class also often assume that class is the only cleavage of importance, implying that other sources of division or conflict are either unimportant or ultimately based on class. However, this preoccupation with class often causes us to ignore other prominent forms of conflict, in particular conflict based on gender or ethnicity.

Most observers have ignored Social Credit's efforts to deal with the position of women in society. As outlined in chapter 5, Aberhart claimed that the implementation of his policies would serve not only to help out with monthly expenses, a significant benefit in itself, as women were largely responsible for the running of the household, but also to raise the *status* of women by lessening their financial dependence on men. Although the issue of the status of women was virtually forgotten by the movement after 1935, the direct appeal to women likely prevented gender from being a divisive issue in the party's drive to attract voters. As for ethnicity, Social Credit made an effort to appeal to all ethnic groups, in part by propagating its message in several languages, including French, German, and Ukranian.

Part of the reason for Social Credit's success, then, was that it presented a program designed to unite groups of people who may have had conflicting interests, or who may have had mutual interests that otherwise would have been ignored. The attempt to unite farmers and workers under the Social Credit banner was very successful; those higher in the class structure, however, largely rejected the appeal. As will be discussed below, this may have been because those higher in the class system had different interests from those in the lower classes. How successful it was in uniting men and women is still largely an open question, as is support for the movement by ethnicity,[11] although open gender or ethnic conflict was not a part of the movement.

So what was the opportunity/threat/deprivation that provided the impetus for the Social Credit movement? The one overriding social problem that cried out for resolution was the Depression. Put in the language of the proposed theory, the Depression caused large portions of the population to suffer both material and psychological deprivation, which followers believed the Social Credit movement could alleviate.

FACTOR 2: IDEOLOGY

An opportunity/threat/deprivation will not lead to organized social action unless there is a system of ideas that explains what is wrong or what is to be gained and how the desired results may be achieved. Also, as Pinard (1983b, 13–15) argues, ideologies strengthen belief in the righteousness of the cause and so inspire people to make personal sacrifices to the movement.

An ideology that combines some uncomplicated fundamentals with an air of mystery and even ambiguity seems to be most effective in reaching a broad audience. It must be simple enough for most people to grasp its basics with minimal time and effort; here the singling out of oppressors is important, as it gives people a clear target for their unrest. Mystery and ambiguity, whether by accident or design, make easy refutation difficult, and also inspire the more intellectually minded to dig deeper into the proposed causes and solutions of the problem.

William Aberhart found his ideology in Social Credit theories. For him, they explained what was causing the Depression and what could be done about it. The villains were clearly identified – financiers – and there was certainly an air of mystery and ambiguity about the program. Below we will consider how he managed to promulgate his chosen ideology, and consider in more detail why it gained broad acceptance.

The chances that a large number of people will adopt a particular ideology depend in part on whether it has a firm grounding in the existing culture. Most members of a society are essentially conservative, in that they will oppose efforts to alter existing cultural practices radically. The civil rights movement in the United States in the 1960s, for example, in pressing for racial equality did not claim to be doing anything radical at all; activists claimed that they were merely implementing the equal-rights provisions contained in the constitution. Social Credit's grounding in Christian, albeit fundamentalist Christian culture was a major asset for the same reason. In the 1930s, having a Christian religious affiliation was a prerequisite to broad social acceptance. As Hiller (1972, 37; 1977, 69–70) has argued, the movement was able to promote social *change* because it was rooted in popular cultural traditions. Like other movements with a close association with religion, Social Credit claimed that the existing social system violated established religious principles; poverty in the midst of plenty was undeniably un-Christian. Members of the movement claimed they were not doing anything contrary to Christianity; in fact, they saw themselves as the only party demanding that Christian ideals be upheld. This illustrates the paradox that a firm grounding in established cultural traditions may allow a movement to contribute to social change.

FACTOR 3: RESOURCES

The importance of resources for any social movement has been recognized by the resource-mobilization school of social movements.[12] Without substantial resources a group of people experiencing opportunity/threat/deprivation, even with a well-articulated ideology, stands little chance of launching a successful movement. What resources did the Social Credit movement have? Several are listed below.

i) Leadership. Charismatic leadership is necessary for any social movement to be successful. William Aberhart provided that leadership, working tirelessly for the Social Credit cause from 1932 until his death in 1943. His leadership was indispensable; in all likelihood, had Aberhart not converted to Social Credit, there would have been no Social Credit Party in the 1935 Alberta election, much less a victorious one. As Irving aptly puts it, the movement was "in essence, a following" (1959, 181).

Aberhart also had a strong coterie of secondary leaders who served him well. Most notable among these was Ernest Manning, who took over the premiership at Aberhart's death. Other important leaders included Edith Gostick, Edith Rogers, Fred Anderson, R.E. Ansley, Joseph Unwin, Floyd Baker, and Alfred Hooke.

ii) Access to Media of Communication. It is now recognized that the amount of media time available to a political party is crucial to its success. Social Credit seems to have had access to more radio time than any other party. Although I am not aware of any records showing the amount of radio time available to the major parties for the 1935 campaign, it is unlikely that any party had more than Social Credit. Aberhart began his radio discussions of Social Credit in 1932 and constantly promoted the cause in his weekly broadcasts thereafter. That he was already a radio celebrity by virtue of his religious broadcasts was an asset as well. Additionally, radio, rather than the print media, was an excellent way to reach the lower classes, as the latter are more likely to be consumers of the electronic media than print. The party also had a widely circulating newspaper, the *Social Credit Chronicle*.

iii) Coalitions. Another resource that a social movement may have are coalitions, which include any organization that supports the movement, whether materially or ideologically. Social Credit managed to embark on a successful mobilization without substantial coalitions, although the movement entered into electoral alliances with Alberta socialists and communists in a few ridings. The absence of major coalitions in the Social Credit movement was very different from the situation of the CCF, which in its early days was a loose coalition of several farmer, labour, and socialist organizations.

FACTOR 4: ORGANIZATION

It is axiomatic that a social movement must have sound organization in order to win public support. Social Credit had a pre-existing organizational structure at the time it began to mobilize as a political movement. Aberhart was the dean of the Prophetic Bible Institute (largely his own creation), whose radio program, building, and followers he enlisted for the Social Credit movement. He expanded on this by fashioning his organization after the UFA system of locals, districts, and constituency organizations, and used the UFA provincial convention as a model for the Social Credit League (Irving 1959, 342). This allowed him to achieve bloc recruitment of farmers through "functional penetration" of UFA organizations (271–4), which involved speaking at UFA-sponsored events, where he often won over virtually an entire local to Social Credit.

Aberhart was one of few social-movement leaders to combine a charismatic personality with a penchant for organization. In fact he was an inveterate and compulsive organizer. "I have been organizing all my life," he once remarked. "There's nothing I'd rather do than organize. It's a hobby with me" (*Edmonton Journal*, 10 August 1939; quoted in Schultz 1959, 20). Before he organized the Social Credit movement, Aberhart took great pride in directing school activities and his lay ministry. During his summers as principal of Crescent Heights High School, for instance, he would go so far as to organize the timetable of every incoming student (20).

FACTOR 5: RESISTANCE

Social movements have enemies and competitors. Resistance as defined here refers to any act that is carried out with the intention of preventing or hindering a social movement from achieving its

156   Social Classes and Social Credit in Alberta

goals. Private individuals or governments may actively oppose a social movement; similarly, a movement may encounter competition – and thus resistance – from a rival movement.

As we learned in earlier chapters, Social Credit faced resistance from the media and various chambers of commerce. This did little to hinder the movement's progress, however; these attempts to dissuade people from supporting Social Credit may even have made the movement appear all the more attractive. None the less, Social Credit encountered insurmountable resistance from federal authorities, which thwarted the implementation of its program. But here again this had its advantages, as the movement could blame its failure on a third party and shift its focus to more conventional goals.

The main social movement competing with Social Credit at this time was the growing social democratic movement, represented by the CCF. By the mid-1930s this movement was discredited in Alberta because CCF-affiliated government of the day used harsh measures against its opponents and seemed unable or unwilling to do anything about the Depression. Thus rightly or wrongly, many Albertans believed that the CCF-oriented solutions had been tried and had failed. Fragmentation within the UFA and Premier Brownlee's scandal didn't help matters either. Looking back on his experiences as a communist in Alberta in the 1930s, Ben Swankey has written that, "to many people the UFA was the CCF in office and they wanted no more of it. The UFA helped to sully the meaning of the word Socialism in Alberta and the CCF never recovered from it" (1980, 35). This situation created a social-movement vacuum that Social Credit was more than eager to fill.

In order to illustrate the notion of competition between social movements suggested here, the concept of a "social-movement economy" will be proposed. It suggests that it is useful to view the political realm as a marketplace since, as in the economic market, the nature and strength of the competition in politics strongly influences both the activity of the competitors and the response of political "consumers": voters, followers, and potential followers. According to the proposed perspective, if there is a demand for social change in the general population, the existing supply of social movements or other agents of social change may be sufficient to satisfy that demand. In such a situation, new movements find it difficult to attract followers. Conversely, a situation in which there is a strong demand for change that is not being met by existing movements or other organizations is one that is very favourable for new movements.

The idea of a social-movement economy helps to explain the success of Social Credit in 1935, when the chief competitor to the movement, the CCF, could not satisfy the demand for social change and so made it possible for Social Credit to attract a huge following. Similarly, it may partially explain the failure of other movements to gain a foothold once the party took power. For the most part, people who opposed conventional economic policies remained committed to Social Credit in 1940; no large unfulfilled demand for non-conventional government remained. Unfortunately for the CCF, the social democratic movement also faced competition from the two traditional parties, the Liberals and Conservatives, who convinced most of the anti–Social Credit voters that the implementation of conventional economic policies rather than major social change would be in their best interests.

To take another illustration, the social-movement economy in California may have caused the Social Credit movement there to suffer the same fate as that experienced by the CCF in Alberta. In that state in the 1930s, a movement led by F.E. Townsend promoted a scheme that would pay two hundred dollars per month to every American citizen over the age of sixty who had never committed a felony. Irving maintains that the Townsend movement "was responsible for the collapse of a rising Social Credit movement in California" (1959, 336). In terms of the model proposed here, the demand for change in the social-movement economy was met by the Townsend movement, which prevented a competitor, Social Credit, from attracting a substantial following.

To sum up the ideas presented under this heading, a social movement will be successful only if it is able to overcome resistance. Part of the reason Social Credit formed the government in 1935 is that it did not encounter strong competition from rival movements. The failure to implement its Social Credit plan resulted from effective resistance from federal authorities.

The general theory of social movements offered here maintains that five conditions must be satisfied in order for a substantial social movement to develop, and that these conditions were present in Alberta in 1935. The Depression created a situation of severe material and psychological deprivation, which was ostensibly explained by the Social Credit ideology. Sufficient resources and organization were available to mount a major mobilization designed to reduce the deprivation, and that mobilization occurred in a social-movement economy in which there was a large unfulfilled demand for change. This explanation combines a focus on small-group behaviour, such as the social-movement leadership and organization, with larger social conditions like opportunity/threat/deprivation and resistance.

158 Social Classes and Social Credit in Alberta

Choices of Individuals: Rational-Choice Theory

Here we will consider the Social Credit phenomenon from the point of view of the individual citizen confronted with the social conditions in Alberta in 1935. Rational-choice theory will be used in an effort to determine why individuals voted either for or against the movement.

Rational-choice theory assumes that human beings are purposeful, goal-seeking, and self-interested. It predicts that people will choose outcomes that maximize their rewards and minimize their costs. Rational choice theorists do not maintain that actors are free to choose any outcome they like; rather, it is recognized that individuals are constrained by limited choices, opportunity costs, the information available to them, and by numerous social structures.[13]

In considering the Social Credit movement from the perspective of rational-choice theory, it is necessary to consider not only what the movement itself offered but also what the other parties were proposing, as an assessment of the rationality of any act must take into consideration the alternatives available. One factor that should be considered in this regard is the general climate of opinion in favour of monetary reform in the early 1930s, something that is rarely mentioned in the various accounts of the movement. According to the Lethbridge Labor Party organization of 1935, "All political parties are advocating some form of monetary reform at the present time. Just how far some of these parties are prepared to go in the direction of reforming the financial system is a matter mainly, it seems to us, of political expediency" (*Lethbridge Herald*, 8 August 1935, 3).

The labour movement itself did not shy away from monetary reform arguments. The CCF's Regina Manifesto of 1933, for example, which Labor championed in the 1935 Alberta campaign, is replete with Social Credit phraseology and ideas. Section 4, for instance, advocates the "improvement of the position of the farmer by the increase of purchasing power made possible by the social control of the financial system." Section 11 reads, in part: "We propose that all Public Works, as directed by the Planning Commission, shall be financed by the issuance of credit, as suggested, based upon the National Wealth of Canada."[14] Similarly, the UFA went to great lengths to explain how the "Aberhart Social Credit plan" would be disastrous for Alberta, yet the UFA Provincial Platform 1935 contains the statement that "such steps ... [will be] taken as may be necessary to bring our entire monetary system under public ownership and control ... [in order to] facilitate the fullest possible use of social credit" (United Farmers of Alberta 1935). And as seen in earlier chapters, the UFA government had appointed Douglas himself as a consultant.

The Liberals also appeared to be in favour of some type of monetary reform. If returned to power in the province, they promised, they would "employ three of the most expert Social Credit Advocates to carry on a full and complete investigation into the proposed schemes of Social Credit for the province, which the Liberal party pledges itself to submit to the legislature for its consideration" (Alberta Provincial Liberal Association 1935, 4). The Liberal Party also made some lofty declarations that would have made Major Douglas proud:

Usury once in control will wreck any nation. Until the control of the issue of currency and credit is restored to government and recognized as its most conspicuous and sacred responsibility, all talk of the sovereignty of Parliament and Democracy is idle and futile ...

The Liberal party stands for a publicly owned national central bank which will, under the control of the government of the nation, issue national currency and credit and manage the monetary system in terms of public need, for the purpose of raising the standard of living of the people and for the further purposes of advancing the economic security of the social system and the stability of the nation. (4)

As seen in chapter 5, shortly after the 1935 election in Alberta, Mackenzie King stated that "Mr. Aberhart has the whole province in his hands and if a Liberal Government is returned to power at Ottawa he will be given the fullest opportunity to work out his plan ... This thing of $25 or $75 a month is just what the world had been looking for for hundreds and thousands of years" (*Montreal Gazette*, 23 September 1935, 1). Also, the Liberal mayor of Vancouver in the early 1930s, Gerry McGeer, was a supporter of Major Douglas, although he argued that Aberhart distorted the Major's ideas. McGeer claimed that "the bankers have us in a prison, with many locks, and only one key can effect monetary reform, which the bankers won't agree to" (*Lethbridge Herald*, 16 August 1935, 1).

With the Labor, UFA, and Liberal parties making what amounted to pro-Social Credit proclamations, albeit while attacking or not endorsing William Aberhart, they implicitly sent the message out to the public that his social credit scheme was not without merit. A similar message had been sent out by the internationally known intellectuals who supported Douglas. Rational-choice theory acknowledges that people act on the information available to them. In the 1930s people were told from a variety of sources that the monetary system should be reformed.

The only party staunchly opposed to any form of Social Credit was the Conservatives. Party leader D.M. Duggan declared that "the time has come for straight-thinking practical people in Alberta to rise against the menace of Social Credit as a provincial scheme without a plan – against the peril of notions which threaten ruin to the province into which have gone the fortunes, the hopes, the hardships, the life-work of our citizens" (Duggan 1935). But supporting the Conservatives in 1935 involved certain liabilities. Many voters, with reason, associated the Alberta Conservatives with the Bennett Conservative government in Ottawa, which, like the UFA, had been in power for five consecutive years of depression and had been widely criticized for its performance. Nor did the Alberta party handle the association with their federal counterparts well. In an era that would be imprinted in the popular consciousness as one of dust bowls and "Bennett buggies,"[15] Conservative candidates like George Green of Lethbridge made statements like: "We stand firmly behind the policy of the Rt. Hon. R.B. Bennett and expect to point out to you the many good things he has done for the western farmer" (*Lethbridge Herald*, 5 August 1935, 3).

An examination of the programs of the parties in competition with Social Credit, apart from their position on monetary reform, will also contribute to an assessment of the rationality of supporting Social Credit in 1935. Both Labor and the UFA favoured the broadly defined democratic socialist program promulgated by the CCF. The Lethbridge Labor Party advocated a "complete change in our social system," pledging to "replace the present capitalist system ... by a social order ... in which economic planning will supersede unregulated private enterprise." It stood for "the establishment of a planned system of social economy for the production, distribution and exchange of all goods and services. Social ownership, development, operation and control of all utilities and natural resources necessary for the public welfare" (*Lethbridge Herald*, 5 August 1935, 3). The purpose of this system, the Edmonton Labor Organization maintained, was to allow the national wealth to become "the property of the Nation" and to "flow into the possession and lives of people in an uninterrupted stream" (*Edmonton Journal*, 12 August 1935, 9). As there would have to be "a transition period before the socialist state is realized," Labor outlined some "immediate objectives": tax reform; using work-camps of unemployed men to perform public works, the men to be paid union wage rates; protecting home owners against foreclosures; "retention and extension" of all social programs; and "control [of] all mines in the province through Government administration" (*Lethbridge Herald*, 5 August 1935, 3).

The UFA's commitment to establishing the co-operative commonwealth was weakened by dissension within the party, in particular the Cabinet's lack of enthusiasm for socialism. This meant that it was sending mixed messages, for in addition to hiring Douglas, the campaign of 1935 was not in keeping with the resolutions endorsing the CCF passed by party conventions. A month before the election was held Premier Reid released the "Manifesto of the Alberta Government," which claimed that the government was performing its duties competently under very adverse conditions and listed a number of social services that it was providing (Irving 1959, 352–4). New policies to be implemented after the election included reducing the minimum age for old-age pensions from seventy to sixty; a program of work for wages for those on relief; reducing interest rates on private mortgages; lobbying the federal government to increase its spending on social services in the province; "reconsideration" of Canada's tariff policies; and more road construction (353–4).

The Liberals emphasized reform in their campaign. Stating that they had conducted a wide-ranging program of consultation with Albertans from virtually all walks of life, they produced "a *Reform Policy, a People's Policy, a Taxpayers' Policy,*" asking Albertans to help them bring about "a *New Start, a New Deal.*" They provided a number of specific proposals, including "fighting for reductions in freight rates"; reducing the cost of government by promoting departmental efficiency and reducing the number of members of the legislature; having the federal government finance all relief costs; industrial development "for the benefit of the people and not for monopolies"; and taking steps to introduce the proposed reciprocity deal with the United States, which had died with the defeat of the federal Liberals in 1911 (Alberta Provincial Liberal Association 1935).

The Conservatives printed the words "Reform," "Recovery", and "Reconstruction" on their pamphlets. Their first stated principle was "the maintenance of the British form of Constitutional and Parliamentary government"; their second, "the retention of those institutions we have till we can change them, with safety, for the better"; and their third, "individual initiative and enterprise with government control to prevent exploitation and abuse." In addition the Conservatives promised various specific programs, such as balancing the budget; reducing the membership of the legislature to save public money; maintenance of social services; a minimum statutory wage rate; and collective bargaining for wage rates (Liberal-Conservative Party of Alberta 1935).

In essence, the Alberta voter in 1935 had to choose one of the following: support the government, which was badly divided, plagued with scandal, and unsuccessful in its handling of the Depression; support Labor (at least in the four constituencies where Labor candidates appeared), which had allied itself with the government by joining the CCF; support the Liberals, who flirted with endorsing Social Credit doctrine and who otherwise offered conventional, and thus to this point futile measures to deal with the Depression; support the Conservatives, who were also orthodox in their approach and who stood behind R.B. Bennett's handling of the Depression; or vote for Social Credit, which in an untried program that was not unequivocally rejected by any party except the Conservatives promised a monthly income supplement, lower prices for consumers, fair wages, and guaranteed prices for farm produce.

The appropriateness of the choice may have depended on the class position of the voter. The most damning criticism of the Social Credit scheme was that it would be inflationary. Those with savings accounts, people holding bonds providing a fixed rate of interest, and creditors would lose in a situation of inflation. For debtors, however, inflation is an *advantage*, as it allows them to pay their debts in inflated dollars. Runaway inflation would have all but wiped out personal debt.

Another aspect of Social Credit that may have influenced voters and must be considered in assessing the rationality of supporting the movement was the party's intention to control the management of privately owned businesses by having all wages, prices, and profits determined by government agencies, and the all-important allocation of "credit" by public need. These departures from the rights of private property and market principles would not have been in the interests of those owning successful enterprises or those otherwise benefiting from the system as it was functioning in 1935.

But what about those Albertans who for years during the Depression literally struggled to stay alive? My conversations with informants who lived in Alberta in the 1930s suggest that the economic situation was so desperate that many people believed Social Credit could not possibly make things worse. The campaign slogan of former Quebec Social Credit leader Réal Caouette, "You have nothing to lose!" aptly describes the mood of many Albertans in the 1930s.

The rationality of supporting Social Credit in 1935, then, largely depended on where in the stratification system the voter found him or herself. Those high in the stratification system had a great deal to lose with the scheme's implementation, those at the bottom much less. As we learned in earlier chapters, those in upper-middle-class and higher positions tended to reject the Social Credit Party, while those lower in the class system embraced it in very large numbers. This suggests that Alberta voters of 1935 were acting with more rationality than they are usually given credit for.[16]

163 An Alternative Perspective

There is another way in which Social Credit's program made sense but which, again, is ignored by most accounts of the movement. The issuance of dividends and subsidies for lower prices may be viewed as similar in some respects to Keynesian economics. Richards and Pratt make this case: "It is important to realize that the call for government to stimulate aggregate demand – by means of public expenditures, fiscal policy, or even the issue of some form of social credit – was in the midst of the depression entirely apposite. The theory of social credit was in that sense an intellectual advance relative to contemporary economic orthodoxy of budgetary constraint and statements of faith in the temporary nature of the current depression" (1979, 33). Richards and Pratt then quote Keynes to the effect that "since [the First World War] there has been a spate of heretical theories of under-consumption, of which those of Major Douglas are the most famous … Major Douglas is entitled to claim, as against some of his orthodox adversaries, that he has not been wholly oblivious of the outstanding problem of our economic system … [Douglas was] a private, perhaps, but not a major in the brave army of heretics … who … have preferred to see the truth obscurely and imperfectly rather than to maintain error, reached indeed with clearness and consistency and by easy logic but on hypotheses inappropriate to the facts" (Keynes 1936, 370–1).

While much of what Social Crediters stood for was inane, technically incorrect, and plainly false, the movement is rarely given credit for raising the issue of the exploitative potential of the banks, or for trying to have financial institutions and bondholders accept a greater share of the losses created by Depression conditions. Few writers propose that the movement actually behaved with some degree of rationality, taking on the powers that be in the interests of the less fortunate. For many scholars, going after the banks as a source of exploitation is a seriously misdirected effort, as they consider the real source of exploitation to be either the capitalist system as a whole or large industrial concerns. The concentration on finance is seen by many intellectuals as a futile attack "against certain sham 'bogeys,'" as Maurice Dobb (1933, 556) put it. At least a partial exoneration of the banks as a possible source of exploitation is suggested by Sam Clark's statement that Social Credit "appealed to western farmers and small-town businessmen who wanted to believe that their troubles resulted from the control of the economy by eastern financial interests" (1982, 352).

The exploitative potential of financial institutions has not been entirely overlooked by social scientists, however. Max Weber, for instance, maintains that the conflict between debtors and creditors may be "real" class conflict, rather than a bogus effort based on false consciousness. He further argues that workers may sometimes overlook the expoitative potential of the banks and other groups:

Since it is quite a general phenomenon we must mention here that the class antagonisms that are conditioned through the market situation are usually most bitter between those who actually and directly participate as opponents in price wars. It is not the rentier, the shareholder and the banker who suffer the ill will of the worker, but almost exclusively the manufacturer and the business executives who are the direct opponents of workers in price wars. This is so in spite of the fact that it is precisely the cash boxes of the rentier, the shareholder and the banker into which the more or less "unearned" gains flow, rather than into the pockets of the manufacturers or of the business executives. (1946, 186).

Similarly, the notion of financial exploitation is evident in C. Wright Mills' critique of Warner and Lunt's *The Social Life of a Modern Community* (1941):

Without a *sigma*, or a more detailed display of the [income] distribution, one cannot know anything whatever about the negatively privileged income classes. Given the credit system (about which nothing is said) as a sanction of social controls, this is all the more regrettable. Not violence but credit may be a rather ultimate seat of control within modern societies ... Were there banks in Yankee City? Who controls them, and whom and what do they control? (1942, 268)

The foregoing is not intended to claim that industrial corporations are not exploitative, or that they are necessarily less exploitative than financial institutions. The point I wish to make is that what went on between the Social Credit movement and the banks was real class conflict. Although the banks were not guilty of all that the movement accused them of, the struggle over interest rates and debt payments was a struggle over who would shoulder the burden of the Depression – those low in the stratification system or those higher up.

Notes

CHAPTER ONE

1 These are W.L. Morton, *The Progressive Party in Canada* (1950); D.C. Masters, *The Winnipeg General Strike* (1950); Jean Burnet, *Next-Year Country* (1951); C.B. Macpherson, *Democracy in Alberta* (1962); J.R. Mallory, *Social Credit and the Federal Power in Canada* (1954); W.E. Mann, *Sect, Cult and Church in Alberta* (1955); V.C. Fowke, *The National Policy and the Wheat Economy* (1957); L.G. Thomas, *The Liberal Party in Alberta* (1959); S.D. Clark, *Movements of Political Protest in Canada, 1640–1840* (1959); and John Irving, *The Social Credit Movement in Alberta* (1959).

2 *Democracy in Alberta* focuses on two social movements: the United Farmers of Alberta, which held office from 1921 to 1935, and Social Credit, which replaced it as the governing party. In this quotation Macpherson is referring to both Social Credit and the UFA.

3 See Hamilton (1982, chap. 2) for a review of this literature.

4 See, for example, Stevenson (1986, 225–6).

5 The reader should know that calling something or someone "petit-bourgeois" is an insult in some circles. Writing about his home town of Croyden, England, Malcolm Muggeridge (1972, 21) states that it "came under the general anathema of being *petit-bourgeois* which, in the vague Marxism which provided our theology, signified contemptible, despicable. We would say of someone we disliked that he was *petit-bourgeois* in precisely the same way that middle- or upper-class boys at that time would say he was under-bred." Cf Macpherson (1962, ix): "Nobody likes to be called *petit-bourgeois.*"

166   Notes to pages 7–24

6 For an analysis of the defeat of Social Credit in 1971 that follows from
the positions taken in this book, see Bell (1993).

CHAPTER TWO

1 All non-prairie provinces retained jurisdiction over natural resources as
a condition of entry into Confederation.

CHAPTER THREE

1 Figures for the male work-force, as opposed to the total work-force, are
cited in this study to avoid the methodological problem of classifying
spouses as members of different social classes. In the 1930s, women
who worked full-time outside the home and had working-class or
farmer husbands were often employed in low-paying, non-manual occupations. A breakdown of the work-force containing both males and
females would classify the husband as working class or agrarian and
the wife as a member of the salaried middle class, yet the couple's orientations and lifestyle would be more in keeping with the husband's
occupation. Also, in the 1930s only a small percentage of married
women worked full-time outside the home. Ideally, data that classify
households by the person, male or female, with the highest-status job
or highest income should be used, but such data are unavailable for the
period in question. Using males only yields a larger percentage of the
labour force in agriculture in Alberta in 1931 – 56 per cent, as against
51 per cent if females are also included.
2 Dobb (1933, 557) also claimed that both Nazism and the British Social
Credit movement expressed the world-view of the petite bourgeoisie,
and referred to Social Credit theories as "satellite creeds" of fascism.
Social Credit in Alberta is sometimes described as having been fascist.
See, for example, Elliott (1980, 23) and Elliott and Miller (1987, 320).
3 Macpherson's figures cover the entire work-force, i.e., males and
females. As noted, the census figures cited in the previous section are
for the male work-force only.
4 Recall that according to Macpherson's figures, in 1941 45 per cent of the
Alberta work-force were petit-bourgeois. Of these, 38 per cent constituted the agricultural petite bourgeoisie, the other 7 per cent the traditional non-agrarian petite bourgeoisie.
5 Other writers have also taken issue with Macpherson's depiction of
Alberta's class structure. Richards and Pratt (1979, 151), for instance,
argue that he does not devote sufficient attention to non-agricultural
economic activities such as coal mining, oil and gas production, and
major urban business interests. They also contend that he underesti-
mates the amount of class conflict that existed in Alberta prior to the

167   Notes to pages 24–9

rise of Social Credit. Richards and Pratt argue that Macpherson is an adept political theorist, but as for *Democracy in Alberta*'s "eluciation of the class structure of Alberta and prairie society generally, the work is flawed and seriously misleading" (150; see also Richards, 1981).

6 Some discrepancies between Table 3.2 and Macpherson's data presented in Table 3.1 arise from the fact that the former is based on the male work-force, while Macpherson's figures include males and females. See n 1 above.

7 Macpherson cites percentages of seats won but not popular vote percentages.

8 The group-government theory claims that each occupational group, such as farmers, labour, business, etc., should be represented in the legislature by its own members. Theoretically, this would give all occupations a voice in government and prevent the exploitation of the less powerful classes that is said to occur in the traditional party system.

9 That is, $.75 \times 11\% = 8.25\%$.

10 That is, $46\% - 8.25\% = 37.75\%$.

11 That is, $39\% - 8.25\% = 30.75\%$.

12 See Bell (1992) for a discussion of the implications of this critique for Macpherson's idea that Alberta had a "quasi-party" system.

13 In the textbook in which the Graysons' article appears (Hagedorn 1983, 521), one finds a cartoon, presumably from the 1930s, showing strings attached to the Canadian Parliament buildings; the strings are held up by a large hand. On the hand is written "Financial Control." Another large hand is shown holding a pair of scissors, which are about to cut the strings. On one scissor blade is written "Labour," on the other, "Farmer." Despite the appearance of the Labour blade, the caption in the book reads: "In 1935, William Aberhart promised Alberta's disillusioned *farmfolk* up to $25 a month for every man, woman and child if they would elect him the first Social Credit premier of Alberta. His new party swept to victory like a prairie fire" (emphasis added).

14 Brym states in a footnote that Social Credit received "some working-class support in 1935, but mainly among unemployed and unorganized workers" (1978, 346, n 10). It would appear from this statement, and from his remarks in the text regarding the typically left-wing ideological position of the working class, that he does not consider working-class support for Social Credit to have been very high. His argument is that the CCF's left-wing orientation derived from the farmers' coalition with the working class, while Social Credit's allegedly right-wing perspective came about through a farmer coalition with the small-town petite bourgeoisie.

15 Elton and Goddard (1979, 56) cite survey data indicating that 58 per cent of those in the "skilled/unskilled labour" category voted Conservative in the 1971 provincial election.

168   Notes to pages 30–1

16 Flanagan is critical of Macpherson's depiction of Alberta's class structure, stating that it is applicable only to the agrarian heartland. "Minus
the cities," he writes, "it is this Alberta which Macpherson described"
(1972, 140).

17 In a chapter on English Social Credit, Macpherson writes that "in the
beginning the very extent and depth of its revolt made the social
credit doctrine attractive to western Canadian farmers whose own
society appeared to be uprooted. The urban outlook of social credit
was secondary; its primary appeal was to those insecure sections of
society, whether independent prairie farm producers or middle class
English city dwellers, whose economic position may be defined as
petit-bourgeois" (1962, 93). He offers no evidence to substantiate these
assertions.

18 Medicine Hat had a population of 10,300 in 1931, Lethbridge 13,489. In
that year 79,197 people lived in Edmonton, 83,761 in Calgary (Canada
1933, 464–82).

19 Medicine Hat was established as a Canadian Pacific Railway station in
1883. Later, natural gas and clay were produced commercially, which
led to the manufacture of pottery, bricks, and tiles. Its economy also
came to include milling, canning, brewing, and some smelting (Gould
1981). Lethbridge had been a coal-mining centre since the 1880s. (The
city is named after William Lethbridge, an early president of a coal
company operating in the area.) Around the turn of the century the
local railway facilities were expanded to include a station and maintenance facilities. In addition to these activities, Lethbridge became a
regional marketing and distributing centre, and was the site of flour-
milling, sugar-refining, brewing, and iron-working industries (Johnston
and den Otter 1985). Brief histories of these two communities are given
in chapter 6.

20 In 1921 Medicine Hat was a large, two-member riding that included a
large section of the countryside in addition to the city proper; it elected
a UFA and a Labor candidate that year. In 1926 the size of the riding
was greatly reduced, with all but a small portion of the countryside
removed. That year it elected a Liberal and a Conservative member; the
UFA did not contest the seat. Medicine Hat became a single-member
constituency in 1930, electing a Liberal – again, there was no UFA candidate, nor did the UFA contest the riding in 1935. Similarly, at no point
in its history did the UFA field a candidate in Lethbridge. An independent candidate represented Lethbridge in 1921, with Labor winning
in 1926 and 1930 (Alberta 1983).

21 Macpherson states that "[Alberta's] population, in 1946 some 800,000,
... is spread out over about 90,000 farms ... , numerous hamlets and
villages, twenty-five towns with populations between 1,000 and 5,000,

169 Notes to pages 31–7

two cities between 10,000 and 15,000, and two large cities of about 90,000 and 100,000" (1962, 10).

22 While Aberhart had made tours of southern Alberta promoting Social Credit as early as the summer of 1933, Edmonton was not organized by the movement until early in 1935 (Irving 1959, 192–3).

23 According to the 1951 census, 12 per cent of the male work-force in greater Edmonton was composed of "employers and own accounts" and "no pays"; the figure for Calgary for that year was also 12 per cent (Census of Canada, Bulletin CT-10, 5–3–1953:12, 14, my calculations). These figures slightly overestimate the presence of the petite bourgeoisie, however, since "employers and own accounts" includes owners of large firms. Of the 12 per cent in these categories, 1 per cent was deducted to account for this. Such data are not available for years before 1951, and are not available for Lethbridge, Medicine Hat, or the smaller communities.

24 See n 21 above. Only four urban centres, the cities discussed above, had populations exceeding 5,000 in 1931.

25 This increase is consistent with Bechhofer and Elliott's contention that, paradoxically, the petite bourgeoisie tends to *expand* during periods of economic decline (1985, 201).

26 In an earlier work Finkel maintained that "Macpherson was correct to identify [Social Credit] as rooted in the petite bourgeoisie" but that it was "nevertheless able to incorporate working class elements because it developed policies and organizational structures that compared favourably in popular democratic terms to working-class parties in Alberta" (1984, 111). He claims that Alberta workers were, as Laclau puts it, "subjected to the articulating principle of a class distinct from that to which [they belong]" (1977, 164). Since Finkel's paper (1984) is devoted to a discussion of Alberta's working class, he makes no attempt to establish the petit-bourgeois "roots" of Social Credit. The issue of whether the Social Credit ideology was an "articulating principle" of the petite bourgeoisie is taken up in the next two chapters.

CHAPTER FOUR

1 Other renowned intellectuals have endorsed Douglas's ideas. Frederick Soddy, a Nobel laureate in chemistry, has said that "science without social credit is sheer suicide" (Munson 1945, 335). Norbert Weiner, who was a professor of mathematics at the Massachusetts Institute of Technology and became famous for his research into cybernetics, stated, "I accept [Douglas] without reservation and see no future for our society unless Social Credit principles are incorporated at an early date" (de Maré 1986, 14).

170 Notes to pages 38–45

2 In explaining why his theories had not been "received with the enthusiasm which at first you might expect," Douglas conceded that "my
own method of communicating information may be to some extent at
fault, although I do not think this is the whole explanation" (1934, 4).

3 Douglas is not alone in claiming that a drastic reduction in the amount
of labour needed for production can be achieved if the existing productive resources are properly utilized. Another social theorist writes that
"human society has an abundance of productive forces at its disposal
which only await a rational organization, regulated distribution, in
order to go into operation to the greatest benefit of all ... given this
kind of organization, the present customary labour time of the individual will be reduced by half simply by making use of the labour
which is either not used at all or used disadvantageously." The theorist
is Friedrich Engels (1975, 251). Elsewhere Engels writes, "The steam
engine and the other new machines have provided modern industry
with the means to achieve a limitless increase in the volume of production in a very short time" (1976, 368).

4 Cf Engels: "Modern industry – and the illimitable expansion of output
which it can achieve – has made possible the emergence of an economy
in which such a volume of the necessities of life can be produced that
every member of society could develop his potentialities to the full"
(1976, 369).

5 Douglas's thought has much in common with Technocracy, and he
makes favourable reference to the work of Thorstein Veblen (e.g.,
Douglas 1922a, 40; 1933, 49). However, Douglas opposes the Technocracy movement itself on the grounds that it advocates too much organization, which he sees as oppressive to the individual (Finlay 1972, 103).
For a discussion of Technocracy and its relationship to Social Credit,
see Atkin (1977, espec. 64–7, 84–6, 114–15).

6 Douglas maintains that without "credit" of some kind, consumers cannot
purchase all of what is produced if goods are sold at cost price or higher.

7 For critical analyses of the Douglas system in addition to those cited
above, see Hiskett (1935) and Lewis (1935).

8 Few of Douglas's critics, it seems, are aware of this.

9 The limit is set by the reserve ratio, which is usually regulated by law.
The lower the reserve ratio, the more the deposit money that can be
created.

10 For a discussion of how banks create money, see Archer (1973, 286–94);
and Smith (1959, 26–7).

11 Veblen takes a similar position: "No large move in the field of corporation finance can be made without the advice and consent of those large
funded interests that are in a position to act as investment bankers; nor
does any large enterprise in corporation business ever escape from the

171 Notes to pages 45–8

continued control of the investment bankers in any of its larger transactions; nor can any corporate enterprise of the larger sort now continue to do business except on terms which will yield something appreciable in the way of income to the investment bankers, whose continued support is necessary to its success" (1921, 47). Veblen also states that "the corporate financier, as a class, came in for an 'unearned increment' of income, on the simple plan of 'sitting tight'" (43).

12 Cf Veblen: "All the costly publicity that goes into sales-costs is in the nature of prevarication; when it is not good broad mendacity; and quite necessarily so" (1921, 111).

13 Cf Marx: "The capitalist gets rich, not like the miser, in proportion to his personal labour and restricted consumption, but at the same rate as he squeezes out the labour-power of others, and enforces on the labourer abstinence from all life's enjoyments" (1967, 594).

14 Engels takes a similar position, claiming that "once production is no longer in the hands of private producers but in those of the community and its administrative bodies, it is a trifling matter *to regulate production according to needs*" (1975, 246). Similarly, until he tried to put his beliefs into practice, Lenin thought it a simple matter to allow the public to control production directly. With the proper groundwork, he states, "it is quite possible, immediately, within twenty-four hours, to pass to the overthrow of the capitalists and bureaucrats, and to replace them, in the control of production and distribution, in the business of apportioning labour and products, by the armed workers, or the people in arms ... Book-keeping and control – these are the chief things necessary for the smooth and correct functioning of [this] ... *first phase* of Communist society ... The book-keeping and control necessary for this have been simplified by capitalism to the utmost, till they have become the extraordinarily simple operations of watching, recording and issuing receipts, within the reach of anybody who can read and write and knows the first four arithmetical rules" (1925, 130–1).

15 Cf Engels: "In the new society it will be essential to take control of all branches of manufacture out of the hands of competing individuals. Industry will have to be run by society as a whole for everybody's benefit. It must be operated by all members of society in accordance with a common plan. Co-operation must take the place of competition" (1976, 369).

16 Technicians also figure prominently in Veblen's thought. Unlike Douglas, however, who places the technicians at the disposal of the community, Veblen advocates that technicians not only run the economy, but also make economic policy: "The situation is ready for a self-selected, but inclusive, Soviet of technicians to take over the economic affairs of the country and to allow and disallow what they may

172 Notes to pages 51–64

agree on; provided always that they live within the requirements of that state of the industrial arts whose keepers they are, and provided that their pretensions continue to have the support of the industrial rank and file; which comes near saying that their Soviet must consistently and effectively take care of the material welfare of the underlying population" (1921, 166).

17 Cf Lenin's plan to have capitalists "converted into employees" of the state (1925, 132).

18 A British Social Credit pamphlet ("Social Credit in Summary," nd) states, "The general effect [of implementing Social Credit] would be *instantly* to raise the destitute above the poverty line, and proportionally improve the condition of every class above them; thereafter progressively to increase the *relative* prosperity of the poor – with the willing assent of the rich. The nominally increased purchasing power of the rich will cease to be effective directly they reach their maximum limit of personal consumption. Many of them are at that limit already; so that their incapacity to absorb more goods in an era of quickening production will automatically cause an overspill, which, in finding its level (as it must) will progressively dispose of the problem of the 'inequitable distribution of wealth.'"

19 Like other writers, Stein does not consider the idea that unions' pursuit of higher wages also stimulates demand, which is beneficial to the petite bourgeoisie and which may give members of this class a favourable attitude towards unions.

20 See Hamilton (1972, chap. 5; 1975, chaps. 2 and 3; 1982).

21 See Douglas (1922b, 39).

22 The Labour committee included many prominent figures of British society, including Sir Leo C. Money, G.D.H. Cole (an Oxford don and socialist writer), Sidney Webb, and J.A. Hobson. It was not a committee of workers.

CHAPTER FIVE

1 Aberhart's concern with price spreads may have stemmed from a Canadian royal commission on this issue that had begun its investigation not long before he began his political campaign. See the *Report of the Royal Commission on Price Spreads* (Canada 1937).

2 Although Douglas was among the critics who chided Aberhart for proposing that social credit be paid for through taxation, Douglas himself was not entirely consistent in his views on taxes. His "Draft Social Credit Scheme for Scotland" does not rule out taxation, stating that "any taxation found to be necessary [is] to take the form either of a flat non-graduated taxation of net income or a percentage *ad valorem* tax

upon sales, or both forms of taxation together" (1933, 212). The larger corpus of Douglas's work, however, clearly indicates that he did not believe that wealth redistribution through taxation could solve fundamental economic problems.

3 Pamphlet, "What Is Social Credit?" (ca 1940), 16.

4 For the standard arguments claiming that the Alberta movement was economically conservative, see Irving (1959, 345–6) and Lipset (1971, 155).

5 Pamphlet, "Social Credit" (1933), 1.

6 Speech, 23 May 1935.

7 For an account of the Alberta Social Credit doctrine that examines its millenarian character and how this changed during the party's long tenure in office, see Flanagan and Lee (1991). See also Morton (1955) on this issue.

8 The Social Crediters were not the only social reformers who believed that major social change could be brought about without causing severe social dislocation. Veblen, for instance, avers that the changeover to a non-market system run by a "Soviet of technicians" "need, in effect, be nothing spectacular; assuredly it need involve no clash of arms or fluttering of banners, unless, as is beginning to seem likely, the Guardians of the old order should find that sort of thing expedient. In its elements, the move will be of the simplest and most matter-of-fact character" (1921, 155–6).

9 Pamphlet, "The Dangers of Aberhart's Social Credit Proposals" (Edmonton Chamber of Commerce 1935), 2.

10 Pamphlet, "Calgary Board of Trade Takes Stand on Social Credit" (ca 1935).

11 Examples of such accounts include Conway (1979, 84) and Macpherson (1962, 221–30).

12 Pamphlet, "What Is Social Credit?" 9.

13 Pamphlet, "Ritual, Women's Auxiliaries, Monetary Reform Groups" (ca 1940).

14 Pamphlet, "What Is Social Credit?" 34–5.

15 Statement of Votes, General Election, 22 August 1935, Provincial Archives of Alberta.

16 See also Johnson and MacNutt (1970, 123, 126).

17 For Macpherson's presentation of this argument, see *Democracy in Alberta* (221–30).

18 Marx and Engels are themselves examples of the phenomenon Taylor describes, and observed that it is difficult to win proletarian support for socialist revolutions. In 1845 Engels gave a series of lectures at Elberfeld in which he outlined what his proposed communist society would be like. After the third meeting he wrote to Marx that, "All of Elberfeld

174   Notes to pages 77–86

and Barmen, from the monied aristocracy to *small shopkeepers*, were represented, the proletariat being the only exception" (1975, 697, n 91, emphasis added).

19 In the Alberta provincial election of 1944 the CCF took 25 per cent of the popular vote (but only 2 of 57 seats). The Labour Progessive (Communist) Party received 4 per cent of the vote, bringing to 29 per cent the total popular vote for socialist-oriented parties in the province (Alberta 1983, 14).

20 Farmers objected to the tariff because it forced them to purchase their farm machinery and consumer goods at tariff-inflated prices, yet their agricultural produce had to be sold in the largely unprotected world market.

21 It should be kept in mind that Macpherson's study is concerned with both the UFA and Social Credit. It is this writer's position that regional grievances were a central component of the Progressive movement (of which the UFA was a part) but not Social Credit.

22 The Farmers' Platform of 1921 is reprinted in Morton (1950, 302–5).

23 Aberhart studied French in order to spread the Social Credit message in Quebec. His desire to establish a social credit system in central Canada is another indication that his movement did not maintain that regional exploitation was the cause of the malaise.

CHAPTER SIX

1 These are not to be found at the Alberta Provincial Archives, the Glenbow Museum and Archives, the Edmonton City Archives, the Calgary City Archives, the Legislative Library in Edmonton, or at the Office of the Chief Electoral Officer. Nor were they reported in local newspapers.

2 Social Credit won 37 per cent of the vote in the constituency of Edmonton in 1935 (N = 37,267). The Liberals took 38 per cent, the Conservatives 13 per cent, the UFA 6 per cent, and Labor 4 per cent.

3 The informants consulted for each city are named in the Acknowledgments. Each group of informants was given a synopsis of the purposes of this study, including the definitions of the social-class categories used. They were then asked to indicate on a large map where concentrations of the various classes would have been found in 1935. A similar method is used by Lipset (1971, chap. 8) in his analysis of the class basis of CCF support in Saskatchewan. H. Quinn (1963, 182–6, 224–9, 265–7) uses a similar ecological method in a study of the Union Nationale, although he appears to have relied primarily on his own knowledge as opposed to that of informants. R. Hamilton (1982) also uses

175   Notes to pages 87–94

the ecological method, although he was able to incorporate census data into his analysis for a few cities.

4 For a discussion of the limitations of ecological analyses, see Robinson (1950) and Hamilton (1982, 500–1, n 6).

5 For a discussion of the transferable ballot system, see Alberta 1983, 193–204.

6 For the 1935 election poll 3 is included in Area 4, and poll 4 in Area 5. In the official record for the 1930 election the results for polls 3 and 4 are recorded together; this combined poll was placed in Area 5 for the 1930 election.

7 These figures include the votes for R.H. Parkin, who had run as a Labor candidate in 1921, was elected as an Independent Labor candidate in 1926, ran as an Independent in 1930, and ran as an Independent Labor candidate in 1935.

8 The author considered using the downtown polls as a measure of petit-bourgeois support. The downtown area contained a number of small businesses, and independent proprietors do sometimes reside on their premises, but *Henderson's Directory* data indicate that many of those who operated small businesses downtown lived (and hence voted) elsewhere. For the record, the only Calgary poll entirely enclosed in the downtown area, poll 14, voted 40 per cent Social Credit ($N = 163$). *Henderson's Directory* was not used as a data source in determining the class composition of the various city neighbourhoods as the number of missing cases was very high and a systematic selection bias could not be ruled out.

The downtown polls in Lethbridge and Medicine Hat were not used as measures of petit-bourgeois support either. In Lethbridge the downtown area was divided among three polling subdivisions, none of which was completely contained in the downtown area. The best coverage was provided by poll 14, only two-thirds of which was downtown. Similarly, in Medicine Hat the best downtown coverage was given by poll 10, only half of which was downtown.

9 The support given to Social Credit by members of the affluent classes deserves further research. G. Hamilton Southam, of the wealthy publishing Southams, recalls his upbringing: "We were taught that it was vulgar to talk of money, unless as an element in economic theory. Father and Uncle Harry [Southam] were strong supporters of Henry George at one time, of Major Douglas in later years. Indeed they invited the latter to Canada – I remember him dining at Lindenelm [the family mansion] – and helped spread Social Credit doctrine across the country" (*Ottawa Citizen*, 23 July 1988, B3). Harry Southam published the *Ottawa Citizen*, his brother (G.H. Southam's father) Wilson the

Calgary Herald. The editor of the *Citizen* in the 1930s, Charles A. Bowman, was a supporter of Douglas.

Irving writes that "in Calgary, socially prominent converts [to Social Credit] were constantly engaged in organizing lectures and study groups in women's circles" (1959, 69–79). At a later point in the book he states: "As interviews with two such men reveal, Social Credit was not without an appeal to the wealthy. In a period when the capitalistic system had obviously broken down, Social Credit (in striking contrast to socialism and communism) promised to 'make capitalism work.' Both of these men, who were animated by humanitarian ideals, repudiated absolutely Aberhart's teaching regarding basic dividends and strongly urged him privately to abandon this aspect of Social Credit doctrine. Yet they were absolutely convinced that monetary reform, along Social Credit lines, was necessary to prevent the overthrow of the capitalistic system by socialists and communists. As they interpreted it, the Social Credit movement was a revolt of Tory radicals. Being members of the social *elite*, they could not afford to be seen in public with Aberhart, although they dined with him privately. It was a great source of satisfaction to him to know that he had recruited at least two men of rank and wealth to the movement. If they could not publicly avow their allegiance to Social Credit, their financial contributions to the cause were not inconsiderable" (249).

John Hugill, who was elected in Calgary as a Social Credit member in 1935 and was Aberhart's first attorney general, was a law partner with R.B. Bennett, legal adviser to the CPR, and was consul for Sweden and vice-consul for the Netherlands. He also held a number of prestigious social positions in Calgary, including the captaincy of the polo club, and wore spats (Elliott and Miller 1987, 206).

10 Includes some areas beyond the city limits. Participation rates for the city proper or by area as defined here are not available.

11 See Pinard (1975, 31–4) for a discussion of the effect of previously apathetic populations on social movements. See Hamilton (1972, 291–5) for a discussion of non-voters in American elections.

12 Informants in both Lethbridge and Medicine Hat stated that before the Second World War very few people in their respective cities were upper class.

13 Figures for the city of Lethbridge itself or the various areas therein are not available.

14 One citizen stated, "I've been here fifty years, and I'm still a newcomer!" Informants also claimed that familial length of residence in the district conferred more status on local citizens than their social class did.

177   Notes to pages 101–8

15 Participation rates for the city proper or by area are not available.
16 In his Table 6.1 Pinard divides the working class into "skilled," "semi-skilled," and "unskilled and service" categories; in Table 6.7 above the three working-class categories have been combined. In his Table 6.1 Pinard divides the respondents into two groups: those in districts within the greater Montreal area and those not in greater Montreal; Table 6.7 above includes all respondents. Pinard classified the self-employed blue-collar workers (artisans, etc.) as "skilled working class"; in Table 6.7 above these have been classified as "small businessmen".
17 With self-employed blue-collar respondents classified as working class.
18 Pinard states, however, that "there are indications that [outside greater Montreal] opposition to social change among small businessmen [defined as not including self-employed manuals] tended to push them towards [the Social Credit] party" (1975, 115). But he adds that, "due to sample size ... we cannot test whether this effect is independent of strains, or whether it is simply an intervening factor which has no effect of its own" (115, n 85). Moreover, although small businessmen outside greater Montreal indicated slightly higher opposition to social security, labour unions, nationalization of industries, and social change in general than did members of other occupations, all differences between small businessmen and other middle-class categories were insignificant, except for the last measure, which had a significance level of .07 (114–15, n 83).

CHAPTER SEVEN

1 Finkel (1989, chap. 3) is a notable exception.
2 Several authors erroneously give 23 August 1935 as the date of this crucial election. The error appears to have originated in the work of Barr (1974, 80), being repeated in Caldarola (1979, 40), Mardiros (1979, 195), and Osborne and Osborne (1986, 120). Lewis H. Thomas (1977, 60) cites 25 August as the date of this election. Barr also appears to have started another chain of errors, citing 23 June 1943 as the date of William Aberhart's death (1974, 118) when in fact he died on 23 May of that year (Calgary Herald, 25 May 1943, 1). Caldarola also gives June 23 as the date of the premier's death (1979, 43); Osborne and Osborne state that he died in June 1943 (1986, 135). Mallory claims that he died on 24 May (1954, 153); Thomas, again an original, cites 20 May (1977, 167). The implications of these patterns of errors for the sociology of knowledge are explored in chapter 9.
3 N.B. James, who was elected as a Social Credit candidate in the 1935 election, has written: "Looking back, I feel that, from the top down, the

178   Notes to pages 108–30

most of us had hoped at the best that we would form His Majesty's Loyal Opposition, and were quite unprepared for the shock of finding that we had to form a government" (1947, 198).

4 In *The Alberta Experiment* (1937) Douglas published all the correspondence between himself and Aberhart from 24 August 1935 to 24 March 1936.

5 The "Report" is contained in Douglas's *The Alberta Experiment* (102–18).

6 Aberhart did not run as a candidate in the 1935 election, claiming that he had no personal stake in the outcome. He was elected by acclamation in a by-election held in the Okotoks–High River constituency on 4 November 1935. Immediately after the general election, however, Social Credit MLAS ratified his leadership of the party, which allowed him to perform his duties as premier-designate.

7 Douglas sometimes learned of a forthcoming letter from Aberhart by reading about it in the London papers.

8 The municipalities themselves were in dire financial straits in the 1930s. In those years municipalities were partially responsible for financing a wide range of social services, such as relief payments and health care, which later came under the jurisdiction of the provincial and federal governments.

9 According to Hooke, who himself was one of the insurgents, only the chairman of the board was an insurgent: "the other four men were recruited from the loyalist ranks" (1971, 125). As many of the key meetings at this time were held in secret, it is difficult to determine who was an insurgent and who was not. Also, some members were reluctant to tell the public which side they were on.

10 The pamphlet is reproduced in Hooke (1971, following 126).

11 The governments of Ontario and Quebec also refused to co-operate with the committee (Mallory 1954, 146).

CHAPTER EIGHT

1 In Edmonton the number of polling places increased from 40 in 1935 to 142 in 1940, so the 1935 poll locations are of little value in determining the location of the 1940 polls. The poll locations for Edmonton are also unavailable for several elections after 1940; when they become available for later years, they do not correspond with the number of polls in 1940, and so are useless in analysing the latter election.

2 The Edmonton constituency results include the city proper as well as some outlying regions.

3 Due to the method used to record the 1940 vote in the official documents, the results for 4 of Calgary's 52 polling places had to be placed in areas different from those used for 1935. In the official record the

results for polls 14, 15, and 16 were calculated together, so this composite figure was included in area 4, where polls 15 and 16 were placed for the 1935 election; in Table 6.1, which shows the results for Calgary for 1935, poll 14 is included in area 3. The results for polls 34, 35, 37, and 38 were recorded together, so this composite result was included in area 3, where polls 37 and 38 were placed for 1935; polls 34 and 35 were in area 5 for the previous election. Polls 47 and 48 are combined in the official record, so this result was included in area 5, where poll 48 was for 1935; for the latter election, poll 47 was in area 3.

4 Participation rates for the constituency of Calgary were 80 per cent in 1935 and 79 per cent in 1940, and the number of eligible voters in the city increased by 11 per cent in 1940. The number of eligible voters in the province as a whole increased by 13 per cent.

5 Polls 71, 72, 73, 74, 77, 78, and 79.

6 Despite the reduction in physical size, the number of eligible voters in the Lethbridge riding increased by 5 per cent over 1935; 83 per cent of all eligible voters voted in 1940, compared to 82 per cent in 1935.

7 The participation rate in the riding in 1940 was 86 per cent, compared to 83 per cent in 1935. The number of eligible voters increased by 10 per cent.

8 There is some controversy over whether the CCF was really a socialist party or merely another manifestation of petit-bourgeois confusion. See chapter 5, 77.

CHAPTER NINE

1 This is not an exhaustive list of the conditions that may have had a bearing on the Social Credit movement, but it does include those most frequently discussed. For an examination of other conditions that may have been relevant, see Hiller (1977).

2 According to Macpherson, "Common relationship to the disposal of labour still tends to give the members of each class, so defined, an outlook and set of assumptions distinct from those of other classes" (1962, 225).

3 See Bell (1992, 94–5).

4 Cf Hamilton (1972, chap. 5), who suggests that the most important dividing line in the American class structure falls between the lower and upper middle classes, the same dividing line as proposed here. Hamilton found key differences in political preference and behaviour with the class structure dichotomized in this way.

5 The following illustrates how western alienation can vary over time. Questioning the validity of Macpherson's "quasi-colonial" notion for the Alberta of the early 1970s, Long and Quo write that "Alberta no longer

has to battle the federal government for natural resources; she now controls and has developed her own natural resources, becoming one of the richest provinces in Canada. Moreover, Alberta voters seem satisfied with having their representation channeled through the traditional national parties. Although Alberta still confronts the national government in the areas of grain marketing, allocation of tax revenue, language rights, and other issues, these conflicts add very little to a party's strength in provincial politics. Conflicts between Ottawa and the provincial governments have been a rather common phenomenon of Canadian federalism in recent years and cannot be considered peculiar to Alberta" (1972, 24–5). Shortly after this piece was written, regional issues again became salient in provincial politics. By the end of the decade regionalism had again subsided, and Roger Gibbins wrote *Prairie Politics and Society: Regionalism in Decline* (1980), the subtitle of which summarizes the main thesis of the book. Shortly thereafter, regional issues were again prominent.

6 See chapter 7, n 2.

7 Stephen Leacock (1936) and D. Smiley (1962) are examples of writers who have made unrestrained efforts to humiliate the movement.

8 Writing about Canadian historians of the 1920s, Mallory states that they "were, whether consciously or not, partisans. They assumed, like the great Whig historians of England, that the reformers, the Liberal politicians, and the apostles of Canadian autonomy about whom they wrote were marching with the destiny of Canada. Their heroes and villains were, as it were, preselected. They painted with strong lights and shadows. They provided, for their time, not only a history but an ideology" (1954, xi). The same may be said of many of those who have written about other historical phenomena, including Social Credit.

9 Cf van den Berg (1988, 492–7).

10 See Alexander and Giesen (1987) for a good general introduction to this issue.

11 Flanagan (1979, 314–19) suggests that French and Ukranian Canadians, who in the 1930s lived mainly in constituencies north of Edmonton, may have had below-average levels of support for Social Credit in 1935, although his data are sketchy. Grayson and Grayson (1974, 302, 309), who examine support for Social Credit in urban areas with a population of 1,000 or more, found that support for the party was not strongly associated with British ethnicity. They report that in the 1935 provincial election the per cent English, per cent Irish, and per cent Scottish variables explained two, three, and four per cent of the variance respectively, with the signs of the regression coefficients being positive for per cent English and per cent Irish, but negative for per cent Scottish.

12 See, for example, McCarthy and Zald (1973).

181   Notes to pages 158–62

13 For an introduction to rational-choice theory, see Friedman and Hechter (1988).

14 The Regina Manifesto is reprinted in Young (1969, 304–13). It is generally believed that intellectuals in Canada, especially those on the left, had nothing but scorn for the concept of social credit. Yet the presence of social credit ideas and nomenclature in the Manifesto, which was written by the League for Social Reconstruction, the CCF's intellectual wing, suggests that a different interpretation is possible.

15 Bennett buggies, named after the prime minister of the day, were automobiles with their engines removed that were pulled by horses. They were created because many motorists could not afford gasoline or maintenance for their vehicles.

16 Also, those higher in the stratification system were more likely to have loyalties to the parties that were in existence before Social Credit. Those lower in the system, and/or previous non-voters, were less likely to have such loyalties and thus were probably more open to Social Credit appeals.

References

Aberhart, William. 1933. *The Douglas System of Economics: "Credit Power for Democracy."* Calgary.

– 1935. *Social Credit Manual: Social Credit as Applied to the Province of Alberta.* Calgary.

– ca 1940. "Premier Aberhart on Agricultural Reform." Pamphlet. Edmonton: Bureau of Information, Legislative Building.

Akin, William E. 1977. *Technocracy and the American Dream.* Berkeley: University of California Press.

Alberta. 1934. *The Douglas System of Social Credit: Evidence Taken by the Agricultural Committee of the Alberta Legislature, Session 1934.* Edmonton: King's Printer.

– 1936a. *Statutes of the Province of Alberta Passed in the First Session of the Eighth Legislative Assembly.* Edmonton: King's Printer.

– 1936b. *Statutes of the Province of Alberta Passed in the Second Session of the Eighth Legislative Assembly.* Edmonton: King's Printer.

– 1937. *Statutes of the Province of Alberta Passed in the Third Session of the Eighth Legislative Assembly.* Edmonton: King's Printer.

– 1938. *The Case for Alberta.* Edmonton: King's Printer.

– 1983. *A Report on Alberta Elections 1905–1982.* Edmonton: Office of the Chief Electoral Officer.

Alberta Provincial Liberal Association. ca 1935. "Alberta's Provincial Liberal Leader." Pamphlet. Provincial Archives of Alberta.

Archer, Maurice. 1973. *Introductory Macroeconomics: A Canadian Analysis.* Toronto: Macmillan of Canada.

184   References

Bakker, J.I. (Hans), and Anthony Winson. 1993. "Rural Sociology." In Peter
S. Li and B. Singh Bolaria, eds., *Contemporary Sociology: Critical Perspectives*.
Toronto: Copp Clark Pitman.

Barr, John J. 1974. *The Dynasty: The Rise and Fall of Social Credit in Alberta*.
Toronto: McClelland and Stewart.

Bechhofer, F., and B. Elliott. 1985. "The Petite Bourgeoisie in Late Capitalism."
Annual Review of Sociology 11:181–207.

Bell, Edward. 1992. "Reconsidering *Democracy in Alberta*." In A. Tupper and
R. Gibbins, eds., *The Government and Politics of Alberta*, 85–108. Edmonton:
University of Alberta Press.

– 1993. "The Rise of the Lougheed Conservatives and the Demise of Social
Credit in Alberta: A Reconsideration." *Canadian Journal of Political Science*
26 (3): 455–75.

Brym, Robert. 1978. "Regional Social Structure and Agrarian Radicalism in
Canada: Alberta, Saskatchewan and New Brunswick." *Canadian Review of
Sociology and Anthropology* 15 (3):339–51.

– 1986. "Anglo-Canadian Sociology." *Current Sociology* 34 (1):1–152.

Burnet, Jean. 1947. "Town-Country Relations and the Problem of Rural Leadership." *Canadian Journal of Economics and Political science* 13:395–409.

– 1951. *Next-Year Country*. Toronto: University of Toronto Press.

Caldarola, Carlo. 1979. "The Social Credit in Alberta, 1935–1971." In C.
Caldarola, ed., *Society and Politics in Alberta*, 33–48. Toronto: Methuen.

Canada. 1933. *Census of Canada 1931*. Vol. 2, *Population by Areas*. Ottawa:
King's Printer.

– 1936. *Census of Canada 1931*. Vol. 7, *Occupations and Industries*. Ottawa:
King's Printer.

– 1937. *Report of the Royal Commission on Price Spreads*. Ottawa: King's Printer.

Clark, S.D. 1954. Foreword to J.R. Mallory, *Social Credit and the Federal Power
in Canada*, vii-ix. Toronto: University of Toronto Press.

– 1959. *Movements of Political Protest in Canada, 1640–1840*. Toronto: University
of Toronto Press.

Clark, Sam. 1982. "Social Movements." In James J. Teevan, ed., *Introduction
to Sociology; A Canadian Focus*, 335–61. Scarborough: Prentice-Hall.

Colbourne, Maurice. 1928. *Unemployment or War*. New York: Coward-
McCann.

– 1934. *Economic Nationalism*. London: Figurehead.

Conway, J.F. 1978. "Populism in the United States, Russia, and Canada:
Explaining the Roots of Canada's Third Parties." *Canadian Journal of Political
Science* 11 (1):99–124.

– 1979. "The Prairie Populist Resistance to the National Policy: Some Recon-
siderations." *Journal of Canadian Studies* 14 (3):77–91.

– 1983. *The West: The History of a Region in Confederation*. Toronto: James
Lorimer.

185 References

– 1990. Review of *The Social Credit Phenomenon in Alberta* by Alvin Finkel (Toronto: University of Toronto Press 1989). *Canadian Journal of Political Science* 23 (2):371–73.

Craven, Paul, and Tom Traves. 1979. "The Class Politics of the National Policy, 1872–1933." *Journal of Canadian Studies* 14 (3):14–38.

de Maré, Eric. 1983. *A Matter of LIFE or DEBT*. Bullsbrook, Australia: Veritas Publishing.

Dobb, Maurice. 1933. "'Social Credit' and the Petit-Bourgeoisie." *Labour Monthly* 15 (9):552–7.

Douglas, Clifford Hugh. 1920. *Economic Democracy*. London: Cecil Palmer.

– 1921. *Credit Power and Democracy*. London: Cecil Palmer.

– 1922a. *The Control and Distribution of Production*. London: Eyre and Spottiswoode.

– 1922b. *These Present Discontents and the Labour Party and Social Credit*. London: Cecil Palmer.

– 1931. *The Monopoly of Credit*. London: Chapman and Hall.

– 1933. *Social Credit*. London: Eyre and Spottisdwoode.

– 1934. *Warning Democracy*. London: Stanley Nott.

– 1935. "First Interim Report on the Possibilities of the Application of Social Credit Principles to the Province of Alberta." Repr. in C.H. Douglas, *The Alberta Experiment*, 102–18. London: Eyre and Spottiswoode, 1937.

– 1936. *The Tragedy of Human Effort*. Stratford-On-Avon: K.R.P. Publications.

– 1937. *The Alberta Experiment: An Interim Survey*. London: Eyre and Spottiswoode.

– 1939. "Whose Service Is Perfect Freedom (VIII)." *Social Crediter* 3 (8):1–2.

– 1942. *The Big Idea*. Liverpool: K.R.P. Publications.

– 1945. *The Brief for the Prosecution*. Liverpool: K.R.P. Publications.

Drache, Daniel, and Arthur Kroker. 1987. "C.B. Macpherson: 1911–1987." *Canadian Journal of Political and Social Theory* 11 (3):99–105.

Duggan, D.M. 1935. "Social Credit." Radio broadcast, station CJCA, 11 Apr. 1935. Provincial Archives of Alberta.

Durbin, E.F.M. 1934. *Purchasing Power and Trade Depression: A Critique of Under-Consumption Theories*. London: Jonathan Cape.

Elliott, David R. 1980. "William Aberhart: Right or Left?" In R.D. Francis and H. Gazevoort, eds., *The Dirty Thirties in Prairie Canada*, 11–31. Vancouver: Tantalus Research.

Elliott, David R., and Iris Miller. 1987. *Bible Bill: A Biography of William Aberhart*. Edmonton: Reidmore Books.

Elton, David K., and A.M. Goddard. 1979. "The Conservative Takeover, 1971–." In C. Caldarola, ed., *Society and Politics in Alberta*, 49–70. Toronto: Methuen.

Engels, Friedrich. 1975 [1845]. "Speeches in Elberfeld." In K. Marx and F. Engels, *Collected Works*, 4: 243–55. New York: International Publishers.

186 References

- 1976 [1847]. "Principles of Communism, November 1847." In W.O. Henderson, *The Life of Friedrich Engels*, 1: 362–79. London: Frank Cass.

Finkel, Alvin. 1984. "Populism and the Proletariat: Social Credit and the Alberta Working Class." *Studies in Political Economy* 13:104–35.

- 1986. "Social Credit and the Cities." *Alberta History* 34 (3):20–6.

- 1989. *The Social Credit Phenomenon in Alberta*. Toronto: University of Toronto Press.

Finlay, John L. 1972. *Social Credit: The English Origins*. Montreal: McGill-Queen's University Press.

Flanagan, Thomas. 1972. "Political Geography and the United Farmers of Alberta." In S. Trofimenkoff, ed., *The Twenties in Western Canada*, 138–69. Ottawa: National Museum of Man.

- 1973. "Stability and Change in Alberta Provincial Elections." *Alberta Historical Review* 21 (4):1–8.

- 1979. "Ethnic Voting in Alberta Provincial Elections, 121–1975." In C. Caldarola, ed., *Society and Politics in Alberta*, 304–21. Toronto: Methuen.

Flanagan, Thomas, and Martha Lee. 1991. "From Social Credit to Social Conservatism: The Evolution of an Ideology." *Prairie Forum* 16 (2):205–23.

Foran, Max. 1978. *Calgary: An Illustrated History*. Ottawa: National Museum of Man.

Fowke, Vernon C. 1946. *Canadian Agricultural Policy*. Toronto: University of Toronto Press.

- 1957. *The National Policy and the Wheat Economy*. Toronto: University of Toronto Press.

Friedman, Debra, and Michael Hechter. 1988. "The Contribution of Rational Choice Theory to Macrosociological Research." *Sociological Theory* 6 (2):201–18.

Gaitskell, H.T.N. 1933. "Four Monetary Heretics." In G.D.H. Cole, ed., *What Everybody Wants To Know about Money*. London: Victor Gollancz.

Gibbins, Roger. 1980. *Prairie Politics and Society: Regionalism in Decline*. Toronto: Butterworths.

Gould, Ed. 1981. *All Hell for A Basement*. Medicine Hat: City of Medicine Hat.

Grayson, J. Paul, and L.M. Grayson. 1974. "The Social Base of Interwar Political Unrest in Urban Alberta." *Canadian Journal of Political Science* 7 (2):289–313.

- 1983. "Social Movements and Social Change." In Robert Hagedorn, ed., *Sociology*. 2nd ed., 507–31. Toronto: Holt, Rinehart and Winston.

Hagedorn, Robert. 1983. *Sociology*. 2nd ed. Toronto: Holt, Rinehart and Winston.

Hamilton, Richard F. 1972. *Class and Politics in the United States*. Toronto: John Wiley and Sons.

- 1975. *Restraining Myths*. Toronto: John Wiley and Sons.

187 References

– 1982. *Who Voted for Hitler?* Princeton, NJ: Princeton University Press.

Hannant, Larry. 1985. "The Calgary Working Class and the Social Credit Movement in Alberta, 1932–35." *Labour / Le Travail* (16):97–116.

Hiller, Harry H. 1972. *Religion, Populism, and Social Credit in Alberta*. Ph D, Department of Religious Studies, McMaster University.

– 1977. "Internal Problem Resolution and Third Party Emergence." *Canadian Journal of Sociology* 2 (1):55–75.

Hiskett, W.R. 1935. *Social Credits or Socialism: An Analysis of the Douglas Credit Scheme*. London: Victor Gollancz.

Hiskett, W.R., and J.A. Franklin. 1939. *Searchlight on Social Credit*. London: P.S. King and Son.

Hooke, Alfred. 1971. *30 + 5: I Know, I Was There*. Edmonton: Institute of Applied Art.

Irving, John. 1959. *The Social Credit Movement in Alberta*. Toronto: University of Toronto Press.

Jackson, Andrew. 1977. "Patterns of Hinterland Revolt: Alberta and Saskatchewan in the Inter-War period." Paper presented at the 49th annual meeting of the Canadian Political Science Association, Fredericton, NB, June.

James, Norman B. 1947. *The Autobiography of a Nobody*. Toronto: J.M. Dent and Sons.

Johnson, L.P.V., and Ola J. MacNutt. 1970. *Aberhart of Alberta*. Edmonton: Institute of Applied Art.

Johnson, Myron. 1979. "The Failure of the CCF in Alberta: An Accident of History." In C. Caldarola, ed., *Society and Politics in Alberta*, 87–107. Toronto: Methuen.

Johnston, Alex, and Andy A. den Otter. 1985. *Lethbridge: A Centennial History*. Lethbridge: City of Lethbridge and the Whoop-Up Country Chapter, Historical Society of Alberta.

Keynes, John M. 1936. *The General Theory of Employment, Interest and Money*. New York: Harcourt, Brace.

Kiser, Edgar, and Michael Hechter. 1991. "The Role of General Theory in Comparative-historical Sociology." *American Journal of Sociology* 97 (1):1–30.

Laclau, Ernesto. 1977. *Politics and Ideology in Marxist Theory*. London: New Left Books.

Leacock, Stephen. 1936. "Social and Other Credit in Alberta." *Fortnightly Review* 146:525–35.

Lenin, V.I. 1925 [1918]. *The State and Revolution*. London: Communist Party of Great Britain.

– 1972 [1895]. "The Economic Content of Narodism and the Criticism of It in Mr. Struve's Book." *Collected Works* 1:333–535. Moscow: Progress Publishers.

Lewis, John. 1935. *Douglas Fallacies: A Critique of Social Credit*. London: Chapman and Hall.

188   References

Liberal-Conservative Party of Alberta. 1935. "The Liberal-Conservative Party of Alberta: Principles and Programme." Pamphlet. Provincial Archives of Alberta.

Lipset, S.M. 1971 [1950]. *Agrarian Socialism*. Berkeley: University of California Press.

– 1981 [1959]. *Political Man: The Social Bases of Politics*. Baltimore: Johns Hopkins University Press.

Long, J.A., and F.Q. Quo. 1972. "One Party Dominance." In Martin Robin, ed., *Canadian Provincial Politics*, 1–26. Scarborough: Prentice-Hall.

Lower, Arthur R.M. 1946. *Colony to Nation: A History of Canada*. Toronto: Longmans, Green and Company.

Lynd, Robert S. 1971 [1950]. Foreword to S.M. Lipset's *Agrarian Socialism*, vii–xii. Berkeley: University of California Press.

McCarthy, J.D., and M.N. Zald. 1973. *The Trend of Social Movements in America: Professionalism and Resource Mobilization*. Morristown, NJ: General Learning Press.

McGoun, A.F. 1936. "Alberta, Economic and Political: I. Social Credit Legislation: A Survey." *Canadian Journal of Economics and Political Science* 2 (4):512–24.

MacGregor, James G. 1972. *A History of Alberta*. Edmonton: Hurtig.

McNaught, Kenneth. 1969. *The Pelican History of Canada*. Markham, Ont.: Penguin Books.

Macpherson, C.B. 1949. "The Political Theory of Social Credit." *Canadian Journal of Economics and Political Science* 14 (3):379–93.

– 1962 [1953]. *Democracy in Alberta: Social Credit and the Party System*. 2nd ed. Toronto: University of Toronto Press.

Mallory, J.R. 1954. *Social Credit and the Federal Power in Canada*. Toronto: University of Toronto Press.

Mann, W.E. 1955. *Sect, Cult and Church in Alberta*. Toronto: University of Toronto Press.

Manning, Ernest. 1936. Speech at the meeting of the Retail, Wholesale and Manufacturers' section of the Edmonton Chamber of Commerce, 10 Jan. Provincial Archives of Alberta.

Mardiros, Anthony. 1979. *William Irvine: The Life of a Prairie Radical*. Toronto: James Lorimer and Company.

Marx, Karl. 1967 [1867]. *Capital: A Critique of Political Economy*, Vol. 1, ed. F. Engels. New York: International Publishers.

Marx, Karl, and F. Engels. 1967 [1848]. *The Communist Manifesto*. Markham, Ont.: Penguin Books.

Masters, D.C. 1950. *The Winnipeg General Strike*. Toronto: University of Toronto Press.

Mills, C. Wright. 1942. Review of W.L. Warner and Paul S. Lunt, *The Social Life of a Modern Community*, vol. 1, Yankee City Series. *American Sociological Review* 7 (3):263–71.

Minogue, K.R. 1976. "Humanist Democracy: The Political Thought of C.B. Macpherson." *Canadian Journal of Political Science* 9(3):377–94.

Morton, W.L. 1950. *The Progressive Party in Canada*. Toronto: University of Toronto Press.

– 1955. "The Bias of Prairie Politics." *Transactions of the Royal Society of Canada*, ser. 3, 49:57–66.

Muggeridge, Malcolm. 1972. *The Green Stick*. Vol. 1 of *Chronicles of Wasted Time*. London: William Collins.

Munson, Gorham. 1945. *Aladdin's Lamp: The Wealth of the American People*. New York: Creative Age Press.

Naylor, R.T. 1972. "The Ideological Foundations of Social Democracy and Social Credit." In Gary Teeple, ed., *Capitalism and the National Question in Canada*, 251–6. Toronto: University of Toronto Press.

Osborne, J.S., and J.T. Osborne. 1986. *Social Credit for Beginners: An Armchair Guide*. Vancouver: Pulp Press.

Paddock, R.F. 1936. "Labour's Victory in New Zealand." *Political Quarterly* 8 (2):260–65.

Palmer, Howard. 1982. *Patterns of Prejudice: A History of Nativism in Alberta*. Toronto: McClelland and Stewart.

Palmer, Howard, and T. Palmer. 1990. *Alberta: A New History*. Edmonton: Hurtig.

Panitch, Leo. 1977. "The Role and Nature of the Canadian State." In L. Panitch, ed., *The Canadian State: Political Economy and Political Power*, 3–27. Toronto: University of Toronto Press.

Pinard, Maurice. 1975 [1971]. *The Rise of a Third Party; A Study in Crisis Politics*. Enlarged ed. Montreal: McGill-Queen's University Press.

– 1983a. "From Deprivation to Mobilization: I. The Role of Some Internal Motives Reexamined." Paper presented at the annual meetings of the American Sociological Association, Detroit.

– 1983b. "From Deprivation to Mobilization: II. Incentives, Ideals, and a General Motivational Model." Paper presented at the annual meetings of the American Sociological Association, Detroit.

Pound, Ezra. 1935. *Social Credit: An Impact*. London: Stanley Nott.

Quinn, Herbert F. 1963. *The Union Nationale: Quebec Nationalism from Duplessis to Levesque*. 2nd enlarged ed. Toronto: University of Toronto Press.

Richards, John. 1981. "Populism: A Qualified Defence." *Studies in Political Economy* 5:5–27.

Richards, John, and Larry Pratt. 1979. *Prairie Capitalism: Power and Influence in the New West*. Toronto: McClelland and Stewart.

Robinson, W.S. 1950. "Ecological Correlations and the Behavior of Individuals." *American Sociological Review* 15:351–7.

Schultz, Harold J. 1959. "Aberhart the Organization Man." *Alberta Historical Review* 7 (2):19–26.

190 References

– 1960. "The Social Credit Back-benchers' Revolt, 1937." *Canadian Historical Review* 41 (1):1–18.
– 1962. "A Second Term: 1940." *Alberta Historical Review* 10 (1):17–26.
Selver, Paul. 1959. *Orage and the New Age Circle*. London: George Allen and Unwin.
Sinclair, Peter R. 1975. "The Saskatchewan CCF: Ascent to Power and the Decline of Socialism." In Sam Clark et al., eds., *Prophesy and Protest: Social Movements in Twentieth Century Canada*, 186–99. Toronto: Gage.
Smelser, Neil. 1963. *Theory of Collective Behavior*. New York: Free Press.
Smiley, Donald V. 1962. "Canada's Poujadists: A New Look at Social Credit." *Canadian Forum* 42 (500):121–3.
Smith, Datus C. 1934. "North Dakota Seeks a Demagogue." *New Republic* 80 (1035):205–6.
Smith, Lawrence. 1959. *Money, Credit, and Public Policy*. Boston: Houghton Mifflin.
Social Credit Party of Great Britain and Northern Ireland. 1937. *Official Report: Alberta; A Documented Record of Mr. John Hargrave's Visit to the Province of Alberta Canada, December 8, 1936 to January 25, 1937*. London.
Stein, Michael. 1973. *The Dynamics of Right-Wing Protest: A Political Analysis of Social Credit in Quebec*. Toronto: University of Toronto Press.
Stevenson, Garth. 1986. "Class and Class Politics in Alberta." In L. Pratt, ed., *Essays in Honour of Grant Notley: Socialism and Democracy in Alberta*, 205–37. Edmonton: NeWest Press.
Swankey, Ben. 1980. "Reflections of a Communist: 1935 Election." *Alberta History* 28 (4):28–36.
Taylor, A.J.P. 1967. Introduction to K. Marx and F. Engels, *The Communist Manifesto*, 7–47. Markham, Ont.: Penguin Books.
Thomas, L.G. 1959. *The Liberal Party in Alberta*. Toronto: University of Toronto Press.
Thomas, L.H. 1977. *William Aberhart and Social Credit in Alberta*. Toronto: Copp Clark.
Tilly, Charles. 1978. *From Mobilization to Revolution*. Reading, Mass.: Addison-Wesley.
Trow, Martin. 1958. "Small Businessmen, Political Tolerance, and Support for McCarthy." *American Journal of Sociology* 64:270–81.
Turner, Ralph H., and Lewis M. Killian. 1987. *Collective Behavior*. 3rd ed. Englewood Cliffs, NJ: Prentice-Hall.
United Farmers of Alberta. 1935. "UFA Provincial Platform 1935." Pamphlet. Provincial Archives of Alberta.
van den Berg, Axel. 1988. *The Immanent Utopia: From Marxism on the State to the State of Marxism*. Princeton, NJ: Princeton University Press.
Veblen, Thorstein. 1921. *The Engineers and the Price System*. New York: Viking Press.

191   References

Ward, Norman. 1955. Review of *Democracy in Alberta* by C.B. Macpherson (Toronto: University of Toronto Press 1953). *Canadian Historical Review* 36 (1):60–1.

Warner, W. Lloyd, and Paul S. Lunt. 1941. *The Social Life of a Modern Community*. Vol. 1 Yankee City Series. New Haven, Conn.: Yale University Press.

Weber, Max. 1946. "Class, Status, Party." In H. Gerth and C.W. Mills, eds., *From Max Weber*, 180–95. New York: Oxford University Press.

Whalen, Hugh. 1952. "Social Credit Measures in Alberta." *Canadian Journal of Economics and Political Science* 18 (4):500–17.

Young, Walter D. 1969. *The Anatomy of a Party: The National CCF, 1932–1961*. Toronto: University of Toronto Press.

– 1978. *Democracy and Discontent*. 2nd ed. Toronto: McGraw-Hill Ryerson.

Index

A + B theorem: *see* Douglas, C.H.

Aberhart, William, 3–4, 7, 13, 14, 15, 16, 18, 38, 43, 80–1, 93, 107, 119–20, 125, 126–7, 130, 145, 147, 159; importance as leader, 154; interpretation of Douglasism, 61–74, 153; organizational skills, 155; relationship with C.H. Douglas, 108–11; relationship with Social Credit Board, 123; support for Hargrave scheme, 116, 121

Alberta Federation of Labor, 15, 17, 29

Anderson, Fred, 154

Ansley, R.E., 154

Backbencher's revolt, 117–19

Baker, Floyd, 127, 154

Barr, John J., 15, 35, 119, 120, 147, 177 n 2

Bennett, Arnold, 37

Bennett, R.B., 81, 109, 112, 144, 160, 162, 176 n 9, 181 n 15

Bourgeoisie: *see* Upper class

Bowen, John, 120

Bowman, Charles A., 176 n 9

Brownlee, John, 12, 13, 16, 156

Brym, Robert, 28, 167 n 14

Burnet, Jean, 28, 33

Byrne, L.D., 119, 123

Caldarola, Carlo, 177 n 2

Calgary, 9, 11, 14, 30, 31, 89–92; 1935 election results, 92–4; 1940 election results, 129–32

Campbell, P.M., 132

Caouette, Réal, 162

Case for Alberta, The, 82–3, 125–6

Centrist theory of the lower middle class, 5–6, 57–8, 74–5, 141, 142, 143

Chesterton, G.K., 37

Clark, S.D., 27, 80, 107, 118–19, 125

Clark, Sam, 28, 163

Classes: *see* Social classes

Cockroft, Charles, 121

Colbourne, Maurice, 38, 67

Commission on turnover policy, 69, 78, 114

Conservative Party
– of Alberta: 9–10, 12, 29, 84, 109, 123, 126, 127, 129, 130, 157, 160, 162; 1935 election platform, 161; 1935 election results, 18, 92–3, 97, 100–1, 103; position on social credit, 16, 159–60
– of Canada: 10, 11, 160; *see also* Bennett, R.B.

Conway, J.F., 27, 74, 79, 139, 148, 173 n 11

Co-operative Commonwealth Federation (CCF), 15, 17, 20, 27, 28, 71, 77, 84, 144–5, 148, 155, 156, 157, 160, 161, 162, 179 n 8; 1940 election results, 130–1, 136–8; *see also* Regina Manifesto

Countryside: 1935 election results in, 102–4; 1940 election results in, 135–9

Covenants: *see* Registration covenants
Craven, Paul, 84
Cross, W.W., 115, 116, 121

Debt legislation, 114–15, 123, 127, 164
Depression, the, 13–14, 81, 84, 141, 144–6, 153, 156, 157, 161–2, 164
Dobb, Maurice, 20, 163
Douglas, C.H., 7, 14, 15, 16, 61, 62, 119, 121, 125, 158, 163; A + B theorem, 39–42; on capitalism, 55–6; on the community, 45–7, 51, 59; on democracy, 47–8; ethno-religious prejudices, 49–50; on money, banks, and credit, 42–5; on national dividend and just price, 40, 65; on production and distribution, 44–7, 50–3; on property rights, 53–5; relationship with Aberhart, 108–11; on socialism, 48; on taxation, 64, 172 n 2
Duggan, D.M., 159–60
Durbin, E.F.M., 41

Edmonton, 9, 14, 17, 30, 31, 86, 129
Elliott, David R., 120, 146
Engels, Friedrich, 170 nn 4–5, 171 nn 14–15, 173 n 18
Ethnicity, 34, 152, 180 n 11

Farmers, 10, 11, 14, 19–20, 21, 23, 26, 29, 144, 146–7, 155, 158; *see also* Countryside, Petite bourgeoisie, United Farmers of Alberta
Finkel, Alvin, 35, 51, 74, 141, 146, 169 n 26, 177 n 1

Flanagan, Thomas, 29–31, 168 n 16, 173 n 7, 180 n 11
Fowke, Vernon C., 82

Gostick, Edith, 74, 154
Grayson, J. Paul, 27–8, 33–4, 35, 180 n 11
Grayson, L.M., 27–8, 33–4, 35, 180 n 11
Green, George, 160
Green Shirts, 59, 63, 108, 115–16; *see also* Hargrave, John

Hamilton, Richard F., 6, 94, 179 n 4
Hannant, Larry, 28
Hargrave, John, 59, 63, 108, 115–16, 121
Hiller, Harry, 153, 179 n 1
Hitler, Adolf, 151
Hooke, Alfred, 112, 123, 154, 178 n 9
Hugill, John, 116, 120, 121, 176 n 9

Imperialism, central Canadian: *see* Regional exploitation
Independents, 123, 129; 1940 election campaign, 127–8; 1940 election results, 129, 130, 132, 134–5, 136–7
Irvine, William, 15, 29
Irving, John, 14, 17, 35, 107, 146, 154, 157, 173 n 4

James, N.B., 177 n 3

Keynes, John M., 163
King, William Lyon Mackenzie, 83, 109, 112, 127, 159
Kitson, Arthur, 55

Labor Party of Alberta, 12, 16, 17, 92, 131, 158,

159, 161–2; 1935 election platform, 160; 1935 election results, 18, 92–3, 95, 97; position on social credit, 15, 16, 158
Leacock, Stephen, 180 n 7
League for Social Reconstruction, 181 n 14
Lee, Martha, 173 n 7
Lenin, V.I., 6, 171 n 14, 172 n 17
Lethbridge, 9, 30–1, 95, 123, 168 nn 19–20; 1935 election results, 95–8; 1940 election results, 132–4
Lewis, Wyndham, 37
Liberal Party
– of Alberta: 9–10, 12, 84, 109, 123, 126, 127, 129, 130, 157, 162; 1935 election platform, 161; 1935 election results, 18, 92–3, 97, 100–1, 103; position on social credit, 15, 16, 159, 162
– of Canada: 9, 10, 11, 161; *see also* King, William Lyon Mackenzie
Lipset, S.M., 19–20, 79, 146, 148, 149, 173 n 4
Lower, A.R.M., 19, 20
Lower middle class, 6, 20, 27; defined, 87; *see also* Centrist theory of the lower middle class, Petite bourgeoisie
Lunt, Paul S., 164
Lynd, Robert S., 149

McCarthy, J.D., 150
McGeer, Gerry, 159
MacLachlan, G.L., 119
McNaught, Kenneth, 27
Macpherson, C.B., 31, 32, 33–4, 70, 107, 141, 146, 147, 148, 149, 174 n 21; on backbencher's revolt and creation of Social Credit Board, 118; on

Douglasism, 50–3, 56; on petite bourgeoisie, 4–6, 20–6, 74–6, 79–80, 87, 148, 168 n 17, 173 n 17; quasi-party system, 167 n 12; on regional exploitation, 4–5, 78–80, 82, 143, 144; on social classes in general, 142–3, 179 n 2

Magor, Robert J., 109, 110

Mallory, J.R., 26–7, 79, 120–1, 177 n 2, 180 n 8

Manning, Ernest, 16, 64, 65, 72, 111–12, 115, 130, 154

Mansfield, Katherine, 37

Mardiros, Anthony, 177 n 2

Marx, Karl, 171 n 13, 173 n 18

Media treatment of Social Credit, 17–18, 121–2, 156

Medicine Hat, 9, 30–1, 98–9, 168 nn 19–20; 1935 election results, 99–101; 1940 election results, 134–5

Miller, Iris, 120, 146

Mills, C. Wright, 164

Minogue, K.R., 76

Monetary reform, public opinion towards, 158

Morton, W.L., 83–4, 145

Muggeridge, Malcolm, 165 n 5

Narodniks, 6

Naylor, R.T., 27

Nazism, 6

New Age Club, 109

Non-Partisan League, 11

Norman, Montagu, 109

Open Mind Club, 109

Orage, A.R., 37, 58

Osborne, J.S, 51, 177 n 2

Osborne, J.T., 51, 177 n 2

Palmer, Howard, 35, 79

Palmer, Tamara, 35, 79

Parkin, R.H., 175 n 7

Petite bourgeoisie: in Alberta, 4–5, 19, 20–6, 27, 31, 74–8, 94, 105–6, 137–8, 139, 141–2, 143, 147; in general, 5–6, 20, 56–8, 59–60, 74–6, 147–8, 165 n 5; defined, 87; see also Countryside, Farmers

Pinard, Maurice, 101, 150, 153

Pound, Ezra, 37

Powell, G.F., 119, 122–3

Pratt, Larry, 163, 166 n 5

Press treatment of Social Credit: see Media treatment of Social Credit

Progressive movement, 11–12, 80, 84, 128, 144, 145

Prophetic Bible Institute, 13, 155

Prosperity certificates, 113

Rational choice theory, 158, 159, 181 n 13

Regina Manifesto, 71, 84, 158, 181 n 14

Regional exploitation, 4, 5, 7, 20, 78–84, 125–6, 140, 141, 143–5, 179 n 5

Regional variation in vote, 103–4, 137–9

Registration covenants, 113–14

Reid, R.G., 16, 161

Religion, 34, 73, 153–4

Richards, John, 163, 166 n 5

Riel rebellions, 144

Robinson, J.L., 134

Rogers, Edith, 74, 154

Ross, C.C., 121

Rutherford, Alexander, 9, 10

Schultz, Harold J., 35, 118–19, 146

Shaw, G.B., 37

Small towns, 23, 27, 28, 30, 34; 1935 election results in, 32–3, 102–4; 1940 election results in, 135–6, 139

Smelser, Neil, 150

Smiley, Donald V., 180 n 7

Social classes, defined, 87–8

Social Credit Board, 72, 117–19, 122, 125, 127

Social movement economy, 156–7

Southam, G. Hamilton, 175 n 9

Stein, Michael, 56

Swankey, Ben, 156

Taylor, A.J.P., 75–6

Technocracy, 170 n 5

Thomas, L.G., 9, 11

Thomas, L.H., 177 n 2

Tilly, Charles, 150

Tower, Graham, 109

Towns: see Small towns

Townsend, F.E., 157

Traves, Tom, 84

Treasury Branches, 124

United Farmers of Alberta (UFA), 11, 12–13, 15–16, 17, 29, 31, 109, 123, 155, 156, 159, 161; 1935 election platform, 160–1; 1935 election results, 18, 26, 103; position on social credit, 15–16, 29, 158

Unwin, Joseph, 122, 154

Upper class, defined, 88

Upper middle class, defined, 87–8

van den Berg, Axel, 180 n 9

Veblen, Thorstein, 170 n 11, 171 n 12, 171 n 16, 173 n 8

Warner, W. Lloyd, 164

196   Index

Weber, Max, 163–4
Wells, H.G., 37
Women, 73–4, 152
Working class, 23, 24, 25,
   28, 29, 56, 77, 91–3, 94,
   95, 97, 99–101, 104,
   105–6, 130–1, 132, 133,
   134, 135, 137–9, 141–2,
   143, 148, 152; defined,
   88

Young, Walter D., 27
Yuill, W.C., 134

Zald, M.N., 150